Implementing Financial Regulation

Implementing Financial Regulation

Theory and Practice

Joanna Gray and Jenny Hamilton

John Wiley & Sons, Ltd

Other Wiley Editorial Offices

John Wiley & Sons Inc., 111 River Street, Hoboken, NJ 07030, USA

Jossey-Bass, 989 Market Street, San Francisco, CA 94103-1741, USA

Wiley-VCH Verlag GmbH, Boschstr. 12, D-69469 Weinheim, Germany

John Wiley & Sons Australia Ltd, 42 McDougall Street, Milton, Queensland 4064, Australia

John Wiley & Sons (Asia) Pte Ltd, 2 Clementi Loop #02-01, Jin Xing Distripark,
Singapore 129809

John Wiley & Sons Canada Ltd, 22 Worcester Road, Etobicoke, Ontario, Canada M9W 1L1

Wiley also publishes its books in a variety of electronic formats. Some content that appears in
print may not be available in electronic books.

British Library Cataloguing in Publication Data

A catalogue record for this book is available from the British Library

ISBN 13 978-0-470-86929-1 (HB)
ISBN 10 0-470-86929-1 (HB)

Typeset in 11/15pt Goudy by TechBooks, New Delhi, India
Printed and bound in Great Britain by TJ International, Padstow, Cornwall
This book is printed on acid-free paper responsibly manufactured from sustainable forestry
in which at least two trees are planted for each one used for paper production.

To Our Families

Contents

Preface

One of the main motivations for writing this book has been the desire to think through the implications of some of the insights provided by recent scholarly work that theorises about regulation and about risk, and to try to apply and "test" these insights, albeit in an admittedly non-scientific fashion, in the practical operating environment of the regulation of the UK financial services sector.

Although there is much written about the application of the risk based supervisory framework in UK financial services, there is little independent consideration of that framework, and its attendant shift in focus from rules to risks. This book attempts to address that shortfall. Against the background of some of this literature we consider how the regulator has extended its reach downwards into the level of the regulated entity to impose direct and specific responsibilities on individuals within firms, especially senior management and individual senior managers. In so doing we analyse this trend against some of the key theoretical literature on regulation and compliance as well as against the notion of "responsibility" within complex organizations, and present a critique of much of the rhetoric surrounding notions of compliance/ethical culture as well as the recent sharpening of mechanisms of management and manager accountability within UK financial regulation. We also present a critique of the impact of some of the 'consumer protection' regulation, such as information disclosure, in the light of the growing literature on, for example, consumer decision making.

We are conscious that in attempting to apply the insights of the theoretical literature to the practice of financial regulation some might
suggest that this book is neither one thing nor the other – neither a
rigorous theoretical analysis nor a rigorous explanation of the operational detail of the regime. However, we would respond that we believe
there should be more cross-over between regulatory theorists and those
familiar with the operational detail of various regulated business sectors.
Unless scholarship has an explanatory power it is open to the classic (and
often unfair) charge that it looks inward and speaks to itself rather than
having any interest, much less relevance, to the world beyond. Attempts
to marry theory and practice are few and far between in legal scholarship,
but the value of any theory must ultimately be its ability to explain.

Inevitably we were selective in those aspects of the regulatory regime
that we have chosen to analyse. We have chosen to confine our analysis primarily to the impact of the policy and actions of the Financial
Services Authority itself, but we acknowledge that there are some significant other areas of the regulatory framework, in the broader sense,
that have the potential to impact on the downward reach of regulation – such as the Financial Ombudsman Service and which would also
benefit from analysis, but these remain for future research.

As ever with any attempt to write in an area of substantive law and
regulation that is subject to constant change and reformulation there
are parts of this work that will look out of date on the literal content
of the law and FSA Handbook once this work appears. The content
of these chapters reflects the state of play in October 2005 and so subsequent developments which would otherwise have been incorporated
into this work do not appear. These include the publication as a House
of Lords Bill in November 2005 of the Company Law Reform Bill at the
start of what is likely to be its lengthy Parliamentary progress. Chapter 2 of that Bill contains provisions which govern the general duties
of directors and provides a statutory statement thereof. No sooner had
the Company Law Reform Bill been published than the Chancellor
of the Exchequer announced, in the December 2005 Pre-Budget Report the Government's intention to do away with the new requirement
for quoted companies to produce an Operating and Financial Review

in which they address and report on some of the broader "stakeholder oriented" issues beyond shareholder value that, as the discussion in Chapter 5 points out, are indicative of a desire to effect a degree of cultural or "mindset" change within companies. However, the reason given by the Chancellor for this decision simply reflects that these concerns and issues will be addressed elsewhere for many companies as they produce Business Reviews in order to comply with the EU Acccounts Modernisation Directive (2003/51/EC).

Another development announced in that same Pre-Budget Report was the Government's intention to produce a Regulatory Reform Order in order to implement those changes recommended by the N2 + 2 Review of FSMA 2000. One of those changes is to remove the need for the FSA Board to give formal approval to all general guidance issued by FSA, so that delegation of this function will be possible in some circumstances, to a committee or even individual staff member at FSA. This might be thought to go some way to meeting the concerns of firms expressed in the most recent Financial Services Practitioner Panel survey discussed in chapter 4 and again in the critique of the operation of regulatory enrolment in chapter 7. However, we would argue that this is unlikely, for the strong concerns expressed therein by firms related to the willingness of FSA to issue guidance in the first place and are more likely to relate to individual guidance than general.

Another important development which is likely to emerge before publication is the FSA's final response to its Consultation Paper 05/10. This feedback is likely to impact on the operation of the regime of "individualised" responsibility for senior managers and other individuals performing key functions within regulated firms discussed in chapter 3. Some initial response was given by the FSA in its "Better Regulation Action Plan" of 2 December 2005 but final feedback will not be given until the position of the Approved Persons regime in Chapter V FSMA under the implementation framework for the Markets in Financial Instruments Directive becomes clearer.

Joanna Gray and Jenny Hamilton
31 January 2006

Acknowledgements

The authors are extremely grateful for the advice and assistance and encouragement received from colleagues within the profession and the academic community, as well as family and friends. In particular we would like to thank Arthur Selman who provided an extremely helpful practical perspective and critique of parts of this book, and Gerald Rose, for identifying additional sociological sources and perspectives. We also want to thank those colleagues at Strathclyde University, Newcastle and Dundee as well as colleagues from other institutions who supported and encouraged us in this endeavour and especially those who reviewed particular chapters and helped us clarify our thoughts, especially Donald Nicholson, John Blackie, Iain MacNeil, and Peter Cartwright. We need also to thank the team at John Wiley & Sons for their generous patience and support.

Finally, to Bruce and Gary, for their tolerance and support.

1

Regulation in context

Financial services regulation has matured considerably in the past 25 years. The current regulator, the Financial Services Authority (hereafter "FSA"), has developed a sophisticated, comprehensive and potentially far-reaching regulatory tool kit through which to implement its objectives.[1] This reflects the fact that the "art" of regulation is now understood to be far more diverse and intricate than when regulation first began to attract academic interest. While it operates within the statutory framework imposed by the Financial Services and Markets Act 2000 (hereafter "FSMA"), there are three aspects of this regulatory toolkit developed by the regulator that we believe are of particular importance and significance. These are the subject of this book, rather than the structure of the regulatory environment for financial services,[2] which needs little explanation and has been extensively described and analysed elsewhere.[3]

[1] See J Black, *Mapping the Contours of Financial Services Regulation* (Centre for Analysis of Risk and Regulation, LSE: London, 2003).
[2] This structure has undergone significant change since the 1980s – from one of little or no regulation of different sectors within financial services industry to "self-regulation under a statutory umbrella" – to full statutory regulation under one "super-regulator".
[3] See, for example, G McMeel and J Virgo, *Financial Advice and Financial Products: Law and Liability* (Oxford University Press: Oxford, 2001); J Hamilton, Financial Services

The first aspect of central importance is the adoption by the FSA of risk-based regulation, and the concomitant development of its risk-based operating framework for supervision. This is of fundamental significance, and provides the context within which analysis and discussion of the two further aspects are carried out. The first of these two further aspects is the trend towards greater regulatory incursion into the internal business management processes and strategies of regulated firms through regulatory tools which address the role of senior managements of firms, and directly regulate individuals within firms, especially senior managers. The second further aspect is the change in regulatory rhetoric and action over the last 20 years to mirror the re-drawing of the boundary between collective and personal responsibility. This has led to an increasing emphasis on financial citizenship and personal financial autonomy.

The centrality of these aspects is in stark contrast to the situation in the early days of the precursor of the FSA, the Securities and Investment Board (hereafter "SIB"). At that time regulation was viewed simply in terms of command and control. Its effectiveness was judged against compliance with prescriptive and detailed rules, and regulators in the financial services sector were left to determine their own broad regulatory objectives.

The rise of risk

In one sense the adoption of risk as the basis of regulation by the financial services regulator is neither particularly unique nor unusual. Discourses around risk have now become commonplace within executive government in the UK.[4] As Fisher[5] has commented:

Regulation, in L Macgregor, T Prosser and C Villiers (eds) *Regulation and Markets Beyond 2000* (Ashgate: Aldershot, 2000), p 243; M Blair, L Minghella, M Taylor, M Threpiland and G Walker, *Blackstone's Guide to the Financial Services and Markets Act 2000* (Blackstone Press: London, 2000).

[4] Although as Black identifies, risk-based regulation has two distinct meanings, one refers to the implementation of internal risk management systems, the other refers to risk-based regulation where sources of risk are regarded as external to the organisation – J Black, The Emergence of Risk-based Regulation and the New Public Risk Management in the UK, *Public Law*, 512–548.

[5] E Fisher, The Rise of the Risk Commonwealth and the Challenge for Administrative Law, *Public Law*, 2003, 455–478 at 455.

One of the central tasks of the UK executive state is now perceived to be the handling of risk...The task of public decision makers is increasingly characterised in terms of the identification and assessment and management of risk and the legitimacy of public decision-making is also being evaluated on such a basis.

Furthermore, risk has become the dominant concept across a range of regulatory spheres from environmental protection and health and safety to other diverse arenas such as health, penology, and child protection,[6] as well as public sector management and finance. It has become the dominant concept in the regulatory reform process itself where regulation has to be proportionate to the risks.[7] As Fisher notes, in some of these spheres a concern for risk has always been implicit, as, for example, in environmental protection, food safety and occupational health and safety. In other regulatory spheres a focus on the concept of risk is relatively recent. Increasingly, however, regulators are required to engage in formal risk assessment and risk management.[8] It is clear now that the language of risk has permeated most areas of executive government. This is so much so that HM Treasury's *Management of Risk: Principles and Concepts*[9] states that "it can now be presumed that all existing [government] organisations have basic risk management processes in place"[10] and further that "every organisation which wants to maximize its success in delivering its objectives needs to have a risk management strategy, led from the very top of the organisation, which is then implemented by managers at every level...and embedded in the normal working routines and activities of the organisation".[11]

---

[6]See, e.g., J Braithwaite, The New Regulatory State and the Transformation of Criminology, in D Garland and R Sparks (eds) *Criminology and Social Theory* (OUP: Oxford, 2000), and P O'Malley, *Risk, Uncertainty and Government* (Glasshouse Press: London, 2004), M Power, *The Risk Management of Everything: Rethinking the Politics of Uncertainty* (Demos: London, 2004).

[7]Better Regulation Action Plan, 24 May 2005, available at http://www.hm-treasury.gov.uk/newsroom_and_speeches/press/2005/press_50_05.cfm. See also Transforming the Regulatory Landscape – Launch of Consultation on Bill for Better Regulation, Cabinet Office, 24 July 2005.

[8]E Fisher, supra, n 5.

[9]Consultation Draft, May 2004 (HMSO, 2004).

[10]Ibid., para 1.3.

[11]Supra, n 9, para. 2.6.

As Fisher observes, however, the notion that risk is now embedded in public decision-making is not a simple case of rebranding past practices with new buzzwords. Instead, risk represents a new way of conceptualising what "public administration" and regulation do. She suggests it is not simply a tool for decision-making, but in fact represents a new way of governing, and adds that "the end result has seemingly been a dramatic evolution in what public administration does and what it is perceived that it should do".[12] This evolution, she believes, has a number of fundamental implications for what is understood to be the role and the nature of the administrative state and the role of non-legal modes of regulating public administration, as well as how to identify good and bad public decision-making. It raises not only questions about the meaning of risk but also questions relating to the ways it is deployed by regulators and administrators, and its implications for citizens.

But it is recognised that the way risk has been embedded varies across public bodies and agencies.[13] Consequently, it cannot be analysed as if it were a uniform and unifying development across administrative and regulatory spheres. Rather each sphere needs to be examined for its specific implications. But in the call for more site specific examination of the embedding of risk it is important not to lose sight of the fact that this embedding is taking place within the context of an embedding of risk generally across a whole range of administrative and regulatory spheres. To ignore this wider context would be to overlook more subtle and broad-based implications of this development, and it is worth therefore analysing why risk has become so central in administrative and regulatory spheres generally. At the same time, risk is a concept that may be taken for granted by those involved in the everyday practices associated with it, and requires to be unpacked before looking at it further in the context of financial services regulation.

---

[12] E Fisher, supra, p 2, n 5.
[13] See, for example, C Hood, H Rothstein and R Baldwin, *The Government of Risk: Understanding Risk Regulation Regimes* (Oxford University Press: Oxford, 2001), P O'Malley, supra, p 7, n 6.

Why risk has become central

Very different explanations are given for why risk has come to be central across government and regulatory spheres.[14] These explanations are, in part, influenced by the different approaches to what risk is, discussed below.

In attempting to account for the emergence of risk as a strategic organising principle in the public sector some commentators have simply pointed towards the particular needs of government. They highlight the need to restore confidence in the aftermath of mismanaged crises (especially responding to particular stimuli such as the collapse of the Barings banking group and BSE), and the need to improve communication with the public, in order to better manage public expectations.[15]

Political scientists, however, convincingly suggest that the adoption of the language and practices of risk reflects a deeper, more complex process, that of "political isomorphism".[16] This is a process of policy transmission such that bodies will adapt to or adopt governance strategies that have a common currency and will alter their practices so as to become more like those around them. In other words, as a strategy or operating principle risk becomes accepted and embedded in one organisation or institution, and so it acquires a currency within other organisations or institutions.

However, given that risk has been conceptualised and utilised in different ways across organisations and institutions, a process of policy

---

[14] And the literature is extensive – see, for example, M Power, supra, n 6; D Vogel, *The New Politics of Risk Regulation in Europe*, Centre for Analysis of Risk and Regulation (LSE: London, 2001), and the references contained within.

[15] M Power, supra, n 6.

[16] P DiMaggio and W Powell, *The New Institutionalism in Organisational Analysis* (University of Chicago Press: Chicago, 1991). See also P Frumkin and J Galaskiewicz, Institutional Isomorphism and Public Sector Organisations, *Journal of Public Administration Research and Theory*, 2004, Issue 3, 283–307, M Lodge and K Wegrich, Control over Government: Institutional Isomorphism and Government Dynamics in Public Administration, *Policy Studies Journal*, 2005, Vol 33, No 2, 213, E Abrahamson, Managerial Fads and Fashions; The Diffusion and Rejection of Innovations, *Academy of Management Review*, 1991, 16, 586–612.

transmission cannot be the whole explanation.[17] Other explanations, primarily from within the socio-cultural disciplines, suggest that the centrality of risk stems from issues connected with control, accountability, responsibility and blame in late modern society. Two prominent theoretical perspectives that address these issues are broadly termed "risk society" theory and "governmentality" theory. The former draws on the work of the sociologists Beck and Giddens.[18] The latter draws on the work of the important French social thinker Foucault.[19]

At the risk of oversimplifying and caricaturing these important and extremely influential perspectives, the approach of "risk society" theorists such as Giddens and Beck is one that identifies what they believe to be broad socio-economic and political changes that have occurred in late modern societies. Among these changes they identify a loss of faith in institutions and authorities and a greater awareness of the limits and uncertainties associated with science and technology. This loss of faith, greater uncertainty and consequent anxiety about the future has arisen, they suggest, because of an increased awareness of the

---

[17]Some suggest that in fact the politics of risk has a long genealogy in government and that in fact what has changed is the way in which it is being deployed – see, e.g., P O'Malley, 2004, supra, p 27, n 13.

[18]See, e.g., the work of Ulrich Beck, and Anthony Giddens: U Beck, *Risk Society* (Sage: London, 1992), U Beck, Risk Society Revisited: Theory, Politics and Research Programmes, in B Adam, U Beck and J Van Loon (eds) *The Risk Society and Beyond: Critical Issues for Social Theory* (Sage: London, 2000), U Beck, The Reinvention of Politics, in U Beck, A Giddens and S Lash, *Reflexive Modernisation: Politics, Tradition and Aesthetics in the Modern Social Order* (Polity Press: Cambridge, 1994), A Giddens, Risk Society: The Context of British Politics, in J Franklin (ed) *The Politics of the Risk Society* (Cambridge: Polity Press, 1998), A Giddens, Risk and Responsibility, *Modern Law Review*, 1999, 62, 1.

[19]See, e.g., G Burchell, C Gordon and P Miller, *The Foucault Effect: Studies in Governmentality*, (Chicago University Press: Chicago, 1991); N Rose, *Governing the Soul: The Shaping of the Private Self* (Routledge: London, 1990); N Rose, *Powers of Freedom: Reframing Political Thought* (CUP: Cambridge, 1999); M Dean, *Governmentality: Power and Rule in Modern Society* (Sage: London, 1999). The Chair Foucault held at the College de France was in "The History of Systems of Thought". This connects with his general concern with the way human beings are sought to be controlled. For an introduction to his work, see P Rabinow, *The Foucault Reader* (Random House: London, 1984); B Smart, *Michael Foucault* (revised ed) (Routledge: London, 2002).

larger scale of risks faced in the 20th and 21st centuries (the period of "late modernity"[20]). This is encapsulated in what has been termed the "risk society"– a society in which most risk is "manufactured", that is, generated by humans as part of the techno-economic development of industrialisation, modernisation and capitalism, rather than externally imposed by nature.

Giddens, for instance, suggests that concern with risk has become ubiquitous because of an increasing awareness of the potential scale of these "manufactured" risks, which are typically unseen, global and potentially catastrophic. There is increasing awareness, too, of the contingent nature of risk assessment and management techniques. Late modern society is not necessarily intrinsically more dangerous than before.[21] Indeed, we now live longer, have better health etc. But for every scientific "breakthrough" there are new uncertainties and new risks to be faced. There is now an awareness at all levels of the "inherent indeterminacies and uncertainties of risk diagnosis" associated with manufactured risk.[22] This contrasts with the position at an earlier period (which Beck calls "simple modernity"), where there was belief in the ability of experts to identify, measure and hence control risks, or at least a belief that with the advancement of science they would ultimately succeed in doing so.

In addition, attempts to try to confine and control these risks increases uncertainty and danger.[23] The near collapse in 1998 of Long Term Capital Management, an investment fund that traded in derivatives – the very instruments created to off-set modern risk – can be seen as a quintessential example of what Beck and Giddens would call modern manufactured risk. Had it not been for the bailout encouraged by US Federal Reserve Bank, its collapse had the potential to unravel the entire

---

[20]Or what some would call "postmodernity". See, for example, D Harvey, *The Condition of Postmodernity* (Blackwell: Oxford, 1989).
[21]Cf. Ulrich Beck – who believes society is facing potentially apocalyptic threats, see U Beck, *Risk Society* (Sage: London, 1992).
[22]U Beck, Risk Society Revisited: Theory, Politics and Research Programmes, in B Adam, U Beck and J Van Loon, 2000, supra, p 219, n 18.
[23]Ibid., p 206.

banking system.[24] As a result, they suggest, we have entered a period of "reflexive modernisation" which involves questioning the outcomes of modernity, including the practices and procedures associated with industry and science.[25] "Risk society" theory suggests that the preoccupation with risk in government and regulatory circles is a response to a general recognition that there are limits to the ability to know or to control the uncertainties associated with late modernity, and to a public wanting to hold public decision-makers to account. Risk is now viewed as a political rather than a metaphysical phenomenon.[26] Giddens, who has been a formative intellectual influence on the development of Labour "third way" ideology, suggests that "[a] good deal of political decision-making is now about managing [these manufactured] risks – risks which do not originate in the political sphere, yet have to be politically managed".[27] For the exponents of the "risk society" thesis, risk governance is not so much associated with control but with the absence of control. In Giddens' phrase late modern society is a "runaway world".[28]

An alternative perspective on the centrality of risk is offered by "governmentality theory". The term "governmentality" is used to refer to

---

[24]The study of the collapse has generated much paper and ink and different reasons put forward for its collapse. See, e.g., F Partnoy, *The Politics of Greed* (Profile Books: London, 2003); M Stein, Unbounded Rationality: Risk and Organizational Narcissism at LTCM, *Human Relations*, 2003, Vol 56(5), 523–540; D MacKenzie, Long-Term Capital Management and the Sociology of Arbitrage, *Economy and Society*, 2003, 32, 349–380; D MacKenzie, Fear in the Markets, *London Review of Books*, 2000, Vol 22, No 8, accessed on-line at www.lrb.co.uk/v22/no8/mack01_.html

[25]A Giddens, Risk and Responsibility, supra, p 6, n 18. Beck describes reflexive modernisation as "self-confrontation with the effects of risk society that cannot be dealt with and assimilated in the system of industrial society": U Beck, in U Beck, A Giddens and S Lash, *Reflexive Modernisation* supra, p 6, n 18. For a discussion of the similarities and differences between Beck's and Gidden's concept of reflexive modernity, see S Lash, Reflexivity and its Doubles, also in U Beck, A Giddens and S Lash, *Reflexive Modernisation*.

[26]D Lupton and J Tulloch, Risk is Part of Your Life; Risk Epistemologies Among a Group of Australians, *Sociology*, 2002, Vol 36(2), 317–334.

[27]A Giddens, Risk and Responsibility, supra, p 5, n 18.

[28]A Giddens, *Runaway World: How Globalization is Reshaping our Lives* (Profile Books: London, 1999).

specific modes of government that have emerged in modern societies in line with liberalist and neo-liberalist discourses.[29] Governmentality theorists are interested in examining the ways in which power is constituted and exercised in liberal and neo-liberal societies. Their interest in risk does not focus on the nature and scale of risks in late modern society, nor does it centre around identifying macro-level transformations in society (transformations governmentality scholars do not necessarily accept in any case[30]). Rather it is centred around the exploration of how the identification of risks associated with certain behaviour or activities provide a means through which to exercise control over populations, groups or individuals in neo-liberal societies. In other words, governmentality theorists are interested in identifying how risk is used as a "tool of governance" to shape behaviours.[31] One of the clearest examples of the use of risk as a tool of governance is in insurance.

The technologies of insurance (statistics, classification and frequency observation) are tools used to make risk calculable and, in making it calculable, it can be used as the basis on which to promote responsible behaviour on the part of the insured, for which the clumsy but apt term "responsibilisation" has been coined. This can be seen, for example, in relation to smoking and other hazardous activities whereby smokers or those who engage in such activities are required to pay higher premiums or denied insurance altogether. This allocation of responsibility in turn enables norms of behaviour to be established, which are then used to encourage voluntary self-regulation,[32] such as, for instance, giving up

[29]D Hodgson, "Know your Consumer": Marketing, Governmentality and the "New Consumer" of Financial Services, *Management Decision*, 2002, Vol 40, No 4, 318–328.
[30]See P O'Malley, 2004, supra p 26, n 6.
[31]P O'Malley, Risk, Power and Crime Prevention, *Economy and Society*, 1992, 252, and P O'Malley, Imagining Insurance: Risk, Thrift, and Life Insurance in Britain, in T Baker and J Simon (eds) *Embracing Risk: The Changing Culture of Insurance and Responsibility* (Chicago University Press: Chicago, 2002).
[32]M Foucault, Governmentality, in G Burchell, C Gordon and P Miller (1991), supra, n 19, F Ewald, Insurance and Risk, in G Burchell C Gordon and P Miller, supra n 19; D Lupton, *Risk* (Routledge: London, 1999) at p 25, M Dean, Sociology after Society, in D Owen (ed) *Sociology after Postmodernism* (Sage: London, 1997), P O'Malley, supra, n 13; D Knights, Governmentality and Financial Services: Welfare Crises and the

smoking. Risk governance in this sense is about using the concept of risk as a means of governing individuals or groups in such a way as to (re)define responsibilities for the outcomes associated with particular phenomena or activities, consistent with an ethos of neo-liberalism which emphasises autonomy and self-help over state intervention.[33]

Examples of this emphasis are not confined to the area of insurance. They can be found across a broad spectrum of fields where the state utilises risks governance in this sense. As O'Malley illustrates, in some jurisdictions drug addicts have been

> recast as "responsible risk takers" who must govern the effects of their risks on themselves and on others. This new governmental image of the drug user no longer represents them as "addicts" enslaved by the drug and cursed with impaired rationality. Rather . . . they are considered rational choice subjects, free to make choices and to take responsibilities, albeit having a "relationship of dependence" with a drug.[34]

In the context of environmental concerns on the other hand, the Australian government has sought to redefine drought to the category of "manageable risk" rather than a "natural disaster", the responsibility for which has been transferred away from the state and on to farmers on the basis of their failure to respond adequately to risk managing deteriorating land conditions.[35] Within the health field Ruhl[36] has drawn attention to how pregnant women are "statistically graded" for risk on the basis of lifestyle and increasingly assigned responsibility for the health of the foetus. Similarly, in the context of criminal behaviour in the UK Batchelor demonstrates that despite their difficult familial and social circumstances young women who offend tend to reject the label of "victim", preferring to focus instead on issues of personal choice and

---

Financially Self Disciplined Subject, in G Morgan and D Knights, *Regulation and Deregulation in European Financial Services* (Macmillan: Basingstoke, 1997).

[33]D Lupton, ibid., p 102.

[34]P O'Malley, 2004, supra p 8, n 6.

[35]V Higgins, Calculating Climate: "Advanced Liberalism" and the Governing of Risk in Australian Drought Policy, *Journal of Sociology*, 2001, 37, 299–316, referred to in P O'Malley, 2004, supra, p 9, n 6.

[36]L Ruhl, Liberal Governance and Prenatal Care: Risk and Regulation in Pregnancy, *Economics & Society*, 1999, 28, 95.

taking responsibility for their risky behaviour.[37] This internalisation of responsibility is a key objective of this form of governance.

It has been suggested that these risks are deliberately conceptualised by the state in ways which conform to neo-liberal ideas about the role of the individual and the role of the state, and in particular neo-liberal ideas about the responsibility of the individual to manage their own risks "free" from state interference.[38] These risks include the risks associated with ill-health, financial security, or personal security risks. Risk, through its ability to "responsibilise" citizens, is described as a form of "government at a distance".[39] In other words, the ways in which risks are conceptualised enables responsibility for the management of behaviours or activities to be (re)allocated away from the state and onto the groups or individuals, in ways that conform to particular political ideologies.[40] The language and practices associated with risk provide an ostensibly neutral and objective basis on which to do so. Risk-governance, governmentality theorists would suggest, can provide a subtle but powerful strategy by which to reshape behaviours and expectations in order to achieve "political" objectives.

Dean[41] describes how this strategy is supplemented through the operation of "technologies of agency" and "technologies of performance". Through technologies of agency such as contract and citizenship,

---

[37]S Batchelor, "Prove me the Bam," Victimisation and Agency in the Lives of Young Women who Commit Violent Offences, *Probation Journal* (Special Edition on Violence), 2005, 52(4), 359–376. See also J Braithwaite, The New Regulatory State and the Transformation of Criminology, in D Garland and R Sparks (eds) *Criminology and Social Theory* (OUP: Oxford, 2000).

[38]See e.g., M Dean, Sociology after Society, in D Owen (ed) *Sociology after Postmodernism*, supra, n 32.

[39]On the importance of the twin concepts of freedom and self-governance in neoliberalism see N Rose, *Powers of Freedom: Reframing Political Thought* (CUP: Cambridge, 1999).

[40]Governance theorists would not however suggest that risk governance is deployed in the same way in every setting but rather that the role to be played by risk will differ depending on the environment in which it is situated – see P O'Malley, 2004, supra, n 6.

[41]M Dean, 1999, supra, pp 167–170, n 19. See also D Hodgson, "Know your Customer": Marketing, Governmentality and the "New Consumer" of Financial Services, *Management Decision*, 2002, 40/4, 318–328.

individuals, groups or organisations are encouraged to become respons-ible and autonomous. In the financial sector this has a certain resonance in relation to current government alerts over the risks associated with re-lying on the state pension to provide financial security after retirement, and the call for "responsible citizens" to make independent pension provision. This risk rhetoric suggests that responsibility for longer-term financial security no longer lies in any collective security provided by the state but lies primarily with the individual.[42]

Similarly, the adoption of a risk-based regulatory strategy by the FSA[43] constitutes a powerful rhetorical framework within which to embed enhanced concepts of senior management responsibility and so to redefine the roles and responsibilities of firms. Technologies of agency are generally accompanied by technologies of performance such as the establishment of, for example, performance standards through which to regulate that autonomy. This is demonstrated in the supervi-sory structure implemented by the FSA which includes an assessment of firms' risk management systems and controls, supplemented by the var-ious principles and standards designed to encourage the development of the responsible firm and responsible senior managers (the subject of Chapters 2 to 5).

Social theorists have also drawn attention to the powerful forensic function of risk. Douglas, for example, suggests that imputations of risk provide a modern, sanitised, and seemingly depoliticised way of attach-ing blame for particular outcomes on particular agencies, organisations or individuals. For Douglas

> The idea of risk could have been custom-made. Its universalizing terminology, its abstractness, its power of condensation, its scientificity, its connection with objective analysis, make it perfect.[44]

As is argued later in this book, it is also a convenient tool for obfuscating and shifting downwards, onto the shoulders of the regulated, politically

---

[42] The implications of this downward shifting of responsibility are discussed in Chapter 6.
[43] Discussed in Chapter 2.
[44] M Douglas, *Risk and Blame: Essays in Cultural Theory* (Routledge: London, 1992), p 15, quoted in *Lupton*, supra, p 48, n 32. See also C Hood, The Risk Game and the Blame Game, *Governments and Opposition*, 2002, 27, 15.

difficult conflicting policy agendas that drive overlapping risk-based regulatory regimes. These conflicts are sometimes unforeseen, but equally sometimes the result of issues not being fully thought through. Apparent depoliticisation through the use of 'risk' then, simply masks and obscures the political.

These theoretical perspectives are not uncontested. "Risk society" proponents in particular have been accused of "grand theorising" and for their tendency to overgeneralise and to perceive late modern risk as universalising in its effects.[45] However, there is now some empirical support for their view that individuals do sense a loss of control over the future; that risk is regarded as a pervasive and inevitable aspect of everyday life; and that there is a need to try to contain this loss of control through careful consideration of risks. However, the evidence also suggests that risk is not always perceived of in purely negative terms.[46]

These perspectives suggest that the increased focus on risk and risk management at the "political" level cannot simply be understood as a pragmatic response to mismanaged crises or to institutional isomorphism.[47] Rather, they reflect concerns emerging at a deeper level around issues of uncertainty and control in late modern societies. Governmentality theorists suggest that the accumulation of knowledge through information and statistics has enabled risk to be used as a mechanism of control. "Risk society" theorists on the other hand would suggest that the shift into risk-based governance reflects a desire to structure decision-making in the face of increased uncertainty, and, moreover, that the contingent nature of our ability to identify and control risks has resulted in a greater sensitivity to risk at both the individual and

---

[45]See, for example, T Baker and J Simon, *Embracing Risk: The Changing Culture of Insurance and Responsibility* (University of Chicago Press: Chicago, 2002), p 21; P O'Malley, 2004, supra, p 176, n 6; A Scott, Risk Society or Angst Society?, in B Adam, U Beck and J Van Loon, supra, n 18; M Cohen, Science and Society in Historical Perspective: Implications for Social Theories of Risk, *Environmental Values – Special Issue: Risk*, 1999, Vol 8, No 2, 152–176.

[46]D Lupton and J. Tulloch, supra, n 26; P Taylor-Gooby, H Dean, M Munro and G Parker, Risk and the Welfare State, *British Journal of Sociology*, 2000, Vol 50, No 2, 177–194.

[47]For the meaning of this term see footnote 16 and accompanying text.

the political (governmental) level. These theoretical strands are not necessarily incompatible, for, as Steele argues, the failure to control manufactured risk does not require rejection of the role of risk as a decision-making resource. Risk as a decision-making resource is in fact extremely resilient and can be adapted to incorporate uncertainty and volatility, as the financial markets in particular demonstrate.[48]

Where these two theoretical strands appear to share common ground is in terms of their assessment of the implications for the relationship between the "state" and the "individual". Giddens in his conception of the "risk society" suggests that the contingent nature of the risks associated with late modernity means that governments cannot automatically assume responsibility for them. Rather individuals have to adopt what he calls a reflexive and calculative attitude to the possibilities presented by modern society and to accept more responsibility for the outcomes flowing from the choices they make. One of the roles of government, he suggests, is to create the opportunity for individuals to engage with government and "experts" in order to better understand the limits of scientific or technical knowledge associated with those choices.[49]

Governmentality theorists on the other hand "look beneath the grand gaze of universal theories such as the risk society" and suggest risk governance is a neo-liberal mechanism of control in that identifying risks enables public decision-makers to allocate responsibility for outcomes in ways that conform with political objectives by, for example, encouraging groups and individuals to take steps to avoid or minimise the

---

[48] J Steele, *Risks and Legal Theory* (Hart Publishing: Oxford, 2004), p 49, but see also S Green, Negotiating with the Future: The Culture of Modern Risk in Global Financial Markets, *Environment & Planning D: Society & Space*, Vol 18, 77–89 who argues that the resilience of risk expertise systems runs counter to Beck's belief that science is beginning to question its rational foundations.

[49] A Giddens, *The Third Way: The Renewal of Social Democracy* (Polity Press: Cambridge, 1998). Beck makes a similar point about the need for reflexivity but whereas for Giddens reflexivity is mediated through expert systems, for Beck the authority of the individual supplants external, "expert" forms of authority. For a discussion of differences and similarities between Giddens' and Beck's concept of reflexive modernity see S Lash, Reflexivity and its Doubles, in U Beck, G Giddens and S Lash, *Reflexive Modernisation*, supra, pp 110–173, n 18.

risks to themselves.[50] It is argued in this book, however, that although regulatory rhetoric appears to bear out this intention to use risk as a governance tool through which to achieve certain political objectives (one of which, we suggest, is to manage and neutralise reputational risk to government), the way in which responsibility is allocated to firms and individuals buries and obfuscates conflicting political objectives once any particular responsibility framework is mapped onto the many others that now pervade social and economic life. Chapter 5 illustrates this obfuscation through the discussion of the various potentially conflicting responsibilities imposed on firms and on specific individuals within firms under FSMA and general company law and corporate governance requirements.

What both of these theoretical explanations agree on is that responsibility for confronting risks and uncertainty is increasingly being devolved downward and away from government. In the context of financial services regulation this is occurring through techniques described as meta regulation, enforced self-regulation or enrolment. It is the aim of the rest of this book to explore and critique this downward shifting more directly in the context of the discussion in Chapters 3, 4 and 5 of downward penetration of financial regulation into firms and within firms, and in Chapter 6 to examine the link between government objectives, financial regulation and the development of the concept of the "financial citizen".

Risk regulation, it is suggested, is therefore about far more than using risk simply as a decision-making tool to, for example, determine the allocation of scarce resources within administrative or regulatory bodies. Risk regulation in general is about far more than the dry and technical implementation of risk assessment and risk management techniques. Rather it has the potential to reshape relationships between those who

---

[50] P O'Malley, 2004, supra, p 9, n 6. Further he notes "[T]hese responsibilising processes seemingly *democratize* government through the mobilizing of risk and uncertainty. Individuals and communities are made free to choose how they will govern themselves in relation to a host of insecurities. Expertise in risk and uncertainty . . . appears in an advisory capacity, often available in a commodified form. We are all to be 'empowered' by the provision of information and skills about how to secure ourselves", at p 175.

govern and those who are governed, to embed norms of behaviour, to attribute blame and to define and delimit both responsibility and accountability.

What is risk?

The issue is one which, of course, is not peculiar to the context of financial services. It is not self-explanatory and has been the subject of considerable discussion and debate, particularly between the techno-scientific community on the one hand, and the socio-cultural community on the other. This debate is reflected, for instance, in the 1992 report for the Royal Society for the Prevention of Accidents.[51] The social scientists and physical scientists called upon to participate in the study of risk were simply unable to agree about the nature and meaning of the concept.[52]

For the techno-scientific community risk has an objective existence. It is, in principle, capable of being identified through measurement and calculation and hence controlled using this knowledge. Debates within this community tend to revolve around the accuracy of the science used to measure and calculate the risk and whether particular risk models are optimally constructed to identify all of the risks and understand how risks occur. The objective nature of risk itself is usually taken for granted.[53]

Socio-cultural theorists on the other hand suggest that far from being a purely objective fact risk is in reality socially constructed and

---

[51] *Risk: Analysis, Perception and Management* (Royal Society: London, 1992).

[52] This led to the presentation of the report in effectively two parts: the first part (Chapters 1–4) representing the views of the physical scientists, the second part (Chapters 5–6) representing the views of the social scientists, and see the discussion in J Adams, *Risk* (UCL Press: London, 1995).

[53] D Lupton, supra, p 18, n 32. Lupton includes within the techno-scientific stream (which she labels the "realist perspective") approaches emerging from fields such as engineering, statistics, actuarialism, psychology, epidemiology and economics (p 17). See also O Renn, Concepts of Risk: A Classification, in S Krimsky and D Golding (eds) *Social Theories of Risk* (Praeger: Westport CT, 1992) for a classification of the various "schools" of risk. See also R Baldwin (ed) *Law and Uncertainty, Risks and Legal Process* (Kluwer: London, 1997).

shaped by cultural belief patterns and societal influences.[54] For this community:

> All knowledge about risk is bound to the socio-cultural contexts in which this knowledge is generated, whether in relation to scientists' and other experts' knowledges or lay people's knowledges. Scientific knowledge, or any other knowledge, is never value free but rather is always a product of a way of seeing. A risk, therefore, is not a static, objective phenomenon, but is constantly constructed and negotiated as part of the network of social interaction and the formation of meaning. "Expert" judgements of risk, rather than being the "objective" and "neutral" and therefore "unbiased" assessments . . . are regarded as being equally as constructed through implicit social and cultural processes as are lay people's judgements.[55]

Socio-cultural theorists, accordingly, emphasise that the very act of risk measurement itself involves value judgements. There are value judgements, shaped by the social and cultural environment, with respect to what to measure, how to measure and how to interpret the results produced.[56]

Furthermore, Young has drawn attention to the role of metaphor in shaping perceptions about risk and suggests that these metaphors help to conceptualise risk in a certain way. In the context of finance, she draws attention to the language used, which refers to risk as "liquid", as "concentrated", and as having varying "levels". All of these terms suggest that risk is a thing apart from the asset or entity to which it is connected, and can therefore be isolated, measured and packaged

---

[54]Within the socio-cultural literature Lupton in fact identifies a range of positions on the nature of risk: from strong social constructionist positions ("nothing in itself is a risk") associated with the "governmentality" perspectives, to the weak social constructionist perspectives associated with the "risk society" ("risk as an objective hazard . . . inevitably mediated through social and cultural processes"), supra, n 32, Chapter 2.

[55]D Lupton, supra, p 29, n 32.

[56]See N Rose, Governing by Numbers: Figuring out Democracy, *Accounting, Organisations and Society*, 1991, 673–692; S Jasanoff, The Political Science of Risk Perception, *Reliability Engineering and System Safety*, 1998, 59, 91–99. As Shrader-Frechette, notes, in the early 1990s cyclamates were permitted and saccharine banned in Canada, while across the border the US adopted exactly the reverse regime – saccharine permitted and cyclamates banned, both based on science. K Shrader-Frechette, *Risk and Rationality* (University of California Press: Berkeley, 1991), as referred to in C Hood, R Baldwin and H Rothstein, *The Government of Risk*, supra, p 5, n 13.

separately from that entity. Risk "exposure" and risk "appetite", on the other hand imply that risk is within our control and simply a matter of personal choice.[57] The power of these metaphors lies in their ability both to help construct and to reinforce a belief in the objectivity and certainty of risk within the financial community. As Knights and Vurdubakis reiterate in the context of discussing risk and insurance that to recognise

> that risk is a construct is not to suggest that risk is a fiction, it is to recognise the need to examine the discursive and practical operations through which the concept becomes attached to the events it purports to describe . . . [I]n itself nothing is a risk. Conversely anything (from a lawsuit to the birth of a child . . .) can be said to be a risk depending on how the event is viewed and analysed.[58]

For socio-cultural theorists risk perceptions are "shared, cultural and symbolic".[59] Membership of groups (such as specialist risk assessment and management teams) and social networks (such as professional organisations) are important for the construction of risk. However, it is possible that even within tightly structured organisations, different shared interpretational frameworks can exist within organisations. Consequently different groups can appear to approach the issue of risk from quite different perspectives.[60]

What these debates draw attention to is not simply the need to be aware of the contested meaning and nature of risk. They also have implications for the way in which the existence of different perceptions of risk are interpreted. For example, different perceptions are often portrayed in the public arena as the result of faulty cognition on the part of one group, for example individual investors as opposed to another, such as financial experts. In this way one group, inevitably the "lay" group, is

---

[57] J J Young, Risk(ing) Metaphors, *Critical Perspectives on Accounting*, 2001, 12, 607–625.
[58] D Knights and T Vurdubakis, Calculations of Risk: Towards an Understanding of Insurance as a Moral and Political Technology, *Accounting, Organizations and Society*, 1993, 18(7/8), 729–764.
[59] D Lupton, supra p 56, n 32.
[60] For empirical research drawing attention to the relationship between risk and "culture", see B Hutter, *Regulation and Risk: Occupational Health and Safety on the Railways* (OUP: Oxford, 2001). On culture and regulation see C Hood, *The Art of the State: Culture, Rhetoric and Public Management* (Clarendon Press: Oxford, 1998).

seen to under- or overestimate or ignore "real" risks. Socio-cultural theorists suggest, however, that these different perceptions may not stem
from lack of understanding, ignorance or a refusal to take "real" risk
seriously. Rather they stem from the fact that risk is not a homogeneous
concept and different perceptions of it arise through the existence of
different interpretive frameworks. It is necessary, therefore, for an appreciation of this to inform our understanding of how different individuals or groups (including "experts") construct, interpret and respond to
different risks.

   Moreover, there is also a need to be aware of the different values that
can be attached to risk. Whereas risk for some is simply a technical and
neutral term referring to the outcome of a probability calculation, risk
for others has come to be associated with the potential for harm, whether
calculable or not.[61] This is the sense in which most regulators use the
concept of risk, concerned as they are to minimise the dangers from excessive risk-taking. But risk-taking can also be valued as positive. It can
be associated with self-fulfilment through, for example, promotion, or
industry recognition or commercial success. Hence it is often valorised.
Business enterprise and risk-taking have been inextricably intertwined
throughout history. The encouragement of risk capital formation and
promotion of an enterprising, risk-taking culture in business and individuals continues to occupy policymakers. In the financial markets, in
particular, risk is not seen as a negative concept. On the contrary, it
is associated primarily with a "good", namely commercial opportunity
and profit-making, and risk-taking is often rewarded handsomely. This
"entrepreneurial" meaning of risk is also evident in current political ideology, which increasingly links entrepreneurship with risk-taking. For
example, the reforms to bankruptcy law introduced under the Enterprise Act 2002 were designed to encourage entrepreneurship through
risk-taking and to reduce the stigma attached to those who fail.[62]

---

[61]Whether it be, for example, the risks associated with nuclear power; MMR vacci-
nations; genetically modified food; or the risks associated with failing to make proper
provision for long-term individual financial security.
[62]See DTI Productivity and Enterprise, *Insolvency: A Second Chance*, CM 5234, July
2001 para 1.1.

Tensions associated with the different values attached to risk may exist not just between different actors, such as regulators and firms. They may also exist within a particular entity, as, for example, between trading arms and compliance sections within firms. In other words, even if different individuals or groups perceive risk similarly, it is possible they will value it differently. Again, in the regulatory context, the existence of these different cultures and values can help to explain why some might be more, or less, receptive to attempts to regulate risk.

Finally, for the purposes of this Introduction, it is important to acknowledge the distinction often drawn between risk and uncertainty[63] (a distinction that arguably lies at the heart of the concept of the 'risk society'). Risk is traditionally associated with probability calculations. That approach to risk is to suggest that an event can be calculated mathematically in terms of probability and so can be predicted and therefore controlled. Uncertainty on the other hand is not capable of measurement and is concerned, therefore, with mere possibilities incapable of calculation but only guesswork or judgement. Uncertainty cannot be controlled because its outcomes are unknown and unknowable.[64] While the term "risk" is often used to refer to risk or uncertainty, one important implication of this distinction relates to the way in which issues are presented for public consumption. Although the distinction between risk and uncertainty is not commonly maintained in the practice of investment and finance (perhaps deliberately so), it points to the need to be aware of the possibility that uncertainty may masquerade in the language of risk in order that "expert" judgements benefit from a greater

---

[63]For a discussion of the distinction between risk and uncertainty see e.g. P O'Malley, 2004, supra, n 6; F Knight, *Risk, Uncertainty and Profit* (Harper & Row: New York, 1965 (1921)) E G McGoun, The History of Risk Management, *Critical Perspectives on Accounting*, 1995, Vol 6, 511–532.

[64]Some would reject any hard and fast division, suggesting that risk and uncertainty are often configured together in varied and complex ways – as in the case of financial products such as catastrophe insurance and exotic derivatives – Ericson and Doyle, Catastrophe Risk, Insurance and Terrorism, *Economy and Society*, 2004, 33(2), 135–173; P O'Malley, 2004, supra p 13 and 24, n 6. O'Malley further suggests that there is no binary divide between risk and uncertainty, rather it is better to regard them as related along multiple axes, at p 19.

appearance of certainty and objectivity. To call something a "risk" suggests the odds are known; to call it an "uncertainty" is to admit to guesswork.

Conclusion

In summary, risk-based regulation is in fact a highly politicised act in which risk is used as a normative tool to delineate accountability, establish norms of behaviour and embed particular conceptions of responsibility. In particular the literature persuasively argues that risk is a tool that can be used to redefine relationships between those doing the regulating and "others", to effect a shift from collective to more individualised responsibility, and also to define the sites and boundaries of that responsibility. At the same time, however, the contested nature of risk, the values attached to it, and the potential existence of different interpretive frameworks inevitably raise questions about the ability of risk to carry the weight of expectations attached to it as a regulatory tool. These same questions are raised, too, given the interpretive frameworks relating to the understanding of the meaning of risk and the approach to it. This book, in its examination of the ways in which the FSA's conception of risk and devolved responsibility is driving and shaping regulatory standards, processes and practice, aims to illustrate both this essential insight *and* this essential critique of its implications in the context of the regulatory environment for UK financial services.

The structure of the book

Chapter 2 takes as its starting point the theoretical perspectives on risk outlined above in order to analyse the risk-to-objectives regulatory framework introduced by the FSA. Although the FSA has published information about this regulatory framework, there has as yet been little independent consideration of it in the light of these perspectives. The chapter explores more closely the reasons for the introduction of risk-based supervision and its design (including how risk is constructed and implemented as a regulatory tool) and asks whose purposes are being served, and how, by its adoption. In doing so it will consider the extent to which it employs a process described as "meta-risk regulation" as a means to harness firms' own risk assessment and management tools into the service of the FSA to reduce the perceived risks to its own statutory objectives. It will also consider the implications of risk-based supervision for the private investor "consumer" of financial services and the way in which these consumers are expected to engage with risk.

Chapters 3, 4 and 5 then move on to focus on the trend towards greater regulatory incursion within the internal business management processes and strategies of regulated firms, through direct regulation of individuals within financial services firms, and in particular of senior managers. Although this direct regulation is set against the backdrop of a risk-based supervisory regime that has the potential to reshape and redefine responsibilities in the name of risk reduction, this trend has its origins in earlier regulatory developments. These developments can be seen against theoretical work specifically relating to the way in which law and regulation have come to attribute responsibility to and within a business organisation. Chapter 3 therefore moves beyond considerations of risk-based supervision. Instead, it looks specifically at the way in which financial regulation has extended its reach "downwards" into the level of the regulated entity to impose specific responsibilities on firms in relation to issues of business organisation, governance and strategy (which might traditionally have been seen as outside the sphere of a regulator's direct concern), and on individuals within those firms, particularly senior managers. It explains the genesis and structure of the FSA Handbook rules and guidance on senior management arrangements, systems and controls (SYSC) as well as the regime for approval, regulation and sanction of people performing what are known as "controlled functions", i.e. key roles, within and on behalf of the firm. It concludes by considering some of the theoretical literature on regulation and compliance, as well as on the notion of "responsibility" within complex organisations and asks how initiatives such as SYSC can be seen in the light of the insights provided by some of that work.

Chapter 4 looks at the evidence about how these new arrangements are being received and implemented into firms. In doing so it draws on both the outcome of FSA disciplinary action since "N2" (1 December 2001), and the results of a small-scale survey of firms undertaken 18 months after N2 into the reception and implementation of the new arrangements. It draws attention to the link between the FSA's ex ante risk assessment of firms, which includes assessment of the control risk components of a firms' "relationship with regulators" and "cultural and business ethics" on the one hand, and ex post assessment of these systems as part of FSA disciplinary outcomes on the other. These provide clear examples of the FSA's view that senior management and its influence on firm culture is the key route into effective regulation within firms.

Chapter 5 then turns to consider the FSA's regime of regulatory senior management responsibilities against both the existing duties owed in company law by the board of directors of a company, and by individual members of it. It will also identify the broader trends in the wider corporate governance arena that shape the appropriate responsibilities of both the board as whole, and of its individual company directors (such as, for example, under the Higgs Report as to Role of Non-Executive Directors, the recent reformulation of the UK Combined Code on Corporate Governance, and, in the US context, the Sarbanes-Oxley Act 2002). It draws attention to a number of potential areas of tension and conflict between these regimes and asks whether the voguish concepts of "compliance culture" and "compliance ethos" are useful aids in understanding the overlap between regulatory expectations; a theme to which Chapter 7 returns.

While Chapters 3, 4 and 5 focus on regulation and the firm, Chapter 6 returns to the discussion introduced in Chapter 2 of the redrawing of the boundary between collective and personal responsibility in the context of the political desire to downshift the responsibility for long-term financial security from the government to the individual citizen. It examines the implementation of the regulatory objectives of "consumer protection" and "public awareness", and in particular the role of information disclosure in developing the model of the "financial citizen". In doing so it considers the potential effectiveness of what is predominantly process, rather than product-based regulation, drawing upon the growing body of literature challenging the model of the rational decision-maker implicit in process-based regulation. It also discusses the extent to which it is possible to align consumer and adviser interests, and considers whether the rhetoric around the risks of consumer savings gaps and the promotion of the financial citizen has negated the opportunity for open political debate on collective versus privatised and individualised responsibility for longer-term financial security.

Chapter 7 returns to and draws together some of the themes addressed earlier in the book to consider more broadly the way in which the FSA, in the context of its risk-based regulatory framework, is seeking to achieve its regulatory goals as set out in its statutory objectives, by effecting cultural and organisational shifts within the financial services industry itself, as well as individual firms and individual managers, to transform them into better, more responsive and open citizens. This chapter considers whether these initiatives, broadly labelled as techniques of "meta regulation", of "regulatory enrolment" or as "enforced self-regulation", are capable of bringing about the results intended or whether they will have unintended effects leading, for example, to a decline of trust and a culture of caution and risk aversion. It also considers the extent to which such techniques gloss over the problem of conflicts in regulatory objectives between different regulatory regimes with different public policy goals to which firms are subject; the resolution of which is being shifted downwards away from politicians and government and onto firms and individuals within firms. It concludes that questions must be asked about the extent to which risk-based supervision and regulatory techniques such as meta-regulation in fact reflect a shortfall in our wider democratic culture.

2

Aligning risk and regulation: FSA's risk-based operating framework

Introduction

That financial markets are built around risk and uncertainty needs no further explanation.[1] At their core is the "identification, calculation, pricing and packaging of risk".[2] In January 2000 the Financial Services Authority (hereafter "FSA") announced that it was adopting risk as the driver for its "business". Risk, but specifically risk to its four statutory objectives, is now used as the trigger for all regulatory activity, including overall strategy and policy development.

With some notable exceptions[3] the principle of risk-based supervision in the financial services sector has attracted relatively little attention,

---

[1] See, e.g., P L Bernstein, *Against the Gods: The Remarkable Story of Risk* (John Wiley & Sons: New York, 1996).
[2] M de Goede, Repoliticizing Financial Risk, *Economy and Society*, 2004, 33(2), 197–217, at 197.
[3] J Black, The Emergence of Risk-based Regulation and the New Public Risk Management in the UK *Public Law*, 2005, 512–548; J Black, The Development of Risk

either from academics or practitioners, perhaps because the language of risk has always permeated this industry sector and therefore its adoption by the regulator considered unremarkable. In January 2000 the FSA outlined what it called its "new" approach to regulating UK financial services, namely one of risk-based supervision, with "risk" being the risk that the FSA will not achieve its regulatory objectives. Risk identification, assessment and risk management are to drive regulatory strategy. On the face of it, within the financial services sector, a central focus on risk is nothing new, some of the previous regulators replaced by the FSA had also begun to introduce risk-based regulation, primarily in response to significant regulatory failures such as the collapse of the Barings banking group, and the Maxwell pension fund scandals.[4] But what is new is that this approach is explicitly articulated as, and focused on, identifying and hence regulating for risks to the FSA's *own* objectives. In other words, risk in this context is not to be understood as risks to others (e.g. risks to the public from fraud or from a systemic loss of confidence) but risk to the FSA's statutory objectives (although the public benefit indirectly as these objectives include "securing an adequate level of consumer protection" and "maintenance of market confidence").

There is much published by the FSA itself on how it has developed and is applying this new risk-based regulatory framework.[5] But there has been little independent consideration of the framework in the light of the extensive academic literature introduced in Chapter 1 that exists examining the concept of risk, why it has come to occupy such a central focus in governmental and policy arenas, and how it becomes absorbed into societal norms and standards of conduct. However, the various

---

Based Regulation in Financial Services: Just 'Modelling Through', in J Black, M Lodge and M Thatcher (eds) *Regulatory Innovation: A Comparative Analysis* (Edward Elgar: Cheltenham, 2005); J Black, *The Development of Risk Based Regulation in Financial Services: Canada, the UK and Australia* (on file with the author).
[4] J Bagge, Senior Management Responsibilities Under the New Regulatory Regime, *Journal of Financial Regulation & Compliance*, 2000, 8(3), 209.
[5] FSA, *A New Regulator for the New Millennium*, February 2000; FSA, *Reasonable Expectations: Regulation in a Non-Zero Failure World*, September 2003; FSA, *Building the New Regulator: Progress Report 2*, February 2002; FSA, *The Firm Risk Assessment Framework* (FRAF), February 2003.

perspectives discussed in the introductory chapter suggest the need to explore more closely the reasons for the introduction of the risk-based regulation, how it is being constructed and implemented, and whose purposes are being served by its adoption. The focus of this chapter is not so much on the mechanics of risk assessment and management but, to borrow a phrase, on "what is being done in the name of risk"[6] specifically in the context of the regulated firm, and the consumer of financial services.

This chapter begins by examining the motivations behind the introduction by the FSA of the risk-to-objectives-based operating framework, in the light of the governance and risk society perspectives already discussed. It then briefly discusses how that risk-based framework is implemented, specifically in the context of the firm. In so doing, it will consider the extent to which the adoption of this framework can be understood as both an attempt to manage public and political expectations and establish boundaries of accountability, and to embed particular concepts of responsibility in the firm and senior management. This discussion will draw attention to the way in which the FSA seeks to enrol firms' own risk assessment and management tools into the service of the FSA, in order to reduce the perceived risks to its statutory objectives. It will suggest that while this strategy has advantages in that it allows the FSA to draw on the expertise of firms, there is also potential danger to the extent that it relies upon a shared understanding of risk. Finally, the chapter considers the implications of risk-based regulation for the private investor consumer, particularly in the context of the broader ideological shift from that of communal responsibility to one of "individual responsibility", and the extent to which they too are also being governed through the technology of risk.

Motivations for the introduction of a risk-to-objectives operating framework

It could be tempting to view the introduction of risk-based regulation in the financial services sector in isolation. Given that financial markets

---

[6]T Baker and J Simon, *Embracing Risk: The Changing Culture of Insurance and Responsibility* (University of Chicago: Chicago, 2002), p 18.

are predicated upon risk and uncertainty it is possible to see risk-based regulation as nothing more than an extension of established industry practices of risk assessment and risk management to the regulatory sphere, and therefore as largely unremarkable. Alternatively, it could be understood simply as an efficient response to resource constraints which necessitate a well-informed understanding of risks to allow for prioritisation of regulatory effort.

There is nothing in the legislation establishing the regulatory regime itself, the Financial Services and Markets Act 2000 ("FSMA 2000"), which explicitly or even implicitly requires the FSA to adopt a risk-based operating framework. Nor is there anything in the formal FSA documentation which provides an explanation of why this approach is used over others. However, as Black in her comprehensive study of the development of risk-based regulation in financial services notes,[7] the first Chairman of the FSA, Howard Davies, was appointed from his position as Deputy Governor of the Bank of England where he had been responsible for banking supervision. The Bank of England had recently developed a risk-based supervisory system in the wake of the Barings Bank collapse designed to provide an objective basis on which to determine strategic priorities. Other financial regulators, who were to be replaced by the FSA, had also used forms of risk assessment to prioritise supervision. However, all of those risk-based systems differed in a number of respects, including their level of sophistication. While the Bank of England's RATE risk assessment system was the most influential in the design of the FSA's framework, it was not a comprehensive risk assessment system in that it focused only on one particular type of risk – systemic risk to the UK banking. As Black identifies, none of these systems (nor the systems developed by overseas regulators) provided a model for the sophisticated comprehensive and strategic model developed by the FSA (named "ARROW").

Although not mandated by the legislation, nevertheless the adoption of a risk-based approach to regulation by the FSA had a number of particular advantages. The FSA represented an amalgamation of nine

---

[7] J Black, The Emergence of Risk-based Regulation, supra, n 3.

previous regulators operating in the financial services sector, with differing functions and powers, as well as different internal cultures that had to be quickly fused into one cohesive body. As Black has commented,[8] in the first instance, developing an appropriate culture for the FSA and a methodology of working became a major priority. Approaching this task from a risk-to-objectives perspective (identifying the threats to its objectives) presented the FSA with a neat way of managing that task. Additionally, the breadth of the FSA's four statutory objectives (maintaining confidence in the financial system; promoting public understanding of the financial system; securing the appropriate degree of protection for consumers; reducing financial crime[9]), and their potential to conflict,[10] made them difficult to implement at a practical level (how does a regulator "maintain public confidence in financial markets"?). For this reason Black notes that it was therefore easier both conceptually and operationally for the FSA to focus attention on the risks to those objectives rather than on how to achieve them. The adoption of a risk-to-objectives strategy was a means of trying to reconcile broad and potentially conflicting regulatory goals.

These were the pragmatic reasons behind the introduction of the FSA's risk-based operating framework. But it is also possible to understand the introduction of this framework in a broader context, namely as a response to greater uncertainty. That uncertainty was, and is, generated not only by the challenges in regulating in an increasingly complex and global financial environment, but also by public expectation that the regulator would clean up the industry, and by political demands for a safe but innovative and globally competitive industry. All these expectations are reflected in the FSA's four statutory objectives, and the underlying statutory principles of "good regulation" contained in section 2(3). Employing risk as its operating framework provides a basis on which to prioritise its activities (towards the greatest risks). It also provides a means to manage public and political expectations. Implicit in

---

[8]Ibid.
[9]Financial Services and Markets Act 2000, sections 3–6.
[10]M Taylor, *Twin Peaks: A Regulatory Structure for the New Century* (Centre for Study of Financial Innovation: London, 1995).

any risk-based regime with limited resources is that priority will be given to the greatest risks, but that not all risks will be addressed. The FSA has made this explicit: firms will be allowed to fail.[11] Risk arguably provides a seemingly objective, "scientific" and rational basis for allowing firms to fail and a means by which to justify regulatory action, or inaction[12] (though whether the public will accept this rationale as sufficient is another matter). But as well as providing an ex post justification for what might otherwise be perceived as regulatory failure, focusing on risks to its objectives also enables the FSA to establish a conceptual boundary around its regulatory role. This boundary effectively enables it to justify the exclusion or limitation of other, more contentious roles, such as that of regulating for distributive goals (arguably not otherwise excluded by its four statutory objectives from its remit). It can provide a neat intellectual basis on which to support a regulatory approach that does not prioritise distributive goals such as social inclusion in banking services.[13]

In implementing its framework the FSA has identified three potential sources of risk: the external environment (including political economic and legal factors), consumer and industry-wide developments, and firms. By focusing first and foremost on those risks to *its* objectives, the FSA has not only acknowledged the limits of its ability to control its external environment but engaged in what Giddens would call a form of reflexivity, actively looking inward in order to try to manage the risks to itself produced by the actions of others over which it has only limited control.[14] But if the adoption of a risk to objectives operating framework

---

[11] FSA, *Reasonable Expectations: Regulation in a Non-Zero Failure World*, September 2003.
[12] And as Black notes in "The Emergence of Risk-based Regulation" (supra, n 3), ARROW featured prominently in the FSA's submission to the Treasury Select Committee and was intended "to provide a defensible basis on which the FSA could answer critics and explain both the actions it took, and more importantly, the actions it did *not* take", at p 545, n 95.
[13] Although it must be acknowledged that the FSA is committed, in carrying out its regulatory responsibilities, to making a positive impact on financial inclusion, and is heavily involved in various financial literacy initiatives designed to encourage citizens to become more financially aware, see, e.g., speech by Callum McCarthy, *Addressing the Issue of Financial Inclusion*, 31/1/2005 at http://www.fsa.gov.uk/Pages/Library/Communication/Speeches/2005/sp225.shtml.
[14] Although in engaging in this reflexivity the FSA is relying on formal risk assessment techniques – techniques associated with a "modern" rather than a "reflexive" society that

is designed to manage public expectations and to establish boundaries of accountability, the design of the framework as it is applied to firms reveals a more normative purpose. This framework, together with FSA regulatory principles and rules, inevitably shapes firms' own internal risk assessment and risk management systems. In so doing, sites of responsibility and accountability are located at and within firms and certain norms of behaviour identified and fostered. As the following discussion seeks to illustrate, risk is being deployed strategically as a governance tool in an attempt to reinforce both firm and individual responsibility for risk. The discussion that follows unpicks the perceptions, attitudes and values implicit in this regulatory framework.

Risk-based supervision and the firm

Firms remain the key focus of regulatory activity and hence considerable attention is paid to identifying the risks-to-objectives that they might pose. As a part of the broader risk assessment process the FSA has developed a "common risk assessment framework" applicable to all firms based upon impact and probability measures. The outcome of this risk assessment process will primarily determine the level of regulatory supervision of individual firms. The starting point in this process is an assessment of the impact that a firm's failure or lapse of conduct will have on the FSA's objectives. This scoring process is based primarily on balance sheet information supplied by the firm and on this basis firms will be scored into one of four categories: low, medium-low, medium-high, high. In general, low impact firms will not be subject to a full risk assessment and will receive much less intensive monitoring.[15] In carrying out this impact assessment the FSA has established impact thresholds for the various regulated sectors such that, for example, a general

---

has come to question the foundations of science and technology including formal risk analysis. As such its approach could perhaps better be described as one of "reflectivity" rather than "reflexivity", see S Green, Negotiating the Future: The Culture of Modern Risk in Global Financial Markets, *Environment and Planning D, Society and Space*, 2000, Vol 18, 77–99.

[15]FSA, *Building the New Regulator: Progress Report 2*, February 2002, Appendix A; FSA, *Reasonable Expectations: Regulation in a Non-Zero Failure World*, September 2003, par 6.6–7.

insurer with a gross premium income of less than £10m will be scored as low impact and therefore low risk.[16] These thresholds, however, are not based upon the application of any independent technical standard, rather they represent value judgements by the FSA (and its judgement alone) about its risk tolerance. As Black identifies, they are effectively the FSA's definition of when a problem becomes important.[17] Firms scored as low impact will receive only baseline monitoring by the FSA, based upon routine sampling of returns and notifications (although they may also receive onsite visits as part of any sector-wide "thematic review"[18]), and will not be subject to any risk mitigation programme.[19] Firms scored above "low impact" will receive a full risk assessment involving a probability assessment. This assessment will focus on assessing the probability of business or control failures occurring within the firm.

Firms are scored by the relevant FSA supervisory staff against a large number of risk elements (currently 45) using detailed assessment criteria. These scores are then aggregated, using an IT package, to produce a risk score for the firm against the seven groups of risks the FSA has identified as constituting the major risks to its objectives.[20] Once the scoring process is complete firms will receive an aggregate score of low, medium-low, medium-high and high risk, and the FSA will then develop a risk mitigation programme for the firm commensurate with this score.[21]

Despite being labelled an impact x probability assessment, the FSA has acknowledged that this assessment is not a scientific process based upon quantitative measures but is based upon qualitative judgement.[22] Recognising perhaps the potential for risk scores to be challenged by

---

[16]FSA, FRAF, supra, Annex 2, n 5.
[17]J Black, The Emergence of Risk-based Regulation, supra, p 547, n 3.
[18]In 2005/06 this thematic work will focus on five areas: conflicts of interest, corporate governance, business continuity, stress testing and market abuse – per FSA Business Plan 2005/06.
[19]FSA, FRAF, supra, para 1.2, n 5.
[20]See FSA, FRAF, supra, n 5, for the seven risk to objective groups, and Annexes 4 and 5 for scoring matrix and summary.
[21]For a full discussion of the firm risk assessment framework see J Black, The Emergence of Risk-based Regulation, supra, n 3.
[22]Per telephone interview with FSA, March 2005.

firms, particularly when issues of judgement (and hence uncertainty) are involved, the scoring process itself is not revealed to firms, only the final scores. Firms receive a letter setting out the FSA's views of the risks posed by the firm, including the impact x probability scores as well as key findings that support those scores where they lead to a probability score of high or medium-high. While firms can identify any factual inaccuracies, the scoring process itself is not open to negotiation.[23]

The role of operational risk

Included in the broad category of "business risks" against which firms will be scored is "operational risk" – the risk of direct or indirect loss resulting from inadequate or failed internal processes, peoples or systems and from external events.[24] As Power states in his discussion of the genesis of operational risk,[25] operational risk has emerged only since the mid to late 1990s as a key component of risk regulation. Previously it was primarily a residual category for risks and uncertainties that were difficult to quantify, measure and insure against. The recent formalisation of operational risk as a central component of banking regulation (particularly in the light of the second Basel Capital Accord[26]) has been heavily contested, primarily around issues of definition, data collection, and the limits to its quantification.

---

[23]FSA, *FRAF*, supra, n 5.
[24]FSA, *FRAF*, supra, Annex 3, n 5.
[25]M Power, *The Invention of Operational Risk* ESRC Centre for Analysis of Risk and Regulation, Discussion Paper 16, June 2003 (CARR: London, 2003).
[26]Basel Committee on Banking Supervision: *International Convergence of Capital Measurement and Capital Standards: A Revised Framework*, Basel II Capital Accord, (www.bis.org). In the context of this Accord operational risk has emerged as an issue only because of technological and structural changes in the banking industry that have globalised aspects of the banking industry (including e-commerce and outsourcing) and are believed therefore to have increased the potential for such risk to arise, see BIS, *Working Paper on the Regulatory Treatment of Operational Risk*, September 2001, available at http://www.bis.org/publ/bcbs_wp8.htm. Organisational risk can be understood in this sense as a modern and global "manufactured" risk of the sort identified by Beck and Giddens.

Power suggests that the emergence of "operational risk" has been as much about a desire to establish certain norms of behaviour – such as embedding managerial responsibility – as it has been about the emergence of any new form of risk. Operational risk has been identified as "an agenda-forming category, whose success lies as much in the catalytic visibility of the issue, as in the details of its implementation".[27] This category is made more visible through the marshalling in support of such paradigm examples as the Barings banking group collapse. In other words, Power suggests that "operational risk" is a way of constructing reality so as to make it amenable to a particular role. Defining a set of problems or issues in terms of "operational risk" provides a new way of problematising issues that in turn provides a new way of intervening in the firm. It enables "the management of operational risk and good corporate governance to connect in such a way as to position . . . 'old' risks [of fraud, legal liability, business disruption and other similar issues] in a new space of regulatory, political and social expectations".[28] At the same time, constructing the collapse of the Barings banking group as a failure of internal management and supervision systems, rather than, for example, as a problem of market structure,[29] has provided a means of re-enforcing and institutionalising this connection. It provides a means of reinforcing firms' responsibilities for mitigating "old" risks, risks that

---

[27]M Power, supra, p 1, n 25.

[28]Power, supra, p 2, n 25.

[29]For a subtle alternative perspective, which points to systemic failures as well as attitudes to, and risks associated with, trading derivatives as contributory causes, see A Tickell, Making a Melodrama out of a Crisis: Reinterpreting the Collapse of Barings Bank, *Environment and Planning D: Society and Space*, 1996, Vol 14, pp 5–33. More generally, for a disscussion of derivatives and their risks see, e.g., B Holzer and Y Millo, *From Risks to Second Order Dangers in Financial Markets: The Unintended Consequences of Risk Management Systems*, ESRC Centre for Analysis of Risk and Regulation Paper 29 (CARR: London, November 2004), who suggest that social and technical connectivities have the potential to heighten the risks associated with derivates. See also D MacKenzie, Globalization, Efficient Markets and Arbitrage, prepared for ESRC/SSRC Colloquium, *Money and Migration after Globalization*, St Hugh's College, University of Oxford, 25–28 March 2004 available at: http://www.sociology.ed.ac.uk/Research/Staff/Mackglobearb-7.pdf.

were they to materialise, would inevitably impact upon regulatory objectives and perceptions of effective regulation.

Risk-based supervision and the alignment of firms' risk management

This inclusion of operating risk as a risk scoring category articulates closely with other aspects of the regulatory regime, namely the statutory requirement that firms have in place appropriate risk management systems as a condition of initial and continued authorisation by the FSA.[30] In addition, binding principles and rules made by the FSA require that firms take reasonable care to control their affairs responsibly and effectively with adequate risk management systems and the requirement to identify appropriate senior management to oversee the establishment of systems and controls, and to ensure rule compliance.[31] Breach may lead to disciplinary action against the firm, while a failure of senior managers to undertake their supervisory roles can result in the imposition of personal financial penalties. Specifically the regulatory framework is designed such that both the firm and senior managers have responsibilities for the design of, as well as compliance with, appropriate internal risk management strategies. The combined effect of the FSA's common risk assessment framework, together with the regulatory requirements that firms have in place their own internal risk management systems, is likely to ensure a degree of convergence between the FSA's risk-based strategy and the risk management practices of the firms themselves.

Firms' own risk management practices will inevitably be influenced by knowledge of the FSA's risk assessment framework, including the "risk elements" the FSA has identified as potential threats posed by firms to its objectives. Indirectly (or perhaps directly, as the FSA retains the last word on the adequacy of design and implementation) firms' policies and practices in relation to risk assessment and risk management are

---

[30]FSMA 2000, Schedule 6, and see further the discussion in Chapter 3 see text accompanying n 19.
[31]FSA Handbook, *High Level Principles for Business*, Principle 3.

likely to be aligned closely with the risks identified in that common risk assessment framework. Otherwise firms risk facing a higher risk score, and consequently greater supervisory intervention by the FSA.[32] The FSA's common risk assessment framework, by which is assessed the risks posed by firms, including operational risk, together with the various requirements imposed on firms to design and implement sound risk assessment and management systems, is an attempt to harness firms' risk management tools directly into the service of the FSA's own risk-to-objectives regulatory strategy.

Meta-risk regulation

Regulation is often conceived of as constituted by command and control strategies whereby the regulator imposes detailed rules and monitors compliance therewith. In contrast, this type of supervisory strategy, identified as "meta risk regulation",[33] draws firms into regulatory processes and seeks to both influence and make use of firms internal risk management and control strategies. Supervision then becomes not so much about the simple monitoring of firms' compliance with regulatory rules, but more about evaluating and monitoring firms' awareness of the risks created by their business and of their internal controls. As Braithwaite explains,[34] meta-risk regulation involves more than the regulator simply becoming more analytical about the risks it must confront; rather

---

[32] In Policy Statement 142, *Building a Framework for Operational Risk Management* (FSA Policy Statement 142) at par 1.5 the FSA note an increasing convergence between the FSA's operational risk methods and the tools used by firms, with emerging practice consistent with the (then) draft PRU 6.1 Guidance.

[33] C Parker, *The Open Corporation: Effective Self-Regulation and Democracy* (Cambridge University Press: Cambridge, 2002), J Braithwaite, Meta Risk Management and Responsive Regulation for Tax System Integrity, *Law and Policy*, January 2003, 1–16. Braithwaite identifies the Three Mile Island near-nuclear meltdown of 1979 as one of the earliest examples of meta risk regulation. He explains one of the causes of that near-meltdown being that plant operators had focused on following rules, rather than on strategic planning. When an emergency arose that was not covered by the rules, operators were unable to cope. As a result, regulatory focus shifted from rule compliance to scrutiny of operators' risk management systems.

[34] Ibid.

it involves seeking to remake the risk management systems of the firms it regulates. "Meta risk regulation" is about the risk management of risk management, and being able to harness firms' own internal risk management systems to achieve regulatory objectives. Thus the focus of the FSA common risk assessment framework is less about assessing rule compliance and more about assessing the adequacy of firms' own risk management practices. In this way, firms are not simply passive recipients *of* risk-based regulation, but are "enrolled" to become active participants *in* it, as their internal systems are shaped, monitored and assessed in order to reduce the risks to the FSA.[35] The Basel II Capital Accord provides another clear example of the operation of meta regulation in that bank capitalisation will not be imposed externally, by regulators, but will be determined by a bank's own internal risk management models, provided these models are judged by regulators to be adequate.

The "risks" of meta-risk regulation?

The FSA has stated that firms who demonstrate a strong management and compliance culture will be rewarded with a "lighter regulatory touch". While one may question whether this would be the case with "large impact" firms, one major advantage of meta-risk regulation is that it should enable the FSA to draw upon the expertise of the industry in an era when the complexity and volatility of modern financial risk call into question the ability of financial regulators to stay one step ahead. For example, banking regulators lack the time and expertise to enable them to effectively evaluate the risk position of large and complex banks. This has prompted the Basel Committee on Banking Supervision (BCBS) to accept that it will allow regulators to rely on banks' own internal risk assessment models in setting bank regulatory capital.[36]

De Goede explains that the Bank of International Settlements first began to encourage the use of risk management models in the mid 1990s

---

[35]Black provides an insightful analysis of enrolment in the financial services context in J Black, *Mapping the Contours of Contemporary Financial Services Regulation* CARR Discussion Paper No 17, 2003.

[36]M de Goede, supra, n 2.

in order to comprehend the risk associated with derivatives. In doing so, it emphasised that qualitative as well as quantitative judgements had to be made; "getting the numbers right is both a science and an art – and it is critical".[37] However, in response to industry resistance to the inclusion of non-quantitative risk factors in the proposed revised Capital Accord, particularly operational risk, the BCBS has shown increasing commitment to the use of quantitative, rather than qualitative measures. In so doing, de Goede argues that regulators will be validating mathematical models used increasingly and routinely by banks as the basis for decision-making, but which are contested as they "entail a legitimation of the normative assumptions concerning nature, time and calculability that are rarely made explicit in financial discourse". These models are attractive to the industry because of the "simplicity of the single risk figure", and their commercial potential to turn future uncertainty into marketable risk, but as de Goede explains, "while pretending to eradicate uncertainty from business ventures, finance identifies and invents more and more possible uncertainties to be hedged".[38] In other words, while "operational risk" is marshalled by regulators to fulfil a particular role in embedding internal management and supervision systems, the industry is potentially undermining that role through its attempts to simplify and repackage risk for commercial purposes.

It is also a truism to say that mathematical risk models only measure what they measure. Power points to the danger that in relying on mathematical models, the extent of the ability to risk models becomes the determinant of what constitutes risk. This he describes as a case of the tail wagging the dog.[38a] In other words what cannot be measured will not be measured. Permitting or encouraging firms to rely on risk modelling systems has the potential to downgrade the value of human expertise and judgement, while at the same time providing a false sense of confidence, leading in turn to greater, rather than less exposure.[39] While

---

[37]Laurence Meyer, US Federal Reserve Governor and BIS member, in a 2000 speech, quoted in de Goede, supra p 211, n 2.

[38]Supra, p 213, n 2.

[38a]Supra, p 12, n 25.

[39]Enron, LTCM and Barings Bank all used VAR risk models. Partnoy reports that just two days before Barings Bank lost $1.4 billion through the Leeson trades, the VAR

Basel II builds in a second pillar of a supervisory review process that requires regulators to ensure the soundness of banks' internal risk rating processes and should provide some checks against poor risk modelling systems, it has been suggested that there is scope for bank "gaming and manipulation" of ratings, as regulators, at best, have information that is no better than that of banks, while banks on the other hand have access to private risk-relevant information that can be excluded from the rating system presented to regulators.[40]

There are other potential dangers inherent in meta-risk regulation. Rather than directly imposing detailed procedural requirements on firms as to the design of their internal risk assessment and management strategies, meta-risk management seeks to leverage off firms' own systems and expertise, in aid of reducing the risks to the FSA's objectives. To be successful suggests the need for a shared understanding of, and culture towards, risk. For the FSA, risk is perceived of as threats to its objectives and hence something to be guarded against. For the industry on the other hand, risk (including uncertainty) represents opportunity and is something to be grasped and exploited. Firms' internal risk assessment and management systems are geared towards the firms' commercial (entrepreneurial) purposes, to providing firms with a competitive edge through maximising the opportunities presented by "risky" business.

At the same time, in the 2003 FSA review of UK insurers' risk management practices the FSA reported that many insurers had defined risk management systems more for the purpose of meeting FSA Guidance than delivering effective risk management and regarded risk management practices as compliance processes rather than as a core business process.[41] Of course uncritical and mechanistic compliance by firms is not an issue specific to meta regulation but can also arise in relation to, for example, command and control-style regulation. One of the perceived advantages of meta-risk regulation, however, is its ability to

for Leeson's portfolio was listed as "zero". F Partnoy, *Infectious Greed* (Profile Books: London, 2004), p 243.

[40] H Benink and C Wihlborg, The New Basel Capital Accord: Making it Effective with Stronger Market Discipline, *European Financial Management*, 2002, 8, 103–115.

[41] FSA, *Review of UK Insurers Risk Management Practices*, October 2003. Available at: http://www.fsa.gov.uk/pubs/other/review_ins_risk.pdf.

shape, but not constrain, internal systems and processes. Black sounds a cautionary note when she suggests that the differences in objectives between the FSA and firms have already posed problems in the implementation of the common risk assessment framework and the ability of firms to understand the assessment given to it, leading her to conclude that "Whilst proponents of meta-regulation are correct to argue that its strength lies in the ability to leverage off firms' own systems of internal control, ... this difference in objectives means that regulators can never rely on firms' own systems without some modification."[42] In other words, the differences between regulatory and firms' own objectives suggest that it may be difficult to ever fully harness firms' own expertise. Insurers, for example, "speculate and gamble", they "thrive on uncertainty". For them, risk has investment potential:

> Insurers make decisions in conditions of uncertainty as a daily routine. Scientific data on risk is variously absent, inadequate, controversial, contradictory and ignored. Insurers impose meaning on uncertainty through non-scientific forms of knowledge that are intuitive, emotional, aesthetic, moral and speculative. Of course the nature of uncertainty and the response to it varies substantially across various types of threat. Insurers confront real empirical variation in these types that is not simply reducible to their own science of actuarialism, technologies, and organisational practices. Insurance is a highly diverse and adaptable industry, with multiple logics and capacities for addressing threats and the limits of their knowledge about them.[43]

An issue must be the extent to which these non-scientific forms of knowledge can ever be fully amenable to risk management systems. It may be that the FSA would have no difficulty about firms grasping opportunities and the risks they carry provided first the firm understands the nature and extent of the risk; second, appropriate precautionary measures were in place to mitigate its impact should the risk materialise; and, third, the risk is "low impact". But risk management ultimately skewed towards controlling threats to regulatory objectives may be anathema to the very uncertainty and creativity that underpin this

---

[42]J. Black, The Emergence of Risk-based Regulation, supra, p 545, n 3.
[43]R V Ericson and A Doyle, Catastrophe Risk, Insurance and Terrorism, *Economy and Society*, 2004, 33(2), 135–173, at 138.

form of decision-making, and reflect the existence of a different culture towards risk than that of the FSA.

The existence of different cultures towards risk, and their implications for risk policy and management, have been explored by the work of cultural theorists.[44] Culture, like risk, is a contested concept. It can be broadly understood in this context as a set of shared understandings which make it possible for groups of people to act together, or as "a contested process of meaning making".[45] Different cultures can exist in a multiplicity of contexts, including within political and regulatory communities, within bureaucracies, and within social groups and organisations, and these cultures will influence perceptions of, and attitudes towards, risk. An influential and distinctive epistemology of risk is offered by the cultural theorists, primarily centred on the grid/group theory developed Mary Douglas,[46] to explain why, and how, different

---

[44]See, for example, M Douglas and A Widlavsky (1982) *Risk and Culture: An Essay on the Selection of Technological and Environmental Dangers* (University of California Press: Berkeley, 1982); M Douglas, *Risk and Blame: Essays in Cultural Theory* (Routledge: London, 1992); M Schwartz and M Thompson, *Divided We Stand: Redefining Politics, Technology and Social Choice* (Harvester Wheatsheaf: Hemel Hempstead, 1992); M Thompson, R Ellis and A Wildavsky, *Cultural Theory* (Westview Press: Boulder Colorado, 1990). For a discussion of the theoretical roots and development of cultural theory see J Tansey and T O'Riordan, Cultural Theory and Risk: A Review, *Health, Risk and Society*, 1999, 1, 70. See also J Lupton, *Risk* (Routledge: London, 1999); S Raynor, Cultural Theory and Risk Analysis, in S Krimsky and D Golding (eds) *Social Theories of Risk* (Praeger Publishers: Connecticut, 1992). For a critique of cultural theory see, e.g., C Lockhart and R Coughlin, Building Better Comparative Social Theory through Alternative Conceptions of Reality, *Western Political Quarterly*, 1992, 793.

[45]S Wright, The Politicisation of Culture, *Anthropology Today*, 1998, 14(1), 7–15 – quoted in C Hall, C Scott and C Hood, *Telecommunications Regulation: Culture, Chaos and Interdependence Inside the Regulatory Process* (Routledge: London, 2000). Concerns that "culture" gets reified and so very static have led to refinements in the concept – for example, Watson suggests culture is a set of ideas, reactions, and expectations that is constantly changing as people and groups themselves change, J L Watson, *Golden Arches East: MacDonald's in the East* (Stanford University Press: Stanford, 1997, p 8). However, the concept of "culture" is contested and there is no single accepted definition. For a discussion see, for example, R Wuthnow, J D Hunter, A Bergesen and E Kurzwell, *Cultural Analysis: The Work of Peter L Berger, Mary Douglas, Michel Foucault and Jurgen Habermas* (Routledge & Kegan Paul: Boston, 1984).

[46]M Douglas, *Cultural Bias* (Occasional Paper 35, London, Royal Anthropological Institute, 1978).

individuals, groups and organisations might perceive risk differently. To explain briefly: in grid/group theory, the term *group* refers to the degree to which an individual is incorporated into social groups. *High group*, then, denotes a high degree of incorporation with the result that more individual choice is subject to group determination. The term *grid* refers to the degree to which an individual's life is subject to external constraints, so *high grid* denotes the greater presence of external prescriptions and hence more limited opportunity for individual negotiation.[47]

Cultural theorists like Douglas have identified the existence of shared interpretational frameworks that enable communities, organisations, groups and individuals to make sense of their social and natural environments. They have also identified the presence of order and pattern in risk-taking behaviour and in the beliefs and biases that underpin it.[48] Specifically, cultural theorists have identified four cultural belief patterns:[49] hierarchists (high grid and high group); egalitarians (low grid and high group); individualists (low grid and low group); and fatalists (high grid and low group).[50] While these typologies are not necessarily immutable or their validity uncontested, cultural theorists would nevertheless argue that individuals are predisposed to one of these typologies in given contexts. In spite of the fact that it may appear at first site to be overly deterministic,[51] the strength of cultural theory is that it offers a theoretical framework through which to analyse why different individuals, groups, organisations and institutions can approach the issue of risk from quite different perspectives.[52] It focuses not so much on the

---

[47]M Thompson, R Ellis and A Wildavsky, supra, n 44.

[48]It is this focus on preference formation that is said to distinguish cultural theory from public choice theories, which focus on preference realisation: M Thompson, R Ellis and A Wildavsky, supra, n 44.

[49]Subsequently refined by J Adams, *Risk* (UCL Press: London, 1995) as "typologies of bias".

[50]In fact subsequently extended by M Thompson, R Ellis and A Wildavsky, supra, n 44, to five – to include the "hermit".

[51]On this point see S Rayner, Cultural Theory and Risk Analysis, in S Krimsky and D Golding, supra, n 44.

[52]While organisational self-interest is not denied in explaining institutional attitudes and responses to risk, cultural theorists would suggest that cultural orientation will

formal structures of, and within, organisations, but on the identification of cultural subgroups that can exist within a group, organisation or
institution and which can cut across formal structures.[53]

In a recent study by Coulson,[54] cultural theory was applied to analyse
the implementation of a centrally developed environmental risk policy
by lending groups within a recently merged major UK bank. In this
bank the environmental policy and procedures were produced by policymakers in a specialist unit responsible for their development. The
main purpose of the policy and procedures was to protect the bank
from liability for environmental damage caused by its borrowers. The
policy and procedures were produced in a handbook and disseminated
to all staff with lending responsibilities within the bank. Grid/group
typology suggests that banks should typically be "hierarchist" organisations, with high grid and high group characteristics in which a high
respect for authority and behaviour closely conforming to bank norms
could be expected. Coulson found, however, that the detailed structure and formality of environmental risk assessment in different sections of the bank varied according to the social relations and cultural
bias displayed within those sections, biases which largely conformed
to the four typologies. For example, she found there existed a group
of individual lenders within the bank (mostly formerly from the larger
pre-merger bank) who considered themselves to be among the elite
group of expert lenders. Members of this group believed they had already proved their lending skill and acumen and so viewed the environmental risk policy and procedures as largely irrelevant to them, basing
their lending decisions instead on the potential for economic gain. This
group displayed the characteristics of "individualists", while members
of traditional local or regional teams on the other hand often displayed
"hierarchist" characteristics in that they were heavily role dependent,

---

shape the style and content of that response. See Raynor in S Krimsky and D Golding,
supra, n 44.

[53] A major challenge for cultural theory remains to identify the different ways of organising – i.e. to identify the cultural boundaries.

[54] A B Coulson, *Environmental Risk Perceptions of Bank Sub-cultures*, Working Paper,
Dept of Accountancy & Finance, University of Strathclyde, 2003.

and formal compliance with the policy was virtually axiomatic, and mechanistic.[55]

Cultural theory suggests then that perceptions of risk, and responses to risk management strategies, are closely related to internal cultures that exist within an organisation. This insight, while perhaps not particularly startling to those who have worked in larger firms or organisations, does suggest that, no matter how strong the commitment to risk management "from the top", there exists a potential for formal strategies to be compromised through the existence of plural rationalities for risk management which reflect very different perceptions of risk and which are shaped independently of formal structures and policies.[56] Cultural theory thus provides an alternative framework through which to anticipate the impact of risk management policies and strategies within firms and cautions against expectations of uniform "buy-ins" to compliance culture or to hasty attributions of blame for compliance failures, despite a shift from command and control structures to meta regulation and regulatory enrolment.

The implications of cultural theory are not limited to firms. For just as firms may be the site of different perceptions of risk, so too may regulators. The FSA is an amalgamation of a number of existing regulators and staff from those regulators were transferred to the FSA in 1998; some from the Civil Service, some from the self-regulatory organisations set up under the Financial Services Act 1986, some from the insurance companies supervisory division of the DTI, and some from the Bank of England. The FSA was acutely aware of the need to develop a common culture across its whole organisation and it was clear that some of those previous regulators had very different attitudes towards risk and regulation. For example, the Securities and Investment Board ("SIB") and the self-regulatory organisations ("SROs") focused primarily on risk to individual investors (a micro approach), through their being tasked

---

[55]For a further study into culture and regulation, see C Hall, H Scott and C Hood, supra, n 45.

[56]Hall, Scott and Hood in their study of telecommunications regulation suggest that organisational structures – sometimes in tension with each other – shape what and how issues are perceived, defining meanings and cognitive boundaries and keeping rival attitudes and beliefs in tension and mediating change, supra, p 199, n 45.

with investor protection. The Bank of England, in contrast, focused on (macro) systemic risk, depositor protection being addressed as an afterthought in that if depositors lost money they could obtain redress through the depositor protection scheme.[57] Regulatory cultural differences were also reflected in the differing approaches to rule-making: the SIB and the SROs first asked "what is the right outcome?" and then devised the rule to produce that outcome; civil servants on the other hand devised their rules with one eye towards their justiciability (i.e. their ability to withstand legal challenge).[58]

The FSA's risk to objectives supervisory framework (the ARROW framework) is implemented by different sections within the FSA. Initially the risk assessment of firms was carried out by sectoral divisions within the FSA; insurance firms by the Insurance Division; banks by the Banking Division, etc. This internal structure was subsequently revised and cross-sectoral sections established (including Major Retail Groups, Retail Firms and Wholesale Firms[59]) incorporating staff from across all of the sectoral divisions.[60] It appears to remain the case, however, that within those cross-sectoral divisions multisectoral teams are not the norm.[61] Hence a large bank is, for example, likely to be risk assessed and supervised by a team consisting of ex-Bank of England staff, providing the opportunity for cultural legacies to persist.[62] However, risk assessments conducted by teams are subject to review within the

---

[57] As initially established under the Banking Act 1979. In a sense this macro approach is mirrored in the ARROW philosophy under which customers of not very well managed or capitalised small firms ("low impact") are considerably more at risk than customers of larger, higher risk (in FSA terms) firms.

[58] Per former senior member of the policy directorate of SIB.

[59] See FSA Organization Chart, available online at: http://www.fsa.gov.uk/pages/about/who/management/who/pdf/orgchart.pdf.

[60] The authors understand that both the ARROW framework and the internal implementation arrangements are currently under review by the FSA.

[61] Telephone interview with FSA senior staff member, April 2005.

[62] In the 2002 Financial Services Practitioner Panel's survey of regulated firms it was reported, in the context of FSA supervisory visits, that while some FSA staff were pragmatic and less rule book oriented, other FSA staff were too checklist oriented (p 81). In the 2004 survey, concerns were expressed over the consistency of application, and variable quality, of FSA staff in relation to supervision and the provision of guidance. Available at http://www.fs-pp.org.uk/surveys_regfirms.html.

sections (the process itself is dependent on the risk category of the firm). At the same time the FSA has addressed the issue of internal consistency by setting up the Regulatory Strategy and Risk Division whose responsibility it is, among others, to monitor the implementation of assessments across divisions and to disseminate good practice etc.[63] But as Rothstein has observed, regulation regimes that comprise multiple components will have their own "microcultures", and these cultures mediate the understanding and attention given to different risk issues. Regulators need to be aware of the potential for what Rothstein describes as systems of "group think" and "ways of working" that can lead to a process of institutional attenuation whereby perceptions of risk are shaped by social and intuitional processes, contributing to ineffective monitoring and enforcement.[64] The Coulson study found that in devolving bank risk policy down to local level the manner in which policy was implemented depended on its interpretation at local level. That in turn was influenced in turn by local subcultures. This may be particularly pertinent in the case of large organisations, including regulators, where policies and strategies are devised a number of steps removed from those responsible for implementation.

In summary, the design of the FSA's risk-based operating framework for supervision aims to give effect to the FSA's regulatory objectives by harnessing firms' internal systems and controls. In other words, this framework constitutes a technology of governance through which firms, as well as individuals within them, are encouraged to develop an active concept of senior management responsibility, and hence accountability, supported in turn by "technologies of performance" that "audit" performance against outcomes determined by the regulator. Despite the illusion of control suggested by the formal risk assessment process, that process represents perceptions of risk (or perhaps more properly "uncertainty") and of values that may well be in conflict and tension with the perceptions, values and cultures prevalent within the regulated

---

[63] See FSA, *Annual Report 2004–5*, par 114.
[64] H Rothstein, *Neglected Risk Regulation: The Institutional Attenuation Phenomenon*, CARR Discussion Paper 7, 2002, p 2. See also C Hood, H Rothstein and R Baldwin, *The Government of Risk: Understanding Risk Regulation Regimes* (OUP: Oxford, 2001).

community. These may, as a result, work against the specific policies and strategies employed by the regulator to mitigate the risk to its objectives, such as those strategies directed at deepening the control and compliance functions of senior management. The effects and impact of these policies and strategies are explored in subsequent chapters.

The risk-based regulatory framework and consumers

Just as risk is deployed as a technology of governance in relation to firms, so too it is clear that it is also being employed as such in relation to consumers, and particularly the private citizen consumer[65] of financial services. Through the implementation of its "consumer protection" and "public awareness" objectives, the FSA is attempting to recast citizens as proactive and risk-aware consumers of financial services and products, who seek the opportunity to secure their financial future through participation in financial markets, and who accept responsibility for the results of the choices they make.

The need for consumer protection is a principal justification for financial regulation.[66] At first glance the specific statutory objective to achieve "an appropriate degree of protection for the consumer" suggests that the regulator should take a proactive, protectionist role, similar to that taken by other regulators such as the Food Standards Agency, or Health and Safety Executive, in order to protect consumers from the harmful effects of activities or industries over which they have little knowledge or control. However, this statutory objective is underpinned by the statutory principles that require the FSA to recognise the differing degrees of risk involved in different types of transactions; the differing

---

[65]Consumer has a specific statutory meaning under the FSMS, s 138(7). It includes any persons who use, have used, or are or may be using, any of the services provided by authorised persons or appointed representatives, and as such, can include market counterparties as well as private retail investors. It is clear, however, that predominant focus of regulatory activity is on the private investor consumer and this discussion is limited to that group of consumers.

[66]See H Davies, *Why Regulate?*, speech of 4 November 1998, available at http://www.fsa. gov.uk/Pages/Library/Communication/Speeches/1998/sp19.shtml.

degrees of experience and expertise that different consumers may have; the need of consumers for advice and information; as well as the general principle that consumers should take responsibility for their own decisions ("caveat emptor").[67] In other words, these principles point to the need for a nuanced approach to consumer protection, balancing consumer protection with a market-oriented approach to regulation that recognises caveat emptor.

The FSA has identified four principal risks that consumers may face: prudential risk; bad faith risk; complexity/unsuitability risk; and performance risk. The FSA has stated that "it has a role to play in identifying and reducing prudential risk, bad faith risk and some aspects of the complexity/unsuitability risk. It is not the FSA's responsibility to protect consumers from performance risk [the risk that investments do not deliver hoped-for returns] . . . providing the firm recommending the product has explained to the consumer the risks involved."[68] Furthermore, the FSA has made it clear that in pursuing a risk-to-objectives approach it will not guarantee a zero-failure regime (firms will be allowed to fail with resultant consumer loss). Its policy and other public documents are replete with references to the need for consumers to accept personal responsibility for their financial security and for the choices they make to achieve it, saying, "[t]he level of protection provided [against these risks] will depend on the sophistication of the consumer . . . [i]t will also reflect the needs that consumers have for advice and information, and the general principle that consumers should take responsibility for their decisions".[69] That consumers are required to accept personal responsibility for their investment decisions is especially significant in the case of low-impact firms, which are subject to baseline monitoring only, even though they might otherwise represent a high probability of failure or misconduct.[70]

---

[67]FSMA 2000, s 5(2)(a)–(d).
[68]FSA, *A New Regulator for the New Millennium*, January 2000, para 12.
[69]Ibid., para 13.
[70]Consumers will of course have access to any relevant legal or regulatory remedies, but on an ex post basis. Ex ante monitoring and supervision, which might have prevented any loss in the first place, will not be the norm.

But while FSA policy might, on the face of it, seem to represent almost an abandonment of the consumer to market forces, analysis of the activities the FSA carries out under both its "public awareness" and "consumer protection" statutory objectives establishes that this is far from the case. What that policy does reveal, however, is a commitment to a specific model of the consumer. Under this model, consumers, including the private citizen consumer, are to become risk regulators in their own right. In so becoming, the FSA believe not only will they reduce the risks to themselves of bad investments, but will also reduce the risk to the FSA's regulatory objectives. Moreover, in reducing these risks, the FSA has indicated this will reduce the need for external regulation of firms. Consumers, as well as firms, are being enrolled into the regulatory task.[71]

Implementation of the consumer protection and consumer awareness objectives

The FSA has identified two main components to its public awareness objective – improving consumer financial literacy and improving the quality of information and advice to consumers. To this end it has devoted considerable effort to developing consumer education and guidance campaigns; in researching consumer decision-making; in developing comparative financial product tables; and in developing disclosure regimes.

In September 2003 the FSA set up a taskforce designed to "significantly raise consumers' capacity and confidence in dealing with financial products".[71a] While these various disclosure and education campaigns can be understood simply in the "market failure" context, as correcting information symmetry and inequality of bargaining power (giving consumers information they want, but cannot readily access in the market),

---

[71]"If capable consumers acting collectively can be a more influential force in the market there could be a consequently less rigorous regulatory regime." Per J Tiner (FSA Chief Executive) Mansion House Speech, September 2003, available at http://www.fsa.gov.uk/Pages/Library/Communication/Speeches/2003/sp152.shtml.
[71a]See www.fsa.gov.uk/financial_capability.

an analysis of FSA research and published papers on these compaigns (of which there are very many) suggest that their underlying purpose is normative – it is not about giving consumers what they want but find difficult to obtain in the market, it is about what consumers *should* want. In other words it is about modelling consumer behaviour towards the acceptance of a particular set of values. These values include the benefits of investing in markets (a theme taken up further in Chapter 6) but also that individuals are ultimately best placed to manage risk. To this end market-based mechanisms such as information disclosure are being deployed to develop in consumers what the FSA believes to be the appropriate skills and values of rational, risk aware and accountable market actors, who can, through their consumption choices, discipline the market against excessive risk-taking.

Consumer perceptions of risk

As part of this process the FSA has commissioned research into consumers' understanding of risk,[72] and has devoted considerable effort to designing information such as "key features/key facts" documents that will give consumers a better understanding of the features and risks associated with investment decisions.[73] What this and other research reveals, however, is that consumers may perceive risk differently from regulators. This has implications for the ability of the regulator to successfully enrol consumers into its risk-to-objectives regulatory process.

While the FSA has identified four principal risks that consumers may face in their financial affairs, research commissioned by the National Consumer Council (NCC) into consumer perspectives on the risks to retirement income identified additional types of risk facing consumers in their investment decisions, including not only complexity and suitability risk but also advice risk, public policy risks, inflation risks and the

---

[72] See, e.g., *Consumer Understanding of Financial Risk*, FSA Consumer Research 33, 2004.
[73] See, e.g., FSA website *Consumer Information: Learn Online – Risk*. Available at http://www.fsa.gov.uk/consumer/11_LEARN/shopping_around/mn_alp_shopping_intro.html.

risks of not investing or saving enough.[74] The complexity of these risks means that risk management by consumers involves risk trade-offs. A consumer decision to save via a deposit account will reduce exposure to investment risk but increase the risk of insufficient retirement savings. Similarly investment in the newer "stakeholder" suite of regulated products might decrease exposure to investment risk, but increase suitability risks where the product is sold without regulated advice. Furthermore, the research revealed that the way consumers approach risks in relation to their retirement income is influenced by their age, personality, gender as well as external influences and perceptions of the nature of risk and its outcomes.

The FSA's own research has revealed that the current disclosure regime through which consumers must be given a "Key Features" (or "Key Facts") document prior to purchase containing a risk warning actually provides consumers with little to assist them to identify what those risks might be, or to understand their own risk profile.[75] Of course it is the role of financial advisers (where a consumer has one) to help the consumer to identify and understand risks. However, the adviser is also a sales person and his or her interests may not be served by being too fastidious about issues of risk. Indeed, as the chairman of the Investment Management Association explained to the recent House of Commons Treasury Committee into restoring confidence in long-term savings, "a lot of the [investment] products which have been designed have been just too complicated for people to understand the risk within them *or even for producers to understand fully the risks that are implicit within them*" (emphasis added).[76] (We would suggest that the Select Committee

---

[74]NCC, *Retirement Roulette, a Case Study of Consumer Perspectives on Risks to Retirement Incomes*, November 2002. The nine risks are: investment risk (equity values may increase or decrease); suitability risk; complexity risk; advice risk; prudential/insolvency risk; performance risk (poor management by the fund); inflation and interest rate risks; public policy risks (e.g. changes to tax regime or other regulatory policies); the risk of not saving enough.

[75]FSA Consumer Research 5, *Informed Decisions*, 2000.

[76]HM Treasury Select Committee Report, *Restoring Confidence in Long-term Savings*, HC 71-1, Vol 1, July 2004, at para 25 and see further *Seymour v. Caroline Ockwell & Co.* [2005] P.N.L.R. 39 where, in a rare judicial scrutiny of investment mis-selling,

recommendation that firms provide consumers with a simple risk rating for each product, while satisfying industry desire for simplicity, is unlikely to assist consumers in this respect. A single numerical indicator of risk can never fully represent the risk and uncertainty associated with financial products.)

Risk, in the financial services context, is presented as having only a financial dimension, divorced from psychological, cultural or social dimensions, and as such is to be managed by consumers through prudent, rational and risk aware investing behaviour. Moreover, this risk is presented as being an intrinsic attribute of financial products themselves (in the same way that calories are an intrinsic attribute of food), and implies that it be controlled through careful selection of the right product. The simple risk statement included in the mocked-up example of the proposed "Quick Guide/Key Facts" document to be given to prospective consumers of certain retail investment products includes statements that "The funds that we offer have different levels of risk . . .", and "Many of our funds invest in shares that can go up and down in value . . . ".[77] This obscures the fact that, for example, share price performance is, in reality, dependent upon the outcome of a myriad of decisions taken by different individuals, often across the globe. Those decisions and their outcomes can only ever be uncertain, no matter how carefully the fund is selected.

What seems missing from the FSA's risk-based strategy for consumers is any recognition of ethical, social or cultural dimensions to risk. As Shah has pointed out in the context of his discussion of the intellectual paucity of the financial models of risk,[78] such models ignore the impact of a risk event occurring (financial loss) on the self-esteem, pride, physical and mental health of the individual concerned, but also perhaps on

---

the court held the adviser liable where she recommended a complex offshore fund administered in the Bahamas to clients whose risk profile was low risk. That the adviser didn't understand the characteristics of the product was no defence. She ought to have advised the clients to seek more specialist advice.

[77] FSA Consultation Paper 05/12, Investment Product Disclosure: Proposals for a Quick Guide at the Point of Sale, July 2005, Annex 2.

[78] A K Shah, The Social Dimensions of Financial Risk, *Journal of Financial Regulation & Compliance*, 1997, 5(3), 195–207.

the family and local community (if, for example, the investment was community based). In other words, the psychological and social impact of financial risk is simply ignored, yet these may have a profound influence on consumers' perception of, and willingness to undertake, risk.

Increasingly, individual citizens are required to accept responsibility for their own longer-term financial security and for the risks associated with that responsibility. But if individuals are to be effective "risk regulators" there is a need, we would suggest, for more comprehensive engagement between the government, the regulator and individuals about risk. The risks perceived *by* individual consumers are not necessarily the same as the risks perceived by regulators *for* consumers. In the context of the issue of investing for old age the NCC in a report on consumer views on risks found that consumers wanted a more open and inclusive debate about the extent to which it is equitable and right for individuals to carry an increased risk burden for their future retirement income.[79] In wanting to make consumers more risk aware what has not been explicitly acknowledged by either the government or the FSA is the ethical dimension to risk implicit in the shift from communitarian to individual responsibility for financial security. It seems that individuals as citizens are well aware that risk is about more than understanding the technical features of various investment products, or of the need to save more. Rather it is a politicised concept, a form of governance that seeks to responsibilise[80] citizens in order to serve the regulator's objectives, but which also facilitates (deliberately or not) the creation of a particular social order in which responsibility for longer-term financial security is shifted downwards, from government to individual.

Conclusion

In seeking to achieve its statutory objectives the FSA focuses on identifying and addressing risks to its objectives. Risk is the driver of regulatory policy and strategy. The FSA has made considerable effort to communicate its regulatory strategy with industry and the public, including

---

[79]NCC, *Running Risks: Summary of NCC Research into Consumers' Views on Risk*, October 2002.
[80]For a discussion of "responsibilisation" see Chapter 1 text accompanying in 31–40.

the realities (faced by all regulators) of determining priorities and balancing resources. As Power nevertheless suggests, a risk-to-objectives approach to governance (including regulation) "contains the seeds for an essentially amoral, inward-looking and self-referential set of practices. It creates and supports a (distracting) consciousness of the organisation as being at risk in the face of the rights and claims of others."[81] It also has implications, as Fisher has commented, for the way in which we judge what is good and bad regulation. One implication is that in attempting to translate regulatory uncertainties and hard choices into the language and practices associated with risk, broader social or political issues or concerns can become displaced or obscured instead by concerns over technologies of performance, and, particularly in the case of consumers, information strategies.

---

[81] M Power, *The Risk Management of Everything* (Demos: 2004).

3

Regulation within the regulated firm: legislation and rules

Chapter 2 set out the broad framework for the supervision of firms, drawing attention to the implications of this framework in terms of the desire to shape firms' internal cultures and processes, and to embed responsibility and accountability. This chapter considers the way in which financial regulation has extended its reach "downwards" into the level of the regulated entity to impose specific responsibilities on individuals within those firms, particularly on senior managers. It explains the genesis and structure of the FSA Handbook rules and guidance on senior management arrangements, systems and controls (collectively known and referred to hereafter as "SYSC") as well as the regime for approval, regulation and sanction of persons performing what are known as "controlled functions", i.e. key roles, within and on behalf of the firm. It concludes by considering some of the theoretical literature on regulation and compliance as well as on the notion of "responsibility" within complex organisations and asking how initiatives such as SYSC can be seen in the light of the insights provided by some of that work.

Forerunners of SYSC: senior management responsibility under the Financial Services Act 1986

Prior to the enactment of the Financial Services and Markets Act 2000 (FSMA 2000) the writing was clearly on the wall for the senior management of firms regulated under the Financial Services Act 1986.[1] The collapse of the Barings banking group in 1995 is now widely accepted to have been as much attributable to a lack of quality, effective internal controls and management systems as to employee deception. It led to new rules and guidance from the Securities and Futures Authority (SFA) designed to make explicit the link between the individual responsibility of a designated senior executive officer for ensuring that the firm discharges its responsibility under the FSA (then the Securities and Investments Board) Principles relating to due skill and care in the conduct of business, and proper internal organisation.[2]

This represented a departure from the traditional concerns and techniques of financial regulation inasmuch as it imposed explicit and specific expectations on a firm's senior executive officers as to *general* management controls and structures within a regulated firm. Hence financial regulation was beginning to concern itself with more than the technical "compliance" obligations imposed by rules and regulations made under the Financial Services Act 1986, and was reaching specifically out of the compliance department and up to and into the boardroom. The prospect of regulatory disciplinary proceedings against designated senior officers of a regulated firm, should that firm suffer serious financial or reputational damage where management failure

---

[1] A Newton, *The Handbook of Compliance: Making Ethics Work in Financial Services* (FT Pitman Publishing: 1998) pp 98–112.

[2] SFA Board Notice 473, May 1998. "Senior Executive Officer" being defined to mean a senior executive director or partner, or equivalent senior executive approved by SFA, who is ultimately responsible for the management of the firm's investment business in the UK. Such a senior executive officer (SEO) became individually registrable as such and was obliged to take reasonable steps to organise and manage the firm in a manner which is designed to ensure that its business is conducted in accordance with regulatory requirements.

has been a cause or contributing factor, began to concentrate minds at a more senior level within regulated firms than the middle ranks of the firm's hierarchy at which the compliance function all too often had operated and had its highest level of access. These 1998 rule changes were accompanied by detailed guidance on the SFA's Fitness and Propriety test. This was designed to strengthen the assessment of the competence and capability of individual applicants to the SFA for registration.[3] The SFA was thus able to have regard to whether a registered person was, at all times, capable and competent effectively to perform the role she was employed to perform.

Guidance was also introduced to assist firms in compliance with what was then Securities and Investments Board Principle 9 (Internal Organisation and Compliance with Regulatory Requirements). The SFA no longer expected firms just to have "adequate management controls", rather the expectation was now that firms "manage and control the business effectively".[4]

The Financial Services Authority (at the time still termed the Securities and Investments Board) had, by the time the SFA's new rules took effect, taken up the senior management responsibility initiative from the SFA.[5] On 1 May 1998 it announced the setting up of a working party to consider the responsibilities of directors and senior management, and to

---

[3]The Self Regulating Organisations operating under the Financial Services Act 1986 all introduced rules at various points in time over the last decade which required certain categories of individuals to be registered and privy to their rules and, ergo disciplinary framework, in the wake of the misappropriation of pension fund monies from Maxwell group companies' funds as a result of fraud and lack of internal controls within Bishopsgate Investment Management Ltd, an IMRO regulated entity. These individual registration rules were the predecessors of the Approved Persons regime now found in Part V FSMA 2000.

[4]This was a rather different and much stricter form of expectation in practice, albeit contained in guidance so that it cannot be, strictly speaking, described as an expectation. Para (1) of Appendix 38 SFA Rules. For example, it included matters such as effective risk management, clear segregation of duties and full reconciliation procedures along with taking reasonable steps to ensure that these work effectively, clear demarcation, communication and acceptance of responsibility for business activities, regular review of the commitments that a business has entered into and proposes to enter into (para 6A, Appendix 38, SFA Rules 1998).

[5]SIB Consultation Paper 109, The Responsibilities of Senior Management, July 1997.

take forward the work that had already been done by financial regulators on this topic. It was this early work, which predated publication of the Draft Financial Services and Markets Bill in July 1998, that laid the foundation stones and provided the conceptual turning point for the introduction of the rules and guidance on senior management arrangements, systems and controls under the FSMA which are discussed in this chapter. The FSA described the rationale for *individual* accountability for a *firm's* compliance thus:

> The benefits of individual accountability … should lead to higher standards of conduct and thus reduce the likelihood of a firm being adversely affected by reckless, negligent or rogue behaviour.[6]

Regulation of the board and senior management as a whole: SYSC

There is no specific legislative basis for the FSA's expectations of senior management contained in FSMA 2000. However, in the early consultation stages on the new legislation HM Treasury emphasised the role of senior management. Although it stressed the new regulatory framework was to be directed at responsibility for business functions, rather than their micro-management at an operational level, stating "it is not the role of regulators to try to run regulated businesses",[7] it was clear that HM Treasury endorsed the emphasis given by the SFA and the FSA to an increased amount of senior management responsibility for firms' businesses and this approach was destined to be reflected in the new legislative framework:

> The boards and senior management of financial services businesses have a crucial role to play in ensuring that effective governance structures, systems and controls are developed and operated … [t]he regulator clearly needs to have some direct influence over individuals in positions of senior management responsibility.[8]

---

[6] The FSA's discussion of the Rationale for Statements of Principle and Code of Practice for Approved Persons (*Policy Statement of High Level Standards for Firms and Individuals*: June 2000), para 4.46.
[7] Chapter 8, Part One : Financial Services and Markets Bill: A Consultation Document, *Overview of Financial Regulatory Reform*. HM Treasury 1998.
[8] Paras 8.3 and 8.4, ibid.

Just what type and degree of influence those words were to import could not be understood by examining in isolation the way in which the primary legislation developed and was justified in debate. This is because, as with so many other aspects of FSMA 2000, the statutory provisions do little more than set the four corners of the framework in which the FSA is then enabled and empowered to develop and apply the content of obligations incumbent on firms and individuals. Detailed reference therefore must also be made to the way in which the FSA developed its thinking on the substantive content of what now form the high level statements on senior management arrangements, systems and controls (SYSC), and this is explained further below.

However, the primary legislative provisions themselves are of importance, along with ministerial statements as to their intended effects.

The relevant legislative provisions that provide the foundation for SYSC, and the Approved Persons regime that supports it and links the responsibilities imposed therein to specific senior managers, are contained in section 2 and Part V FSMA 2000 respectively.

Section 2(3)(b) FSMA includes in the list of factors to which the FSA must have regard in discharging its general statutory functions "the responsibilities of those who manage the affairs of authorised persons". As has been noted in Chapter 2, the various factors enumerated in subsection 2(3) came to be described in debate on the legislation as "principles of good regulation" designed to "condition the way the FSA goes about meeting [its] objectives".[9]

The FSA has set out its own view of the significance of this principle on the role of management, containing within it protection of the business "space" from that of the regulatory in terms of continued autonomy, but carrying as the price for this autonomy explicit and defined senior management responsibilities.

> A firm's senior management is responsible for its activities and for ensuring that its business is conducted in compliance with regulatory requirements. This principle is designed to guard against unnecessary intrusion by the regulator into

---

[9]See, for example, Lord McIntosh of Haringey concluding for the government at the Lords Committee Stage debate on Clause 2, 16 March 2000, *Hansard* (HL).

firms' business and requires us to hold senior management responsible for risk management and controls within firms.[10]

Throughout the extensive consultation on its Handbook, which the FSA has engaged in on a continuing basis since 1998, it has adopted the practice of couching specific proposals for rules, guidance and codes of conduct in terms of these general principles as well as its four statutory objectives. This forging of explicit linkages between detailed, specific prescription, and the high level policy objectives and constraints on regulatory action, is welcome not only in terms of its democratic discipline, but also for the opportunity it offers to the regulated to assist with developing their own interpretation of specific rules in specific circumstances.

The FSA's general rule-making power

Both the SYSC rules themselves and FSA Principle 3 (from which they flow)[11] are made pursuant to the FSA's power to "make such rules applying to authorised persons with respect either to their carrying on of regulated activities or to their carrying on of activities which are not regulated activities, as appear to be necessary or expedient for the purpose of protecting the interests of consumers".[12] Thus the SYSC rules enjoy a broader remit for their application and operation than merely the regulated activities of firms. However, the policy driver behind the rules is limited to the consumer protection statutory objective of the FSA, so it is the "risk to consumers" discussed in the previous chapter that provides the *raison d'être* of SYSC.

The detailed guidance included throughout SYSC (and indeed many other parts of the FSA's Handbook) owes its legislative origin to the very wide power given the FSA by section 157 to issue many different forms and levels of guidance. The issuance of guidance was not made subject

---

[10] A *New Regulator for a New Millennium* (FSA, January 2000), p 10.
[11] FSA Principle 3 provides "A firm must take reasonable care to organise and control its affairs responsibly and effectively, with adequate risk management systems."
[12] Section 138 FSMA.

to the same detailed consultative, publicity and cost/benefit analysis constraints as was the FSA's general rule-making power. The practical effect of this is it is likely that the FSA will continue to seek to develop and refine the obligations imposed by SYSC by the use of guidance rather than rule amendment in the future, as far as it is able to.

Financial Services Authority Handbook

It is at the level of principles, detailed rules, codes and guidance in the FSA's Handbook that a fuller picture begins to emerge of the implementation of financial regulation at the firm, intra-firm and individual level. The statute itself sets out little more than the broad framework within which the FSA will supply the content of both individual senior manager's and firm's regulatory obligations and the monitoring, reporting and enforcement context in which those obligations will play out.

Principles for business

Ever since the 1990s "New Settlement" in financial services regulation ameliorated the worst excesses of legalism committed in the name of the Financial Services Act 1986, there has been increasing emphasis laid on a clearly principled approach to financial regulation. FSMA 2000 added a new layer of abstraction, that of clearer policy or objective orientation of regulation, which the FSA has developed at an operational level through its risk related approach to the discharge of its statutory functions discussed in the previous chapter. However, the role of principles (even though they are now strictly speaking in legal terms "rules") is in no way diminished. Since December 2001 all regulated firms, whatever the nature of their regulated activities, have been subject to the 11 FSA Principles for Business forming part of Block One of the Handbook.[13] The FSA has described these as "a general statement of the fundamental obligations of authorised firms under the regulatory system". The

---

[13]These Principles along with related rules and guidance are contained in Block One, FSA Handbook, and are given the prefix PRIN.

FSA's expectation is that senior management, along with all employees within the authorised firm, ensure that all 11 of the Principles inform and colour their day to day conduct as well as their approach to, and decision-making in, difficult or novel situations. However, there is one Principle in particular that is of most concern to senior managers and it is to this Principle that the detailed rules and guidance of SYSC are directed. Principle 3, subtitled "Management and Control", requires with deceptive simplicity:

> A firm must take reasonable care to organise and control its affairs responsibly and effectively, with adequate risk management systems.

Two important changes, made by the FSA from an earlier draft of this Principle, were the insertion of the requirement to take reasonable care in order to emphasise that this Principle in no way is designed to impose strict or absolute liability on the firm, and the insertion of the word "responsibly" in order to emphasise the linkage between this important Principle and the more detailed rules and guidance in SYSC.

SYSC

The rules and guidance on Senior Management Arrangements, Systems and Controls which bear the prefix SYSC apply to firms but compliance with them is, as will be seen to be, of direct importance to certain designated individual senior managers or executives.[14] The purpose of the rules and guidance relating to SYSC, the FSA describes as threefold:

(1) to encourage firms' directors and senior executives to take appropriate practical responsibility for their firms' arrangements on matters likely to be of interest to the FSA because they impinge on the FSA's functions under the Act;

(2) to increase certainty by amplifying Principle 3 ... ; and

(3) to encourage firms to vest responsibility for effective and responsible organisation in specific directors and senior executives[15]

---

[14]They also comprise Block One, FSA Handbook.
[15]SYSC Guidance G1.2.1(1).

The matters likely to be of interest to the FSA are defined as those which bear some relation to its four statutory objectives, so a firm's arrangements relating to matters purely internal to it and its owners are outwith the scope of SYSC.

As well as being designed to amplify and thus provide greater certainty as to the meaning of Principle 3 of the Principles for Business, the SYSC rules and guidance assist the FSA and firms in the interpretation of the Qualifying Conditions for Authorisation.[16] Guidance on these Authorisation Conditions refers to issues of board organisation, risk management systems, etc., in the context of assessing the competence and prudence of a firm's management and hence its suitability to be authorised.[17]

Significant requirements contained in SYSC are as follows:

Apportionment of responsibilities

Rule 2.1.1 obliges a firm to:

> take reasonable care to maintain a clear and appropriate apportionment of significant responsibilities among its directors and senior managers in such a way that:
>
> – it is clear who has which of those responsibilities; and
> – the business and affairs of the firm can be adequately monitored and controlled by the directors, relevant senior managers and governing body of the firm.

Allocation of responsibility to one or more designated individuals

Rule 2.1.3 obliges a firm to:

> appropriately allocate to one or more individuals, in accordance with the SYSC rules on how such allocation should be made, the functions of dealing with the apportionment of responsibilities outlined above and such individual or individuals must also assume responsibility for oversight of establishment and maintenance of the firms' systems and controls.

---

[16]Schedule 6, para (4) FSMA.
[17]COND 2.5.7G.

Recording the apportionment

Rule 2.2.1 requires that a firm must make a record of the arrangements it has made to satisfy the rules on apportionment of responsibilities among directors and senior management as well as allocation of responsibilities to designated individuals, and take reasonable care to keep this record up to date.[18] When responsibilities are reapportioned the record must be updated with a reasonable degree of contemporaneity and, where responsibilities are shared between individuals, it must be clear who is to do what, in order to avoid the problem of essential responsibilities evaporating into the vacuum left by a gap in demarcation.

Systems and controls

With regard to the regulation of a firm's systems and controls Rule 3.1.1 of SYSC requires a firm to:

> take reasonable care to establish and maintain such systems and controls as are appropriate to its business. Guidance accompanying this rule lists as factors relevant to the nature and extent of the systems and controls that are appropriate for a firm to operate the following:
>
> – the nature, scale and complexity of its business;
> – the diversity of its operations, including geographical diversity;
> – the volume and size of its transactions; and
> – the degree of risk associated with each area of its operation.
>
> The firm should carry out a regular review of its systems and controls in order to determine appropriateness on a continuing basis.

This rule is accompanied by a catalogue of reasonably detailed guidance entitled "Areas Covered by Systems and Controls", which the FSA has identified as typically falling within the terms of the obligation

---

[18]The record must be kept for six years from the date on which it was superseded by a more up to date record. Guidance accompanying this rule makes clear that this record does not need to be in any particular format ordained and approved by the regulator. Indeed it is possible to constitute this record through joinder of relevant internal business records such as organisational charts, diagrams, project management documents, job descriptions and terms of reference of committees provided that the firm takes reasonable care to keep them up to date and they link clearly to the firm's main functions.

in Rule 3.1.1.[19] The guidance indicates the areas of business function and potential risk to be covered by a firm's systems and controls. These include not only (and most obviously) internal organisation and the role of the compliance function, but also risk assessment, management information, employees and agents, the role of the audit committee and internal audit function, business strategy and provisions for business continuity. A general record-keeping requirement forms part of the SYSC rules although obviously more detailed and specific record-keeping requirements occur throughout the FSA Handbook.

Each and every one of these areas identified by the guidance to Rule 3.1.1 is highly significant in itself. The FSA has drilled down to and beneath the coalface of operational risk that, as the example of Barings showed, can be the source of hazard to the regulated themselves as well as to the FSA's own regulatory objectives and is, by virtue of its very opacity, such an intractable type of risk for regulators acting alone to counter.[20] These paragraphs then are the real "guts" of what SYSC is all about in practice. Scrutiny of these by the FSA forms a large part of its risk related approach to supervision. Examples of firms' falling short of required internal systems and controls standards in the context of disciplinary and enforcement action brought by the FSA are discussed in the next chapter.

Compliance

Rule 3.2.6 obliges a firm to:

> take reasonable care to establish and maintain effective systems and controls for compliance with applicable requirements and standards under the regulatory system and for countering the risk that the firm might be used to further financial crime.

Guidance accompanying this rule emphasises the importance of an independent, well-organised, adequately resourced and empowered compliance function which, depending on the scale, nature and complexity

---

[19]SYSC G3.1.2(3).
[20]M Power, *The Invention of Operational Risk*, ESRC Centre for Analysis of Risk and Regulation (CARR) Discussion Paper No. 16 (CARR: London, 2003).

of the firm's business, may well be appropriately separated from the firm's business functions. Compliance staff should be sufficiently independent to perform their duties objectively, and yet this regulatory constraint may conflict with a firm's own need and likely preference to have compliance staff who know the business well and "fit" with the overall culture of the firm. The Guidance suggests that as well as adequate resources the compliance function should have unrestricted access to relevant records as well as ultimate recourse to the firm's governing body. In other words, the compliance unit has to have its own short and direct reporting line to the seat of strategic decision-making.

SYSC rules upgrade the status within the regulated entity of the head of the compliance function to governing body level. Rule 3.2.8R requires that a firm which carries on designated investment business,[21] must allocate, to a director or senior executive, the function of having responsibility for oversight of the firm's compliance and for reporting to the governing body. "Compliance" is given a tightly defined meaning. For the purposes of this rule "compliance" means compliance with requirements and standards contained in the Conduct of Business and Collective Investment Schemes sourcebooks. It had been proposed in an earlier draft of the rule to have a much wider definition of compliance to include compliance with the Principles for Business, Part VIII of FSMA (which sketches out the parameters of the market abuse regime and the penalties attaching to it), and the FSA Code of Market Conduct, along with section 390 FSMA which replaces (with some amendments) the previous criminal prohibition in section 47 Financial Services Act 1986 on misleading statements and practices. However, the FSA narrowed the scope of the definition in response to concern expressed during consultation on the breadth of the definition of compliance responsibilities.

Guidance accompanying Rule 3.2.8R makes clear that this narrow definition of compliance is not intended by any means to be exhaustive of the responsibilities such a director or senior executive may have, simply that compliance with those standards form the minimum

---

[21]Regulated and ancillary activities relating to investments specified in Part III of the FSMA 2000 Regulated Activities Order SI 2001/544.

necessary content for an individual engaged in the "Compliance" function. This should not, however, be taken as connoting any FSA approval for loading the director or senior executive up with so many other functions, or potentially conflicting and distracting responsibilities, that it compromises her ability to perform the compliance function. The adequate resourcing and ability to perform duties objectively, as asked for by the FSA guidance to Rule 3.2.6 (the general compliance rule), applies to the head of the compliance function equally as to her staff. Thus the inclusion of a discrete and tightly defined compliance function in SYSC, and insistence on a certain level of seniority for that function, is designed to ensure a level of robustness and seriousness for the compliance function, which may not have been accorded it within all firms hitherto. It is also a necessary complement to the FSA's decision to include "Compliance Oversight" as a "controlled function" under the Approved Persons regime.[22] Therefore there is a clear linkage between the individual's responsibility under that Approved Persons regime, and the discharge of individual responsibility with regard to the firm in the broader context of SYSC.

Who is to "carry the can" overall?

Who then are the appropriate individuals to be designated with ultimate responsibility for the firm's compliance with SYSC? SYSC contains fairly detailed rules and guidance in tabular form[23] on how the allocation of the functions of apportionment of management responsibilities and oversight of systems and controls should be made. The FSA has described the main purpose of this guidance as being "to ensure that these vital functions [apportionment and oversight] are viably discharged by identified individuals".[24] Earlier proposals for an evidential provision which would have presumed compliance with the requirement of

---

[22]FSA Consultation Paper 53, June 2000, *The Regulation of Approved Persons: Controlled Functions* paras 4.9–4.10. FSA Policy Statement: *The Regulation of Approved Persons: Controlled Functions (February 2001). Feedback to Consultation Paper 53 and Final Text of Rules and Guidance* paras 3.2.2–3.2.9 and para 4.9.

[23]SYSC R2.1.4 Guidance 2.1.5–2.1.6.

[24]FSA *Policy Statement on High Level Standards for Firms and Individuals*, June 2000 para 3.14.

"appropriate allocation" of these two functions if such allocation were made to one or two individuals, met with the criticism of overprescription from some industry consultees. In an era when business cultures differ so much, with flatter and less hierarchical decision-making structures in which management responsibilities are more diffuse and may extend beyond two individuals alone, such a presumption on "appropriate" allocation might have proved unworkable, and contrary to the spirit of section 2(3)(b) FSMA 2000 which provides that the FSA must have regard to the responsibilities of those who manage authorised firms.

Regulators seeking to "reach" their rules right inside a regulated entity to track those with real rather than "de jure" responsibility are faced with the same barriers of legal personality and jurisdictional difference that have long confronted the common law. The SYSC rules on allocation of responsibility take account of where, and how, a regulated firm sits within an overall group structure of which it may be a part, as well as who within that group has ultimate responsibility for the management strategy which affects that firm's systems and controls.[25] The widespread existence of matrix management structures within (often international) groups is thus responsible for the complexity of the SYSC rules and guidance on allocation, and their effect is sometimes inevitably "veil piercing" in the sense that the allocation need not be made to the chief executive of the firm itself but can instead be made to:

> a director or senior executive responsible for the overall management of the group, or a group division within which some or all of the firm's regulated activities fall.

The FSA summarises the broad effect of its allocation rule as being:

> – firms may allocate the relevant SYSC functions to one individual or to a group of individuals, provided that the allocation is appropriate;
> – individuals can be selected from the firm or the group (where the firm is part of a group), or a combination of these;
> – where there is a chief executive he or she must be one of the individuals to whom the functions are allocated unless an appropriate individual of greater seniority from elsewhere in the corporate group is substituted.

---

[25]SYSC 2.1.4–2.1.6.

To the extent that the guidance on allocation of functions indicates that it is appropriate to allocate the apportionment and oversight functions to a firm's chief executive[26] then it also makes clear that this normal expectation "does not require the involvement of the chief executive or other executive director or senior manager in aspects of corporate governance if that would be contrary to generally accepted principles of good corporate governance".[27]

From these rules and guidance it is possible to identify a potential danger for the chief executive of a firm that is a member of a group in which overall management issues are decided elsewhere in the group. It is that chief executive who will be more likely to be the designated individual to whom SYSC functions are allocated than more senior individuals within the group, especially where they are outside either the UK or the regulated industry itself. She therefore carries the responsibility, yet cannot ultimately determine many of the issues pertinent to her discharge of that responsibility. Regulatory risk is thus distilled under SYSC, concentrated and located on the shoulders of one individual *within* (indeed at the heart of) the regulated entity. This process, which is discussed in more depth in Chapter 5, is referred to hereafter as "individualisation", a clumsy yet apt word for a key phenomenon in the regulatory process. It is likely that compensation packages and contractual employment arrangements will come to reflect this new category of individual risk but, as is discussed in the next chapter, recent FSA rule changes prohibit firms insuring individuals against personal regulatory fines.[28] This "individualisation" of risk arises from the fact that there is a clear link between the designated individual or individuals

---

[26]Guidance 2.1.6 Question & Answer makes clear that this is the normal expectation.
[27]The Answer to Question 14 in the Table of Questions and Answers on Allocation that forms the Table in Guidance 2.1.6 gives the example of the recommendation in the Combined Code on Corporate Governance that the board of a listed company should establish an audit committee of non-executive directors to be responsible for oversight of the audit. That aspect of the oversight function may therefore be allocated to the members of such a committee without involving the chief executive.
[28]GEN 6 and ENF 13.1.1G introduced this prohibition on insurance against financial penalties into the FSA's Handbook on 1 January 2004. These changes are explained and discussed further in Chapter 5.

under SYSC and their separate and more general individual responsibilities under the Approved Persons regime. Failure to discharge their responsibilities under SYSC is imported into that regime and can, in certain circumstances, attract sanction under Part V FSMA. This is now examined below.

Regulatory sanction of the individual in respect of her role in organisational failures

We have seen how regulation has opened the door of the regulated business entity itself (corporate veil piercing as traditional company lawyers term this "look-through" process) and how it has imposed specific obligations on the senior management of the regulated entity. However, regulation does not stop there, but rather casts its eye around the boardroom, then below it to the next tier of management, and indeed below that to many other individual functions within that firm. It then goes on to visit individual standards, obligations and codes of behaviour on many of the individuals within that entity by way of the construction, under Part V FSMA 2000, of a regulatory and enforcement framework. Breach of this bespoke "individualised" regulatory framework can and does result in direct action against named individuals. This is veil piercing at its most extreme in the sense that any protective corporate veil of the business entity is nigh on invisible as regulation surrounds individual employees, officers and contractors of the regulated entity; seeks to shape their conduct; and, where necessary, wields its stick through sanction and discipline. The closest (but far from exact) parallel is the regime for the disqualification of directors of limited companies[29] in the UK, and the perspective offered by that regime is discussed in Chapter 5.

The legislative basis of the direct regulation of individuals within authorised firms

Part V FSMA 2000 provides the framework for the imposition of a self-contained regulatory and disciplinary framework applicable to a

---

[29]Company Directors Disqualification Act 1986.

number of various designated categories of individuals, including senior managers. An authorised person must take reasonable care to ensure that no individual performs a "controlled function" without FSA approval.[30] Approval is subject to the FSA's being satisfied that the individual who will perform it is fit and proper. Although the FSA has power to specify the exact categories of controlled functions, such functions must fulfil one of the three conditions set out in section 59, subsection (5) of which provides:

> that the function is likely to enable the person responsible for its performance to exercise a significant influence on the conduct of the authorised person's affairs, so far as relating to the regulated activity.

Thus, by definition, senior managers are carrying out a controlled function subject to the Approved Persons regime.

The FSA has power to issue statements of principle accompanied by a more detailed interpretive code of practice and these form the substantive content of the Approved Persons regulatory regime.[31] An individual's failure to comply with a statement of principle (and in determining the fact of compliance the accompanying code of practice comes into its own) can result in disciplinary action being taken against her by the FSA. Such action can also be taken on the basis of that approved person being "knowingly concerned in a contravention by the relevant authorised person [firm] of a requirement imposed on that authorised person by or under the Act".[32] One or two examples of such action are considered further in the following chapter. The FSA has the power to impose a financial penalty or to publish a statement of misconduct in either of these two circumstances.

Some comfort might be gleaned by individuals worried about hawkish regulatory disciplinary policy in respect of their actions (or inactions), since the FSA may only take disciplinary action against an approved person if, as well as there being the appearance of misconduct, it is also satisfied that "it is appropriate in all the circumstances to take

---

[30] Section 59 FSMA.
[31] Section 64 FSMA.
[32] Section 66(2)(b).

action against him".[33] The FSA has made it clear that this requirement will operate as an internal filter, so that it pursues disciplinary action against individuals only where it is proportionate and appropriate to do so in the light of a number of clear and explicit factors.[34] However, it is also worth drawing attention to the potential width of section 66(2)(b) – the "knowingly concerned" basis of disciplinary action against an individual for his role in her employer's non-compliance. Although attention might focus on the new detailed Statements of Principle and Code of Practice for Approved Persons, it must not be overlooked that a sufficiently culpable role in the authorised firm's non-compliance with the Act or with the FSA Handbook can also trigger direct individual disciplinary action. This is an example of legislative use of the device of accessory liability (which the FSA's predecessor to the Securities and Investments Board used to some effect in the past[35]), to provide, for the first time, an explicit statutory basis for *individual* discipline for failures by the firm, as opposed to sanction of the firm itself.[36] This is one route by which the individual senior manager's role in her firm's inadequate compliance with the rules and guidance on SYSC can rebound on her as an individual. The other route is provided by the explicit linkage between the Principles and Code of Practice for Approved Persons and SYSC firm obligations and is discussed below.

An alternative to, or perhaps an outcome of, disciplinary action under section 66 against an approved individual is provided by the prohibition order. If the FSA takes the view that an individual is not a fit and proper person to perform, or to continue to perform, controlled functions then it has the power to impose a prohibition order, which may take a limited or more general form, prohibiting the approved person's future performance of functions in connection with the carrying on of regulated

---

[33]Section 66(1)(b).
[34]See Guidance, paras 12.4 and 12.5, FSA Draft Enforcement Manual (August 2000).
[35]For example, s 6(2) and s 61(1) Financial Services Act 1986. See *SIB v. Pantell SA (No 2)* [1993] 1 Ch 256, *SIB v. Scandex Capital Management* [1998] 1 All ER 514.
[36]For an example of its recent use see *Financial Services Authority v. Fradley (trading as Top Bet Placement Services) and another* [2004] All ER (D) 297.

activities by authorised persons.[37] The nature of regulatory discipline of individuals in the financial sector, its basis in principle and code as opposed to "strict law", and its effect on an individual's livelihood, are evidently rich questions for human rights lawyers and these have been considered elsewhere.[38]

The Approved Persons regime and the "controlled functions"

The individual or individuals to whom a regulated firm has allocated the SYSC functions are, by virtue of that fact, brought into the self-contained regulatory regime for Approved Persons established by Part V FSMA 2000. The FSA has built further upon that legislative framework and carved out specific categories of individual responsibility, which the legislation terms "controlled functions",[39] all of which it has subjected to further controls and a supporting disciplinary framework.

Of the 27 functions currently specified,[40] 20 are "significant influence" functions[41] and are further subdivided as follows ("CF" being Controlled Function): Governing Body Functions (*Director, Non-Executive Director, Chief Executive, Partner, Director of Unincorporated Association, Small Friendly Society, Sole Trader*); Required Controlled Functions (*Apportionment and Oversight under SYSC, EEA Investment Business Oversight, Compliance Oversight, Money Laundering Reporting Officer,*

---

[37]Section 56 FSMA.
[38]The June 1999 Second Report of the Joint Committee on Financial Services and Markets Bill (HL Paper 66, HC 465) provides an interesting starting point for analysis of the relationship between regulatory discipline and human rights law. Also see D F Waters and M Hopper, Discipline, Enforcement and Human Rights: Regulatory Discipline and the European Convention on Human Rights – A Reality Check, in E Ferran and C Goodhart (eds) *Regulating Financial Services and Markets in the 21st Century* (Hart Publishing: 2001).
[39]Section 59(3) FSMA 2000, see Consultation Paper 53 (The Regulation of Approved Persons: Controlled Functions, June 2000) and subsequent FSA Policy Statement, February 2001, for useful background on the development and scoping out of these functions.
[40]SUP 10.4.5R.
[41]Section 59(5) FSMA 2000.

Appointed Actuary); Systems and Controls Functions (Senior managers undertaking the following roles: *Finance, Risk Assessment, Internal Audit*);[42] Significant Management Functions (these are senior managers who, despite being below the governing body still exercise significant influence over the conduct of the firm's affairs by virtue of what they do).[43] Interestingly, the FSA has recently consulted on proposals to reduce the scope, and hence the number, of its required categories of controlled functions for the purposes of Part V approval.[44]

These then are (at the time of writing) the controlled functions in respect of which an authorised firm must take reasonable care to ensure are not performed by unapproved individuals (at least in relation to the firm's regulated activities). Many individuals employed or working within regulated firms fall into more than one category, but approval must still be sought for each function for those who wear more than one hat. Such individuals must take careful and detailed cognisance of the way in which the Statements of Principle and Code of Practice apply differently to their discharge of these different tasks. They cannot apply a holistic approach to them all but must consider each individually. If the proposals in the recent consultation come to fruition it will be possible to move staff around jobs within two merged wider generic "systems and controls" and "significant management" controlled functions, without the need for approval of each change of role.

---

[42] As far as this subcategory is concerned the FSA does not prescribe that the individuals performing these functions need be members of the governing body of the firm but where they are not it is the individual who reports thereto who is performing the controlled function, thereby ensuring that no layers are leapfrogged and individual responsibility for regulatory efficacy stays at or near the top of the firm.

[43] Significant Management (Designated Investment Business) – senior managers who head up a category of investment services activities; Significant Management (Other Business Operations)–senior managers who head up a category of non-investment service activities; Significant Management (Insurance Underwriting); Significant Management (Financial Resources) – essentially senior managers responsible for making material decisions on the firm's own financial resources and commitments; Significant Management (Settlements) – senior managers responsible for back office functions.

[44] FSA Consultation Paper 05/10, *Reviewing the FSA Handbook*, July 2005, Chapter 3.

Controlled functions and SYSC

One of the most important, intended and likely effects of the SYSC rules and guidance considered above is the individualisation of firm-wide regulatory risk. In this respect it is the "Apportionment and Oversight" and "Compliance Oversight" controlled functions that provide the link between responsibility of the firm and the responsibility of identifiable individuals. Hence, the success or failure of the firm in its compliance with Principle 3 and SYSC has a *direct* impact upon the success or failure of the relevant individuals in their own compliance with the Approved Persons regulatory code promulgated under Part V FSMA. This, to put it crudely, ensures that the buck for the firm's performance against the SYSC standards does actually stop with particular individuals and does not disappear into the mists and gaps of collective board responsibility, or evaporate in the face of claims by those at the top of an organisation of their lack of knowledge of what was really going on deep within the underbelly of the firm.

The Rules and Guidance relating to Controlled Functions under the Approved Persons regime mesh seamlessly into those that comprise SYSC so that the Apportionment and Oversight Controlled Function is defined as:

acting in the capacity of a director or senior manager responsible for either or both of the apportionment and oversight functions set out in SYSC Rule 2.1.3.[45]

---

[45]SUP Rule 10.7.1. Accompanying guidance links into the concept of appropriate allocation in SYSC. In response to points made to the FSA during consultation that the chief executive role should automatically include the Apportionment and Oversight Function ("A&O function") the FSA has stated:

> The senior management arrangements, systems and controls rules state that where there is a chief executive she must be approved for the A & O function whether alone or jointly with others. The number of people who may be approved for the A & O function will depend on the size and complexity of the firm. The FSA's principal concern is that too many individuals sharing this responsibility risk the possibility of responsibility falling between the cracks. The FSA expects most firms to have just one or a few individuals in the A & O function and would look carefully at arrangements with greater numbers.

In relation to the Compliance Oversight function the FSA was at pains to emphasise that responsibility for compliance with conduct of business rules and collective investment scheme rules is the minimum content of that function and that it should not be taken by firms as a signal to overly compartmentalise the role of compliance. Indeed the FSA applauded:

> a move by some of the larger firms, to adopt a more holistic approach to the role of compliance whereby it oversees all the various requirements and standards that apply to a firm. By narrowing the compliance role for the purposes of the Approved Persons regime, the FSA does not wish to discourage firms from widening the role of compliance. Such further responsibilities will not be brought within the compliance oversight function for the purposes of the Approved Persons regime.[46]

A less literal and compartmentalised approach within the regulated entity to the arrangement of the compliance functions would thus appear to be a trend that meets with regulatory approval. This is an important point in the context of the growing emphasis on "compliance culture" in a wider theoretical and policy context in financial regulation, and beyond in regulatory law generally, and is developed further in the discussion of "compliance culture" in the concluding chapter. Suffice it to say, in this more explanatory and practical context, that firms taking such an approach do not thereby expose the senior individual with ultimate responsibility under SYSC for a wider and more broadly defined portfolio of compliance responsibilities, to a concomitant wider range of individual risk under the Approved Persons regime. That would be a positive barrier to the development of bolder new holistic approaches to compliance and the development of compliance culture that the FSA

The chief executive function does not automatically include the A & O function. This is because [it] may be performed by more than the CEO and therefore a separate function is required. The emphasis of SYSC is that the A & O function is required in all firms (except EEA passporting branches), whether or not they have a CEO (Paras 3.69–3.70, *Policy Statement on Regulation of Approved Persons*, February 2001.

To have required the CEO role to automatically encompass the A&O function in all cases would have been to detract from the ability of firms with different management matrices to make an allocation of this key controlled function in a way that is appropriate to the firm in question.

[46] Ibid., Para 4.9.

appears keen to encourage. The addition of the word "Oversight" to the compliance oversight function was intended to emphasise the necessary seniority of this function and that it is not a function to be performed by junior compliance staff undertaking day-to-day compliance responsibilities. As to what exactly constitutes "oversight" the FSA has described it as:

> being satisfied that the business has suitable systems and controls; being satisfied that sufficient resources are assigned to compliance activities; where unsatisfied, the individual must have ultimate recourse to the governing body.[47]

Statements of Principle and Code of Practice applicable to approved persons

The substantive content of the individual regulatory framework set up by Part V FSMA 2000 comprises the Statements of Principle and Code of Practice for Approved Persons, along with guidance as to the "Fitness and Properness" criteria that the FSA employs when granting initial approval. The recent FSA consultation on reducing and simplifying the scope of the Part V controlled functions does not recommend any changes to the substance of this individualised regulatory framework.[48]

The Statements of Principle (SPs) themselves are interlaced with detailed evidential provisions provided by the Code of Practice for Approved Persons as well as Guidance. These principles require all Approved Persons to act with integrity and due skill, care and diligence; to observe proper standards of market conduct in carrying out their controlled functions; to deal with the FSA and other regulators in an open and cooperative way; and to disclose appropriately any information of which the FSA would reasonably expect notice.

In addition to these core obligations those Approved Persons performing significant influence functions must, in relation to that function, also: take reasonable steps to ensure that the business of the firm can be controlled effectively; exercise due skill, care and diligence in

---

[47] Ibid., Para 3.72.
[48] FSA Consultation Paper 05/10 *Reviewing the FSA Handbook* (July 2005) para 3.67 chapter 3.

managing the business of the firm; and take reasonable steps to ensure that the business of the firm complies with the regulatory requirements imposed on that business.

It is these final three Statements of Principle (5–7) that are of most importance to senior managers in shaping how they go about their tasks and exercise their management and, if applicable, governing responsibilities. These three are of particular importance too for the designated senior manager or managers performing Controlled Function 8 to whom the allocation of SYSC functions of Apportionment and Oversight has been made.

Just how far does their individual responsibility for the acts and omissions of the firm stretch? The greatest worry for such individuals will be the risk of the FSA taking disciplinary action against them, or seeking a prohibition order, in respect of shortcomings of the firm's compliance under SYSC caused by others within the firm over whose actions the individual had no control. The provisions of the Code and Guidance accompanying the Statements of Principle are of particular assistance here.

Code of Practice provisions and Guidance of particular relevance to SYSC obligations

The Code of Practice for Approved Persons provides assistance in determining whether an individual approved person's conduct complies with a statement of principle. It sets out types of conduct which the FSA sees as non-compliant with the statement of principle, and factors which, in the opinion of the FSA, are to be taken into account when determining such compliance or non-compliance.[49] Statements of Principle 5–7 applying to those holding significant influence functions are buttressed by the following specific evidential provisions in the Code:

- whether he exercised reasonable care when considering the information available to him;
- whether he reached a reasonable conclusion which she acted on;

---

[49] APER (Statements of Principle and Code of Practice for Approved Persons), Block One, General Provisions, FSA Handbook. See CP53 (2000) and FSA *Policy Statement on High Level Standards for Firms and Individuals* (February 2001).

- the nature, scale and complexity of the business;
- the role and responsibility of the approved person performing a significant influence function; and
- the knowledge he had, or should have had, of regulatory concerns, if any, arising in the business under his control.

Despite the inclusion of a reasonableness standard within the first of these two factors (and indeed in the wording of the Statements of Principle themselves), this still should not be seen as an automatic let-out from responsibility of the approved individual for the acts and omissions of others. These standards enable the FSA to unravel specific aspects of the individual's conduct in relation to her knowledge (or lack thereof) of regulatory issues within the business, and to assess the reasonableness of her conduct at each stage of a particular unfolding scenario. If the way in which the general law on company directors' duties has developed recently, and appears to be moving, is anything to judge by, then it is likely that the standard to emerge will be more objective than subjective.[50]

Of particular importance to senior managers trying to gauge the extent to which their conduct may be said to be non-compliant with Statements of Principle 5–7 are the following Code provisions:

SP5. Effective Organisation of Business

Evidential Code provisions and accompanying Guidance make clear that (inter alia) a failure to take reasonable steps to apportion responsibilities clearly among delegates constitutes non-compliance with SP5. Examples given by the FSA of such failure include the implementation of confused or uncertain reporting lines, authorisation levels or job descriptions and responsibilities. Specific linkage between the Statements of Principle for Approved Persons and the SYSC is provided by the clear statement that if the individual approved person tasked

---

[50]See Law Commission Consultation Paper No 153: *Company Directors: Regulating Conflicts of Interest and Formulating a Statement of Duties* (1998) and DTI Consultation Document No 5, *Modern Company Law for a Competitive Economy: Developing the Framework* (March 2000), Chapter 3.

under SYSC 2.1.3R(1) with dealing with the apportionment of responsibilities under SYSC 2.1.1R fails to take reasonable care to maintain a clear and appropriate apportionment of significant responsibilities among the firm's directors and senior managers, then that is an instance of non-compliance with SP5. Examples of such non-compliance given by the FSA are a failure to review regularly the significant responsibilities which the firm is required to apportion under SYSC 2.1.1R, and failure to act where that review shows those significant responsibilities have not been clearly apportioned. Once again we see the FSA's emphasis is not just on the need to review or be aware of matters but also equally on the need to take follow-up action.

The onus is also on the approved person to ensure that the individuals taking responsibility for aspects of the business under her control are actually suitable to the task. In judging whether or not the approved person has taken reasonable steps to ensure such suitability the Code lists three factors that demonstrate the standard has not been met: failure to review competence, knowledge, skills and performance of staff to assess their suitability to fulfil their duties despite evidence that their performance is unacceptable; giving undue weight to financial performance when considering suitability; and allowing managerial vacancies that put at risk compliance with the firm's regulatory obligations to remain, without arranging suitable cover for the responsibilities.[51] Accompanying Guidance provides a reminder of the inversely proportional relationship between riskiness of business strategy and tightness of controls. Other Guidance as to clarity of job descriptions, reporting lines, and assessment of individuals' suitability, point to a climate in which "Know Your Staff" is as much of an internal norm within regulated firms as "Know Your Customer" became a consequence of the Financial Services Act 1986.

SP6 Due Skill, Care and Diligence

The Code's Evidential provisions and the Guidance which fleshes out Statement of Principle 6 provide a highly specific regulatory formulation

---

[51]Evidential Provisions 4.5.8 and 4.5.9, Code of Practice for Approved Persons.

of the standard of care to be expected from an individual approved person exercising a significant influence function. Careful attention needs to be paid to the provisions on delegation. The degree to which delegation can be safely relied on to exculpate a senior manager from disciplinary risk is of crucial importance to her whole approach to, and performance of, her senior management responsibilities. In relation to delegation in particular (and it must be emphasised that delegation is not the only issue of relevance to due skill, care and diligence – other types of conduct are also included within this part of the Code), the FSA singles out a number of types of conduct as non-compliant with SP6 including:

- delegating the authority for dealing with an issue or a part of the business to an individual or individuals (whether in-house or outside contractors) without reasonable grounds for believing that the delegate had the necessary capacity and/or competence and/or knowledge and/or seniority or skill to deal with the issue or to take authority for dealing with part of the business;[52]
- failure to take reasonable steps to maintain an appropriate level of understanding about an issue or part of the business that she has delegated to an individual or individuals (whether in-house or outside contractors).[53]

The Evidential provisions of the Code are explicit on the extent to which the FSA will see failure to supervise and monitor performance of delegates as conduct which is non-compliant with SP6, and on the extent to which failure to follow up on warning signals being given out from an area of delegated business, will also fall short of SP6.[54] The quality of the initial delegation decisions taken by an approved person will be a relevant factor in determining that approved person's compliance with SP6. Therefore it simply will not be open to a senior manager to rely upon delegation to a new, inexperienced and relatively

---

[52]Evidential Provision 4.6.5, ibid.
[53]Evidential Provision 4.6.6, ibid.
[54]Evidential Provisions 4.6.7–4.6.9, ibid.

junior or problematic member of staff (or contractor). A much greater and continuing focus on the quality of decision-making about delegation, within or outwith the firm, is called for. Because the impact of a delegate's acts and omissions on his principal's potential regulatory responsibilities under Part V FSMA is an uncomfortable area of individual risk for approved persons, the FSA has given reasonably detailed Guidance upon both the circumstances in which delegation is appropriate, and on the continuing responsibilities of the approved person where an issue has been delegated.[55] The Guidance makes clear that the FSA envisages that approved persons may delegate the investigation, resolution, or management, of an issue or authority for dealing with a certain part of the business, to individuals who report to her or others. This provides some implicit regulatory basis for internal delegation and outsourcing of discrete tasks and functions.

Legal advisers and compliance consultants may be heartened by the Guidance's exhortation to approved persons to consider taking external legal advice where such is not available in-house and where an issue for resolution via delegation raises questions of law or interpretation.[56] Approved persons may take some comfort from the fact that the FSA makes clear in this guidance that such a person will only be in breach of SP6 if she "fails to exercise due and reasonable consideration before she delegates the resolution of an issue or authority for dealing with a part of the business and fails to reach a reasonable conclusion. *If he is in doubt about how to deal with an issue or the seriousness of a particular compliance problem, then, although he cannot delegate to the FSA the responsibility for dealing with the problem or issue, he can speak to the FSA to discuss his approach*" (emphasis added).[57]

It would be interesting to know to what extent regulated individuals take advantage of the FSA's apparent willingness to act as a sounding board for internal management decisions that impinge on compliance. If the evidence considered in the next chapter from the December

---

[55] Guidance 4.6.13 and 4.6.14, ibid.
[56] Guidance 4.6.13(3), ibid.
[57] Guidance 4.6.13(4), ibid.

2004 Financial Services Practitioner Panel Survey into the FSA's performance is anything to go by, then the indications are that such guidance is not as forthcoming or as clear as the regulated community would like.

SP7 ensuring firms' compliance with regulatory requirements

The Evidential provisions and Guidance that buttress this Statement of Principle 7 provide a further pillar in the regulatory system to accompany the SYSC rules and guidance on the establishment and maintenance of systems and controls within a regulated firm. These pinpoint the individual responsibilities under the Approved Persons regime of those designated with individual responsibility under SYSC for the firm's establishment and maintenance of those controls. It is a breach of SP7 on the part of such persons to fail to take reasonable care to oversee the establishment and maintenance of such controls within the firm.[58] This provides the "bite" for SYSC – the incentive for the designated individuals under SYSC to actually take their responsibilities thereunder seriously – and not to see it as a mere paper exercise in senior management flowcharts. This is the mechanism whereby the incentives towards compliance by both the firm and individual managers are aligned and pointed in the same direction. Real regulatory risk of individual disciplinary action will arise for those individuals who do not exhibit the necessary standard of care and focus towards their firm's systems and controls. Further examples of behaviours which the Code prescribes as evidence of non-compliance with SP7 include an approved person's:

- failure to take reasonable steps to monitor (either personally or through a compliance department or other departments) compliance with the regulatory requirements of the business in respect of its regulated activities;

In other words it is not sufficient just to set up and resource a compliance department in the manner envisaged by the SYSC rules and guidance,

---

[58]Evidential Provision 4.7.3, ibid.

but it must also be used to monitor on an ongoing basis the extent to which compliance is actually happening within the business.[59]

- failure to take reasonable steps to adequately inform himself about the reason why significant breaches (whether suspected or actual) of regulatory requirements in respect of the firm's regulated activities may have arisen;

The FSA is looking for follow-up of, and a genuine senior management desire to, understand the reasons for non-compliance within the firm. Failure to investigate systems and procedures failures and, where appropriate, to obtain expert opinion can be taken as evidence of such lack of follow-up.[60]

- failure to take reasonable steps to ensure that procedures and systems of control are reviewed and, if appropriate, improved following the identification of significant breaches (whether suspected or actual) of the regulatory requirements of the business relating to its regulated activities;

An unreasonable failure to implement, in a timely manner, recommended improvements is to be taken as evidence of such failure.[61]

Obviously, it is core to the performance of the Compliance Oversight function (Controlled Function 10) that whoever performs that function has the most immediate individual responsibility for ensuring that appropriate compliance systems and procedures are in place. But the Code of Practice makes clear that such an approved person (who will also be expressed to be responsible for compliance under SYSC 3.2.8R) must take reasonable steps to ensure that this is so.[62]

Tucked away in Guidance to this part of the Code is the important regulatory expectation of approved persons performing significant functions, that they will ensure all staff (whether within the Approved Persons regime or not) are aware of the need for compliance.

---

[59]Evidential Provision 4.7.4, ibid.
[60]Evidential Provisions 4.7.5–4.7.6, ibid.
[61]Evidential Provisions 4.7.7 and 4.7.8, ibid.
[62]Evidential Provision 4.7.10, ibid.

Crossing boundaries by SYSC and the Approved Persons regime: regulation at work within the regulated business unit

The greater "intrusiveness" of SYSC and the Approved Persons regime are but two concrete illustrations of a reconceptualisation in what we mean by "regulation". Such a reconceptualisation is evident in recent theoretical literature on regulation. It is beyond the scope of this work to provide a detailed account of that literature but rather to select from it those contributions that appear to the authors to offer the most useful insights into implementation of UK financial regulation. Indeed the discourse on "regulation" has come a long way since academic debate first got going on issues such as justifications for regulation (private interest versus public interest), regulatory rule design (degrees of specificity and enforceability), and the appropriate balance between "statutory" and "self" regulation.[63] Demarcating where "public" ended and "officialdom" no longer intruded and where the real business of private enterprise could begin were, for a while, central concerns, as was the cost/benefit analysis of regulatory intervention in debates about financial regulation in particular.

The work of Ayres and Braithwaite was probably the most successful in moving this debate on from these "preliminary" concerns.[64] Their analysis, rather than concentrating on where regulation should begin and end and how much it should cost, took as a given the fact that regulation, in one form or another, was here to stay. Yet it had much else of potential interest to scholars and policymakers alike. Ayres and Braithwaite argued that in order to determine if regulation was achieving its desired outcomes, a greater understanding was urgently needed about regulation's inner workings, its interaction with the regulated,

---

[63] Good descriptions of these earlier debates exist in Ogus, *Regulation: Legal Form and Economic Theory* (OUP: Oxford, 1994), R Baldwin, H Scott and C Hood *A Reader on Regulation* (OUP: Oxford, 1998), R Baldwin and H Cave, *Understanding Regulation* (OUP: Oxford, 1999), Part I, all of which works contextualise those debates in light of more recent thinking.

[64] I Ayres and J Braithwaite, *Responsive Regulation: Transcending the Deregulation Debate* (OUP: Oxford, 1992).

and the processes (both within regulator and regulated) that produced (or did not produce) regulatory compliance. In developing their idea of "responsive regulation" that admits for more subtle and effective regulatory processes and "games" than the traditional hierarchy of "command and control"[65] they argue for an alternative model of "enforced self-regulation" which they present as:

> a middle path between self-regulation and command and control government regulation . . . [E]nforced self-regulation means that firms are required to write their own set of corporate rules, which are then publicly ratified. And when there is a failure of these privately written [and publicly ratified] rules, the rules are then publicly enforced.[66]

The realisation that regulation has moved far beyond "command and control" to develop more diffuse and subtle strategies of influence has won widespread recognition among regulatory practitioners and theorists, and terms such as "de-centred", "smart" and "risk related" regulation represent the new orthodoxy.[67] The introduction of the SYSC requirements around FSA Principle 3, with their emphasis on the need to have, record and maintain robust and effective internal systems and controls within the authorised firm, can most certainly be viewed as an example of enforced self-regulation. The "public ratification" element is provided by the inclusion of the need to comply with SYSC as part of the threshold conditions for a firm's gaining, and keeping, authorisation.[68]

---

[65] I.e. at its simplest the Regulator commands the Regulated to obey certain specific rules and where this does not happen sanctioning (often criminal) will follow. There are of course many variations of command and control regulation but the basic model is discussed by Baldwin and Cave in Chapter 4, Understanding Regulation, supra, n 63 (who give an account of the dangers, such as over legalism, with which it is often associated).

[66] I Ayres and J Braithwaite, supra, p 6, n 63, and Chapter 4.

[67] *Reducing Administrative Burdens: Effective Inspection and Enforcement*, Hampton Review (HM Treasury, 2005) for how far regulatory practice has moved and see R Brownsword, Code Control and Choice: Why East is East and West is West, *Legal Studies*, 2005, 25(1), 1–21 for width of scholarly acceptance of shift away from command and control.

[68] Schedule 6 FSMA and guidance on conditions for obtaining and keeping authorisation contained in COND 2.4G (FSA Handbook).

Power, in his discussion of regulation's increased reliance on internal controls in the broader context of the reinvention of governance across public and private sectors, charts the move away from traditional command and control. He detects a consensus in the work of leading theorists towards the emergence of formalised "regulatory layers" which have resulted in "...the internalisation of control mechanisms and the validation of their integrity by internal and external audits".[69]

Another characteristic of FSA Principle 3 and its amplifying rules and guidance contained in SYSC, which is interesting in light of broader scholarship on regulation, is the rule design employed therein.[70] With frequent use of terms such as "adequate", "effective" and "robust" these rules provide good examples of the type of shift to outcome-oriented and effects-based performance standards that have been evident in UK financial regulation since the recasting of the then SIB Handbook under the "New Settlement" in 1992.

As for the way in which Principle 3/SYSC is designed to affect the internal workings of an authorised firm, as well as those considerable numbers of individuals within it who are now directly harnessed to the FSA's regulatory objectives through the Approved Persons regime, recent work from Black provides some insight here. Her work has been leading thinking on how regulation in the financial services arena particularly is a much less monolithic, and a far "smarter", concept than traditionally viewed.[71] As was explained in the previous chapter,[72] Black's "de-" or "multi-" centred analysis of regulation assumes powerful explanatory force when mapped onto SYSC with its view of regulation as an essentially fragmented process taking place "in many rooms", and

---

[69]M Power, *The Audit Society: Rituals of Verification* (OUP: Oxford, 1997) p 55.
[70]The different ways in which regulation can be used to set standards is discussed in Baldwin and Cave, supra, n 63 Chapter 9.
[71]J Black, Decentring Regulation: Understanding the Role of Regulation and Self-Regulation in a "Post-Regulatory World", *Current Legal Problems*, 54 103–146 and J Black, *Mapping the Contours of Contemporary Financial Services Regulation* ESRC Centre for Analysis of Risk and Regulation (CARR) Discussion Paper No 17. (CARR: London, 2003).
[72]See text accompanying n 31 in Chapter 2.

having enrolled many different and diverse actors into its tasks. In her description of what she shows is now a much expanded regulatory toolkit at work within UK financial services regulation; she identifies as the fourth and fifth tools in the kit the "technologies" and design of organisational and decision-making processes.[73] One example of the former at work, she argues, is the emergence of strategies of "meta regulation" whereby a regulator audits a firm's own design, conduct and audit of its own compliance processes.[74] In her analysis of the employment within the regulatory toolkit of organisational and decision-making processes, she cites guidance on internal controls (in a corporate governance context but the point applies equally well with the FSA's SYSC rules and guidance) as examples of "using processes more explicitly as an instrument to reach a desired end: processes have to be put in place but the regulation also specifies the type of outcome that should result, and imposes liability in certain circumstances when it does not."[75]

In moving her analysis of contemporary financial services regulation on from the model of an expanded toolkit to illustrate how the more amorphous and shifting "enrolment analysis" might be visualised, Black provides examples of a wide range of regulatory actors who are enrolled in one capacity or another into the task of financial regulation, and she drills down into practical examples of how some of these actors might deploy their capacities and be seen as a regulatory resource. Her analysis respects no national/supranational or public/private divides, and regulatory actors include the Basel Committee on Banking Supervision and other international financial institutions, consumer groups, trade associations, knowledge intermediaries (such as accountants, lawyers etc.) and for the purposes of this chapter, most importantly, firms themselves and certain individuals within those firms. The examples of individual actors she gives (compliance officers, executives, back office and front office staff) are all most likely to be formally and legally enrolled into financial services regulation through the Part V FSMA Approved Persons

---

[73] J Black (2003) CARR Discussion Paper 17, supra, n 71 pp 6–7.
[74] Discussed in previous chapter, see n 22, Chapter 2, and accompanying text. See also C Parker, Reinventing Regulation within the Corporation: Compliance-Oriented Regulatory Innovation, *Administration and Society*, 32(5) 529–565.
[75] J Black (2003) CARR Discussion Paper 17, supra, n 71 p 7.

regime and, in the case of those individuals to whom the Apportionment and Oversight and Compliance Oversight Controlled Functions
have been allocated, their enrolment and alignment to desired regulatory outcomes is deliberately designed to be particularly strong.

Black's description of the practical processes of enrolment provides
some insight into how the bespoke individual regulatory framework
that is the Approved Persons regime should operate. It should operate
by involving and incentivising multiple individual actors with their own
regulatory agenda. She gives the example of the deployment of a regulatory official, or knowledge professionals (management consultants), to
provide leverage to compliance staff to, for example, convince management to take an issue seriously, or of the importance of implementing
change. In the same way the SYSC rules, in the way in which they
combine to operate with the Approved Persons regime, are designed
to provide exactly the same kind of cross-fertilisation, cross-leveraging
and internal persuasive discourse on an ongoing basis within the firm.
Call it "enrolment" or regulatory trickledown, it is now crystal clear that
regulatory scholars, and indeed those concerned with practical compliance, must be increasingly and more forensically concerned with what
is going on within regulated firms. This is where regulation is now firmly
embedded.

One final and more philosophical question arises as to how the whole
notion of "responsibility" is being employed by financial regulation
within SYSC (responsibility of the firm) and the Approved Persons
regime (individual responsibility). Those interested in the construction
and justification of appropriate criminal law frameworks for corporate
actors have had to grapple with this question and ask whether or not
the moral and public catharsis that criminal sanction carries with it
sits appropriately, or indeed justly, when applied to complex corporate
persons or indeed, individual(s) within that organisation.[76] Bovens provides a thoughtful analysis of some of the fundamental questions that
must first be considered before "responsibility" is imposed on complex
organisations themselves, and indeed on any individual or individuals
who form part of such organisations, in respect of the outcomes that

---

[76] C Wells, *Corporations and Criminal Responsibility* (Clarendon Press: Oxford, 1993).

arise from its actions.[77] He identifies "the problem of many hands" as a problem of modernity which bedevils attempts to impose responsibility for organisational deviance in the context of complex, multilayered, multidivisional, and often multinational, corporate organisations. He then goes on to unpick the slippery concept of responsibility by asking "What do I mean when I ask who is responsible for the conduct of complex organisations?"

He employs Hart's classic vision of responsibility having four components: Cause (responsible for), Accountability (being responsible to), Capacity (having the capacity to be accountable) and Task (responsibility flowing from performance of a particular task).[78] Many elements of SYSC and the Approved Persons regime have at least the final three of those (some might argue they are deliberately vague on "cause" being outcome-oriented performance standards). He adds one more component of his own, responsibility as virtue or value judgement (behaving responsibly). He develops this analysis much further by dividing "responsibility" into two types "passive" and "active":

> In the case of passive forms of responsibility, one is called to account after the event and either held responsible or not. It is a question of who *bears* the responsibility for a given state of affairs. The central question is why *did* you do it? In the case of active forms, the emphasis lies much more on action in the present, on the prevention of unwanted situations and events. Above all, it is a question of responsible acting, of taking responsibility, of behaving responsibly. The central question here is "what *is* to be done?".[79]

He shows that there is in fact much connectivity between the two notions and that one feeds the other. For example, decisions of, and sanctions imposed within, the forum for accountability, such as before a regulatory disciplinary committee, court or tribunal (passive), can influence behaviour and exhort management to more virtuous and responsible behaviour within an organisation (active). The extent to

---

[77]M Bovens, *The Quest for Responsibility: Accountability and Citizenship in Complex Organisations* (Theories of Institutional Design Series: Cambridge, 1998).
[78]Hart, H L A *Punishment and Responsibility: Essays in the Philosophy of Law* (OUP: Oxford, 1968).
[79]M Bovens, supra, n 77 p 27.

which this happens in the context of responsibility within UK financial regulation is assessed in the next chapter's review of disciplinary actions against firms under SYSC, and against individuals under Part V FSMA. Although those subject to SYSC and the individual discipline regime in Part V FSMA may well think of them as little more than mechanisms for increased, and role specific, regulatory accountability (passive), it is clear that the FSA had, and continues to have, the development of active responsibility for regulatory compliance in mind in their intro-duction. For example, the encouragement of a "culture of compliance amongst senior management in authorised firms" was stated as a core belief by the FSA when it introduced the SYSC rules and guidance.[80]

The shift over a decade ago to a more principled regulatory code and away from detailed rules, and the continuing and growing emphasis on organisational culture and in particular management's contribution thereto, which, as the next chapter shows, increasingly appears in public statements about regulatory enforcement, bear out that these regulatory mechanisms are employing the notions of responsibility actively, as well as in the more familiar (to lawyers anyway if not ethicists) passive way.

If active responsibility in this context is about the encouragement of a "compliance culture" within regulated firms, what do different regula-tory actors mean by that? The concluding chapter attempts closer and critical analysis of that question.

---

[80]FSA Consultation Paper 35, para 5 (December 1999).

4

Senior management regulation: evidence and practice since N2

Discussion in the previous chapter has focused on how and why the internal organisation of regulated firms, and functions within them, are now clearly structured around and harnessed to the FSA's regulatory objectives. This chapter considers the FSA's approach to its powers that reach within the regulated entity. What the FSA considers appropriate standards from senior management, both as a body and individually, can be gleaned as much from its general public statements and exhortations, along with its exercise of its enforcement jurisdiction, as from the rules and guidance already considered.

This chapter also considers evidence as to how the arrangements contained in both the SYSC and APER sections of Block One of the FSA's Handbook have been received and implemented into firms. It does this by drawing on the outcome of disciplinary action taken by the FSA since N2 against firms in relation to rule breaches under SYSC.[1] It also reviews the FSA's enforcement actions taken against individuals

---

[1] Pursuant to ss 205–206 FSMA 2000.

in management positions within authorised firms where it has sought prohibition orders[2] or to levy a financial penalty or impose a public statement of censure.[3] This growing body of "enforcement jurisprudence" provides a kind of regulatory common law, albeit of much more limited precedent and predictive value than judge-made law, into regulatory expectations of senior management as a *corpus* and senior managers in their individual functions.

Finally, it presents and discusses the results of a small-scale survey of firms undertaken 18 months after N2 which attempted to elicit views into how the new arrangements are being received and implemented into firms, along with the most recently available Financial Services Practitioner Panel and the British Banking Association surveys into the perceptions of various aspects of the FSMA 2000 regulatory regime (including some which pertain to these aspects of the relationship between the FSA and firms).[4]

The FSA's disciplinary action and senior management arrangements, systems and controls

What is said below about the FSA's enforcement action to date must be viewed in light of changes likely to unfold following the recent recommendations of the FSA's own review of its enforcement processes and practices.[5] The review was established in response to growing concern about aspects of enforcement by the FSA which, to some extent, crystallised in critical comment made by the Financial Services and Markets Tribunal in the Legal & General Assurance Society

---

[2] Pursuant to s 56 FSMA 2000.
[3] Pursuant to s 66 FSMA 2000.
[4] Financial Services Practitioner Panel Second Survey in 2002, Third Survey in 2004 (www.fs-pp.org.uk) and British Bankers Association Membership Survey on the Effectiveness of the Regulatory Framework 2003 (available at www.bba.org.uk).
[5] Enforcement Process Review: Report and Recommendations (FSA, July 2005). Its terms of reference *"to review the use of, approach to and decision-making process for supervisory actions and enforcement actions to address breaches of regulatory requirements and, where appropriate, to make recommendations"*.

reference.[6] The Legal & General reference itself is discussed further in the final chapter but at this stage suffice it to say that the FSA was at pains, in its discussion of the enforcement review's recommendations, to point out that the tool of disciplinary enforcement has been used highly selectively since N2 and that it is far from being an enforcement-led regulator.[7]

However, that very selectivity is itself yet another strategy of regulatory enrolment as the FSA states that it sees its use of the enforcement tool as being a weapon in the armoury of risk-based supervision. Enforcement outcomes are intended as much to be a wider regulatory messaging to firms, individuals and industry sectors as they are intended to affect the individual or firm themselves.[8] The Final Notices summarising the outcome of enforcement action taken by the FSA are published regularly on its website and closer scrutiny of its reasons for taking the action it took in any particular case reveals the bases upon which it is making decisions as well as how it is employing extant guidance in the Enforcement section of the Handbook. Patterns in the FSA's expectations of firms and senior management undoubtedly emerge, despite the huge differences in the types, size and nature of the firms who are the subjects of enforcement attention.

There is value in identifying behaviours that actually ground the breaches of Principle 3 and SYSC themselves as well as any recurrent emphases and messages given by the FSA about what is "good" or "bad" behaviour from a firm or individual (in the sense of what contributed to, or minimised, the size of financial penalty imposed). From a regulated firm's and senior management's perspective this should provide some guidance as to expected standards and behaviours of prophylactic value in order to avoid enforcement attention. Or at least should such action occur, then it provides some guidance as to how to act in order to minimise the disciplinary penalty and reputational damage

---

[6]*FSA v. Legal & General Assurance Society,* decision of the Financial Services and Markets Tribunal (18 January 2005).
[7]FSA Enforcement Review, supra, n 5, paras 4.4–4.5.
[8]Ibid., para 4.9.

that might result. On a more theoretical level, in light of changing and changed perceptions of the regulatory mission in UK financial services regulation,[9] it is possible to ask quite what flavours "enrolment" into the regulatory mission of the various regulatory actors (firms and key individuals) who, to use yesterday's "Command and Control" language, exist in a "subordinate" relationship to the FSA, at the bottom of the regulatory apex. To what (if any) extent is it possible to discern attempts to develop a more active concept of responsibility, what Bovens termed "responsibility as *virtue*",[10] in the FSA's pronouncements and disciplinary actions against firms and individuals?

Regulatory rhetoric and senior management responsibility since N2

From 1 December 2001 onwards there has been consistent and increasing emphasis placed in speeches from senior figures within the FSA, as well as in its discussion and policy papers, on the centrality to the post-N2 regulatory framework of the responsibilities of the role of senior management and the SYSC high-level obligations.

It is not just in the FSA's shaping of the passive component of the meanings of senior management responsibility (i.e. the announcement of outcomes of enforcement action concerning public accountability of firms and actors) where this increased emphasis on the role, responsiveness and commitment of senior management is apparent. For it is also built into the FSA's own risk-based operating framework (the "ARROW" framework discussed in Chapter 2) which is designed to operate as an ex ante regulatory mechanism. The "good" scoring within that framework of those component risk to objectives (RTOs) which pertain to senior management and issues of compliance and controls culture, builds incentives whereby concerned and committed

---

[9] J Black, *Mapping the Contours of Contemporary Financial Services Regulation*, ESRC Centre for Analysis of Risk and Regulation (CARR) Discussion Paper No 17 (CARR: London, 2003).

[10] M Bovens, *The Quest for Responsibility: Accountability and Citizenship in Complex Organisations* (Theories of Institutional Design Series: Cambridge, 1998), Chapter 3 at p 6, and Part III.

managements score lower on control risks RTOs. This is a clear attempt to develop and reward a more active responsibility.

In the various documents over the past three years in which the FSA has sought to develop and explain its risk-based operating framework, it is clear that, over time, as the framework has developed and been tested by the FSA, it has become more bullish on the role of senior management's commitment. That commitment as well as actions and a firm's broader compliance culture are key components of that cluster of Risks to Objectives termed "Control" risks within the ARROW framework. As already explained, a firm's ARROW score under this new framework is partly dependent on the FSA's assessment of probability of risks to objectives occurring. In the first of its Progress Reports on Building the New Regulator (which followed the ground-breaking "New Regulator for the New Millennium" document)[11] firm-specific Control risks were identified as marketing, selling and advice practices; organisation: systems and controls; and board, management and staff.

Other than, some might argue unhelpfully, exhorting firms to keep their risk assessment by the FSA or "ARROW score" confidential, the FSA gave little detail in its hypothetical case studies about the impact on probability scores of board behaviour, management practices and broader organisational cultural issues. However, in 2002 the FSA's second Progress Report added, without specific comment, a new dimension to the components of Control risk. In addition to the four identified the previous year, it stated that a firm's "Business and Compliance Culture" formed one of the risk group clusters of Control risk.[12] It is pertinent to ask just how the "and" is being used here. Conjunctively or disjunctively? For a firm's "business culture" can be different to its compliance culture and just how the FSA goes about making this assessment at this ex ante stage is less than clear, although the increasing attention that the concept of "culture" is receiving at the ex post enforcement stage may shed some insight here.

---

[11] FSA Progress Report: *Building the New Regulator I* (2001); see also FSA *New Regulator for New Millennium* January 2000.

[12] Para 41, *Building the New Regulator: Progress Report II*, FSA, February 2002.

In making its probability assessments of those firm-specific clusters of risk termed Business and Control risks, the FSA employs some 40 different risk elements within the matrix it uses.[13] Unsurprisingly, within the Control risk category of the assessment matrix, the 18 specific risk elements relating to the "Organisation", "Internal Systems and Controls", and "Board, Management and Staff" risk clusters map directly onto the areas dealt with in Chapters 2 and 3 of SYSC, respectively Senior Management Arrangements,[14] and Systems and Controls.[15] However, there are at least three risk elements being used by the FSA in assessing Control risks that do not appear in SYSC in either rule or guidance form. One is "quality of management" (under the Board, Management and Staff category), although it is open to debate that this is inextricably linked to a firm's ability to comply with SYSC and hence no need for it to be explicit therein. The other two are within the new category of Control risk, namely "Business and Compliance Culture", and comprise a firm's "relationship with regulators" and its "cultural issues and business ethics". All of these are capable of impacting upon the seven groups of risks to objectives used to arrive at scoring and hence capable of exerting a greater influence on final score than some of the other risk elements. They are all characterised by a degree of indeterminacy and are highly contestable concepts but they form a key part in determining the intensity of the FSA's supervisory relationship with a firm. This is so even though they neither appear explicitly within rules and guidance to SYSC, nor (at least in the case of compliance culture/business ethics and quality of management) are they in themselves capable of grounding enforcement action against a firm.

---

[13]See Probability Assessment Matrix Appendix B, *Building the New Regulator: Progress Report II* ibid.

[14]Risk elements comprising organisation risk cluster are broken down by the FSA to encompass clarity of legal/ownership structure: jurisdiction/characteristics of controllers and group entities and "relationship with the rest of the group". The risk elements comprising the Board, Management and Staff risk category again appear influenced by SYSC as risk elements and include corporate governance, human resources policies and procedures and allocation and definition of management responsibilities .

[15]For example, Internal Audit, Business Continuity, Outsourcing/Third Party Providers (presumably here the FSA must be looking for reasoned compliance with SYSC guidance on delegation), Management Information, Compliance Arrangements.

It is of course not at all surprising that a regulator should choose to employ a wider perspective on the components of risk for ex ante supervisory purposes than it would or indeed could choose to try to minimise and control through the use of rules and standards in a Handbook. For Handbook changes must be consulted upon and withstand review and legal challenge. It is hard to imagine that risk factors such as "quality of management" or "compliance culture" would ever have been acceptable in a rulebook form that could trigger enforcement consequences. However, as the rest of this chapter illustrates, in instances where firms are facing disciplinary action then, although this is not grounded by rules, these same factors are being cited by the FSA in disciplinary contexts as having been a significant influence on the outcome of such actions.

In its discussion of how it aims to incentivise well-managed firms and penalise poorly managed ones through varying the intensity of supervision,[16] and in the emphasis placed on the commitment of management to identification and control of Control risks,[17] the FSA provides yet another example of its increasingly public view of senior management and its influence on firm culture as *the* key route (or point of "enrolment") into effecting regulation within firms.

The fact that there have been some 45 "Dear CEO" letters[18] since N2 on matters of pressing regulatory concerns further illustrates this point. Each of these letters provides a reminder about who the FSA regards, and indeed SYSC requires, to carry ultimate regulatory responsibility for firms' compliance. Almost every other speech or presentation given by the FSA's senior figures and divisional heads has not missed a chance to hammer home the centrality of senior management responsibility to almost every part of the mission of financial regulation. The Building

---

[16]Para 68, Incentives and Senior Management Responsibilities, FSA *Progress Report – II* supra, n 12.

[17]Ibid., p 22.

[18]As at August 2005 ranging from matters as disparate as financial promotions for spread-betting firms (July 2004) to financial reporting (four on reporting in 2003). Usage of this penetrative technique has increased over time since N2 and "Dear CFO" letters have been addressed from the FSA to Finance directors, with the same technique being employed for heads of compliance too.

Societies' Association were warned:

> Suppose a society were to issue an advertisement for a product that didn't meet the requirements to be fair, clear and not misleading. If we [the FSA] were to pick up on this, whom do you think we would hold responsible? The promotions manager? The society's legal adviser? The advertising agency? The correct answer is none of the above. Our view is that it is the senior management of the society that are responsible for ensuring that our regulatory requirements have been complied with.[19]

While the insurance industry were recently warned:

> A central maxim of the regulatory doctrine for the UK, the onus of responsibility that we place on the senior management of all financial services firms is a cornerstone of our regulatory approach. What this means in practice is that we [the FSA] expect a firm's senior management to take responsibility for ensuring that it complies with the regulatory requirements – both in terms of our high level principles for business and the detail of specific rules on capital adequacy and the way in which they treat their customers... we see Boards and senior management as running the industry and have imposed on them very clear regulatory requirements as to what they need first to deliver.[20]

Indeed the then outgoing chairman of the FSA in his last public address as such chose to express his "biggest disappointment of [his] time at [the] FSA has been the failure of firms, and particularly their senior management, to learn the lessons of past mis-selling".[21]

Both the current chairman and chief executive have continued this emphasis. The chief executive, for example, in development of the "Treating Customers Fairly" theme (discussed in Chapter 6), reminds senior management that theirs is the ultimate responsibility for the firm's compliance with Principle 6 (The fair treatment of customers), and that proper discharge of this responsibility may require some deeper-level effort from them and "change leadership" than they might perhaps realise. In the context of an example drawn from the need to ensure that

---

[19]Speech by Philip Robinson, Director Deposit-Takers Division of the FSA to Building Societies Association (17 July 2003).
[20]Speech by David Strachan, Sector Leader for Insurance at the FSA to International Insurance Society Conference, London, 12 July 2004.
[21]Howard Davies, then chairman and chief executive FSA, addressing the FSA's Annual Meeting, July 2003.

financial promotions are clear, fair and not misleading, he argues that some firms' managements are still seeing compliance with this as being within the province of a separate compliance department checking off against rules, without realising that the very principle itself requires a customer-focused empathy that it is down to them to develop and lead:

> [F]or a more principles based approach to supervision to work effectively, senior management in some firms will need to *change their mindset*... and should not think that meeting regulatory responsibilities is a matter for compliance departments alone. (emphasis added)[22]

In all of these foregoing descriptions we see emphasis laid on what Bovens termed "passive" accountability, task and capacity components of responsibility. The FSA's current chairman, in discussing the FSA's approach to the accountability aspects, emphasised the more active "virtuous citizenship" aspects of senior management responsibility when he expressed as a central concern of the FSA's enforcement policy that:

> A central concern of the FSA is that proper behaviour – respect for the law and its derived regulation – is the responsibility of the senior managers of firms, not with their general counsel or their compliance officer.[23]

Then, having gone on to cite some of the recent specific examples of enforcement action against senior management and managers considered below in the next section, he added that he saw such action as "an obvious means of motivating senior management to meet the standards they are obliged to follow".[24]

More recently, the FSA's head of asset management has challenged senior management in the fund management sector to treat the "Treating Customers Fairly" agenda as a strategic business goal in itself and embed it into their firm's culture.[25] Finally, it is worth noting that the role of senior management and, to a lesser extent firms' compliance

---

[22]Speech to SOFA conference, John Tiner, chief executive of the FSA, November 2003.
[23]Speech by Callum McCarthy, chairman FSA from 2003 to date, on the FSA's Enforcement Policy (29 June 2004).
[24]Ibid.
[25]Speech by Dan Waters, head of asset management at the FSA to Investment Management Association Conference, 16 June 2005.

culture and ethics, have received increasing levels of attention in the FSA's annual reports which review its activity on a number of fronts such as enforcement, strategic thematic work, supervisory activity and developmental work. The commitment of the FSA to reminding firms' senior management of the extent of their responsibilities now being firmly embedded into a range of regulatory processes is clear from a range of indicators. These include a description of the FSA's strategic aims vis-à-vis firms "to ensure that regulated firms and their senior management understand and meet their regulatory obligations".[26] At the same time, the use of recent enforcement action taken under all of SYSC, the Listing Rules and Part V FSMA backs up this rhetoric with a demonstration of a will and ability to target those behind corporate veils of regulated entities.[27]

The FSA has highlighted in a recent annual report how non-executive directors can and have played a key role in its supervisory processes through intervention in, and challenge to, firms' management.[28] Likewise, the FSA's recent statement that the "Treating Customers Fairly" agenda should be built into firms' business strategy by senior management, and aligned with firms' core business objectives, further illustrates enrolment in action.[29] In its most recent annual report the FSA again spells out the incentive to senior management to see themselves cast in a co-regulatory role along with the FSA.[30] Such frequent and public emphasis given by the FSA to senior managements' regulatory responsibility as distinct from, but ultimately, driving that of the firm, is a deliberate attempt to render a dim and distant memory the type of compartmentalisation that characterised the early days of the pre-FSMA 2000 regulatory regime whereby "regulatory issues" were seen as contained and containable in terms of the firm's strategy and organisation. It seeks to do this by building regulation into board strategy and management culture.

---

[26]FSA Annual Report 2002/2003, Chapter 3.
[27]FSA Annual Report 2003/2004, p 16.
[28]Ibid.
[29]Supra, n 27 p 27.
[30]FSA Annual Report 2004/2005, p 17.

It is interesting to note that in evidence to the Treasury Select Committee, the FSA Chief Executive appeared to have appreciated that the next stage of this challenge to effect cultural change was to effect much broader-based and more diffuse regulatory "enrolment" within the firm. In answer to a question from the committee chairman on how to move regulation forward he said:

> [T]he real issue for the big [and presumably less big? –] players is how they convert the strong sentiments and good works of their top management through the tens of thousands of people who work in their organisations, and make it real at the coalface to the customer. That is the challenge for them and that is the one we are willing to work with them [again note the language of enrolment and "co-regulation" –] to try and help resolve.[31]

The further percolation of regulation inside and around the regulated entity into the interstices of "culture" and "ethics" is seen in many other sector- and non-sector-specific regulatory and legal spheres, and more generally in corporate governance and company law initiatives and is discussed further in the following chapter.

Disciplinary action taken for breaches of SYSC rules

In November 2003 the FSA announced the outcome of disciplinary action taken against St James's Place UK plc, St James's Place International plc and St James's Place Unit Trust Group Ltd (the St James's Place companies) which operated as a marketing group, previously trading as the J. Rothschild Assurance group, registered with the Personal Investment Authority (PIA) until N2 and subsequently supervised by the FSA. The principal activity of the first two of these companies was the provision of a range of investment, pension, life assurance and protection products, with St James's Place Unit Trust Group Ltd acting as a collective investment scheme provider, advising and arranging collective investments. The companies employed a distribution and

---

[31] John Tiner, Chief Executive of the FSA, in response to Q 1914 HC Treasury Select Committee Minutes of Evidence (23 June 2004) to Eighth Report 2003–2004, HC 71-I.

marketing network of over 1000 individual Appointed Representatives often recruited from other product providers. Both pre- and post-N2 conduct of business regulation contained safeguards, including record-keeping and transaction monitoring requirements, against the potential consumer detriment that could arise from new Appointed Representatives approaching their former clients and recommending "replacement sales" which were driven more by the desire to earn commission from sales for their new principal rather than the responsibility to give suitable advice and make suitable recommendations.

Having found evidence of non-compliance with these record-keeping and monitoring requirements the FSA imposed a financial penalty of £250 000 on each of the three St James's Place companies involved in this investigation. The FSA gave details of the conduct of the companies that triggered the enforcement action:

> serious record-keeping inadequacies in connection with recommendations made to customers by their Appointed Representatives to surrender and replace existing investment contracts that had previously been arranged by competitor product providers ["replacement sales"] and their monitoring of these transactions. In particular deficiencies in the content and implementation of St James's Place's [companies] procedures for monitoring replacement sales failed to detect, and prevent, serious deficiencies in record-keeping in connection with replacement sales. As a result of these deficiencies it was necessary to obtain further information in order to determine whether the replacement sale was suitable for the investor.[32]

The relevant conduct spanned 1 January 2000 to 13 January 2003, and the further shift to outcome-oriented performance standards that the FSMA regime heralded is clear from a detailed reading of the FSA's expression of the rule transgressions in the two different eras for financial regulation. Those breaches identified in the post-N2 period are described as (inter alia):

> SYSC Rule 3.2.6 in that [the companies] failed to take reasonable care to establish and maintain effective systems and controls for compliance with applicable requirements and standards under the regulatory system: and the FSA Principle

---

[32] FSA Final Notices for St James's Place UK plc, St James's Unit Trust Group Ltd, St James's Place International plc (24 November 2003) at paras 3.1–3.2.

3 in that [the companies] failed to take reasonable care to organise and control its affairs responsibly and effectively, with adequate risk management systems.

This post-N2 regulatory exhortation is marked by a much higher level of abstraction and generality that focuses on the firm's own responsibility for running itself in such a way as to ensure compliance, than was evident in its pre-N2 equivalent. The previous FSA's Principle 9 required a firm to "organise and control its affairs in a responsible manner and to have well-defined compliance procedures". The post-N2 language of adequacy and effectiveness is deliberately designed to focus the enquiry on "Did what was done [or not done] work in terms of regulatory objectives? What result or outcome did it have? How did the firms' systems or standards perform?" A very different enquiry from "well-defined procedures", this type of requirement expects an extra and more dynamic compliance effort from the firm to stress test, review and re-engineer if necessary, procedures that may have otherwise been well defined and "responsibly" (in an active sense) put in place. Post-N2 Principle 3 is by its very nature capable of having far more of an "intrusive" (using the word neutrally) effect "within" the firm than its predecessor pre-N2.

Pure rule design apart, from the point of view of the growing emphasis on the role of senior management and their behaviour as being a key determinant to the regulatory treatment of the firm, it is significant to note that one of the five factors in the conduct of the companies identified by the FSA as particularly serious was the FSA's implication that senior management had failed to react in a timely and effective manner to regulatory guidance issued in 1994 on replacement sales. This failure contributed to the seriousness of the breach, and fed into the FSA's justification of a significant financial penalty.[33]

The same potential for the behaviour of senior management to impact on the outcome of the FSA enforcement action was illustrated by the FSA's disciplinary action taken against Abbey National Asset Managers Ltd ("ANAM") in December 2003. A financial penalty of £320 000 was levied for the firm's breaches of the FSA Principle 2 (due skill, care and

---

[33] Ibid., para 3.6(2).

diligence) and SYSC Rules 3.1.1 and 3.2.6. The relevant systems and controls failures were described by the FSA as:

> [failure to] act with due skill, care and diligence in addressing the concerns raised in connection with the Risk Mitigation Programme . . . project which was initiated in July 2002 to ensure the effectiveness of systems and controls in ANAM and [other Abbey Group companies.] While recognising the complex nature of the manual processes in place within ANAM, the divisional compliance function was critical of ANAM's failure to meet project deadlines and the poor quality of work undertaken for the [Risk Mitigation] project. As a result, it took ANAM three months longer than planned to put its process and controls documentation in place . . . [failure to] act with sufficient urgency in addressing serious concerns about the systems and controls in place on the fund management desks which were raised in two compliance reports in late 2002. It took up to nine months to address these concerns fully. Compliance monitoring resource available to Abbey National's Life Division . . . , of which ANAM forms a part, was significantly below budgeted headcount from about March 2002 to June 2003. The resource available was insufficient to maintain adequate compliance oversight from November 2002 and may have contributed to control failings in ANAM. ANAM allowed a situation where compliance oversight was not being maintained to continue for eight months after concerns were first raised by divisional compliance. ANAM did not have sufficient management information to allow it to identify, measure, manage and control risks of regulatory concern that affected ANAM between [N2] and June 2003.[34]

Once again, emphasis was laid upon the lack of alacrity of senior management's response to compliance problems once they surfaced and, in enumerating factors that contributed to the penalty levied, the FSA emphasised the seriousness of the SYSC failures. The FSA identified the firm's underresourced and poorly performing compliance function as a key failing for the purposes of SYSC. So too was the failure of senior management to fully appreciate, and be ready for, the changes within the firm's organisational structure and internal systems that N2 and the application of SYSC entailed. The FSA singled out the fact that the firm did not conduct its own assessment of the status of its systems and controls in readiness for or at N2, in order to ensure that they complied with SYSC requirements. Implicit in this criticism is the expectation that regulatory change that affects rules and processes designed to apply

---

[34]FSA Final Notice for Abbey National Asset Managers Ltd (9 December 2003).

within firms, demands a more "enrolled" and proactive response from such firms. Other instances where firms' inadequate internal systems and controls were subject to sanction under SYSC Rule 3.1.1 have included cases where senior management have failed to respond in "a timely and effective manner to guidance regarding the handling of mortgage endowment complaints where it had a reasonable opportunity to do so".[35] This contributed to a financial penalty of £675 000 for Friends Provident Life and Pensions Ltd in circumstances where internal mortgage endowment complaints-handling systems were overwhelmed by sheer volume and hence failed to function effectively. The failure of Interdependence Ltd to keep adequate records in relation to its pension fund withdrawal business (a business which itself was inadequately monitored and controlled in breach of the FSA's Principle 3) also attracted sanction under SYSC 3.1.1.[36]

In relation to the action against Friends Provident, another of the factors used by the FSA to justify a significant financial penalty was that the compliance failures were a result of systemic, rather than ad hoc, weaknesses in the firm's procedures. In the case of Interdependence Ltd the fact that the firm already had two previous regulatory fines (one in respect of similar control issues) was taken into account. The FSA's guidance relating to enforcement allows for the firm's disciplinary record and compliance history to be taken into account.[37] In attempting to unpick the concept of "compliance culture" undertaken in the next chapter, and what it might mean to different regulatory actors, a firm's compliance history can be seen as one of its possible components.

In fining Leopold Joseph & Sons Ltd in respect of breaches of SYSC Rule 3.1.1 for its failure to take reasonable care to maintain adequate systems and controls for monitoring adherence to credit limits,[38] the FSA considered SYSC guidance on delegation. It reminded the firm that, although SYSC permits a governing body to delegate functions,

---

[35]FSA Final Notice Friends Provident Life and Pensions Ltd (15 December 2003) para 3.4(g).
[36]FSA Final Notice Interdependence Ltd (8 June 2004).
[37]ENF 13.3.3(6)G FSA Handbook.
[38]FSA Final Notice Leopold Joseph & Sons Ltd (1 June 2004).

nonetheless the discharge of functions by a delegate must still be monitored and supervised.[39] Under the FSA's guidance on how "reasonable care" is to be gauged ("what the firm knew or *ought to have known*"), lack of management information at the relevant time the firm's standard of conduct falls to be judged, does *not* constitute any excusing factor. Indeed, the FSA based part of its evidence of breach of SYSC 3.1.1R on the fact that SYSC guidance further requires a governing body to base its risk identification, controls and management upon sufficiently timely, reliable and relevant management information.[40] Once again it was the lack of follow-up from senior management to being made aware of the need for extra credit limit monitoring on two separate occasions, and to having been informed two years later that the director to whom it had discharged the review function to control credit risk had not carried out reviews for several months, that contributed to the FSA's measure of seriousness of the breach.

Wholly inadequate compliance arrangements at Carr Sheppards Crosthwaite Ltd from N2 until October 2003 in terms of insufficient and confused demarcation of roles, responsibilities and reporting lines, resulted in a penalty of £500 000.[41] The compliance manual was incomplete and inadequate, and monitoring activity was confined to conduct of business regulation only, with the business failing to monitor compliance with the Approved Persons regime and SYSC. The fact that the firm failed to "ensure the appropriate involvement of senior management in its compliance arrangements", and the fact that it failed to appreciate and therefore implement the extent of the changes brought about by N2, were viewed by the FSA as contributory to the seriousness of the breaches of both SYSC 3.1.1 and 3.2.6.

At the end of 2004 AXA Sun Life plc and Bradford & Bingley plc were both subjected to financial penalty for breaches (inter alia) of SYSC Rule 3.2.6 in relation to faulty information flows upwards to

---

[39] SYSC Guidance 3.2.3.
[40] SYSC Guidance 3.2.11.
[41] FSA Final Notice Carr Sheppards Crosthwaite Ltd (19 May 2004).

senior management.[42] This shows that responsibility for failings under SYSC can extend equally to instances where senior management did not know of compliance failings occurring lower down within business structures, as when they do know, yet respond inadequately.

Similarly Cantor Index Ltd was found to have contravened SYSC Rule 3.2.6 due to insufficient engagement by its senior management with the establishment and functioning of financial promotions approval systems.[43] More recently there has been a flurry of disciplinary actions by the FSA in relation to firms' contravention of financial promotion rules. The financial promotion regime has been given greater emphasis in enforcement over the past year, in line with the FSA's "Treating Customers Fairly" priority. In all of these enforcement actions the FSA saw non-compliant, unclear and misleading financial promotions as evidence of failure to establish and/or implement effective systems for financial promotion approval (and, in some cases, record such approvals) which, in turn, were clearly evidence of shortcomings SYSC 3.2.6R (and, in the case of two of these firms, of SYSC 3.1.1R too).[44]

Senior management engagement and reaction as a regulatory "positive" in an enforcement context

In an enforcement context changes in senior management, along with commitment and prompt engagement with the issues that gave rise to the disciplinary action, have been singled out by the FSA as having had a positive impact on its decisions.

For example, Abbey National plc's weaknesses in identification and gathering of key management information which would have shown

---

[42] FSA Final Notice Bradford & Bingley plc (22 December 2004), FSA Final Notice AXA Sun Life plc (21 December 2004).

[43] FSA Final Notice Cantor Index Ltd (30 December 2004).

[44] FSA Final Notice Highbury Financial Services Ltd (3 March 2005), FSA Final Notice Courtover Investment Management Ltd (29 April 2005), FSA Final Notice City Index Ltd (22 March 2005).

defects in the wider compliance and internal control environment within the Abbey Group at the material time, was viewed by the FSA as in breach of SYSC 3.2.6.[45] A £2 million financial penalty was levied in respect of that breach along with breaches of money laundering rules. However, in emphasising the impact on the sanction of Abbey's conduct following the contravention the FSA indicated that this very high fine could have been substantially greater. It pointed to the fact that senior management led the remedial conduct swiftly, openly and effectively: "Abbey National's senior management took prompt and effective action to address the issues raised by [the Group Internal Audit Report] as soon as [its findings] became known" and "Abbey National's senior management demonstrated at the highest level its willingness to co-operate fully with the investigation and ... desire to resolve this matter as expeditiously as possible". This provides a clear illustration of how the "passive" accountability through the public sanction aspect of responsibility is being varied and fine-tuned in order to reward and promote the more "active" sense of responsibility in the encouragement of a more "enrolled" and "virtuous" management that will take up the regulatory baton within the firm.

In the same vein, the quick and effective response from the senior management of the firm's parent company, as soon as they were notified of problems, in particular its replacement of its founder directors with a wholly new management team, was highlighted by the FSA as a positive influencing factor when it imposed a financial penalty of £175 000 on Berkeley Jacobs Financial Services Ltd for breaches of various Personal Investment Authority (PIA) and Adopted Financial Intermediaries, Managers and Brokers Regulatory Association (FIMBRA) Rules between December 2000 and N2, and breaches of various of the FSA's Conduct of Business rules (financial promotions, suitability and transaction confirmation for customers) along with breaches of SYSC 3.1.1 and 3.2.6 between N2 and June 2003.[46] A higher penalty may well otherwise have resulted.

---

[45] FSA Final Notice Abbey National plc (9 December 2003).
[46] FSA Final Notice Berkeley Jacobs Financial Services Ltd (11 February 2003).

Senior management's reliance on others

Interesting points were raised in the disciplinary action taken by the FSA against CFS Independent Ltd over the extent to which a firm's senior management may rely on the advice of outside experts in the context of its obligations under SYSC.[47] The firm in question (an advisory and discretionary management firm with some 50 private clients and £8 million under management) had, in the FSA's view, failed (inter alia):

> to take reasonable steps to ensure that senior management received prompt notification of employees' personal account transactions in designated investments, or that it maintained records by which its management could identify such transactions . . . and . . . to ensure that it had in place a written policy for the allocation of investments when it aggregated a customer order with an own account order, and did not maintain appropriate records of its allocations of investments in relation to aggregated orders.

The FSA saw these specific failings as evidence of a wider inadequacy in systems and controls in relation to essential administrative and back office functions, and of deficiencies in awareness and management of risks. The firm, however, had argued that as a relatively small firm in what was to it a new area of its business, both it and its senior management had relied upon external advice. They argued that they had been justified in so doing and, since it was a small firm with one person exercising all the relevant senior management and oversight controlled functions, it had done what it could, in taking and relying on such external advice, to ensure that regulatory aims and objectives were met. In other words it argued that it had used techniques of enrolment of others to ensure that it was doing all it reasonably could to further regulatory objectives and minimise risks to those objectives in its particular business context. On one reading of this enforcement action one might take the view that this argument may have persuaded the FSA to reduce the level of financial penalty (£25 000) from what it had proposed initially. But the FSA was careful to spell out the limits of what it

---

[47]FSA Final Notice CFS Independent Ltd (7 September 2005).

saw as appropriate delegation of regulatory responsibility, and how this firm had gone beyond them:

> The degree of reliance placed by CFS and its senior management on others was extremely high. Indeed CFS's management had sought recommendations of appropriate procedures from external sources, and sought to implement these, without gaining sufficient understanding of the underlying regulatory issues and obligations themselves. In particular, the degree of CFS's reliance on a custodian, to ensure that CFS's regulatory obligations were met, was unreasonable and inappropriate.[48]

A recent and high profile enforcement action was brought by the FSA against Citigroup Capital Markets Ltd under the FSA's Principles 2, 3, SYSC 3.1.1R and 3.2.6R in relation to a trading strategy it executed in 2004 in the market for European Government Bonds.[49] The fact that this action (which resulted in a total financial penalty of some £14 million) was brought under the FSA's Principles and SYSC rules only, is itself worth noting, since most instances of SYSC disciplinary action to date have involved breaches of other more specific rules from elsewhere in the FSA Handbook, and not just the more general performance and outcome-oriented standards of SYSC and the FSA's Principles alone.

The FSA detailed the management systems and controls failures within Citigroup which it saw as responsible for allowing an unacceptably risky trading strategy to be both formulated and executed, without the approval or knowledge of senior management or of the compliance, risk management or legal functions within the firm. The FSA identified problems in information gaps and escalation flows between the trading floor and senior management, as well as inadequate supervision and training of traders. There were distinct echoes of the "bad old days" of financial regulatory compliance under the Financial Services Act 1986, with senior management and the control functions of the firm existing in a wholly separate but parallel universe to the market or customer facing functions from where most risk to regulatory objectives arises.

---

[48] Ibid., para 5.5.
[49] FSA Final Notice Citigroup Global Capital Markets Ltd (25 June 2005).

Within these two universes were differing levels of understanding of, and "buy-in" to, the importance and goals of regulatory compliance. The relative ease with which the FSA was, in the post-N2 regulatory environment, to levy a significant penalty on Citigroup without the need to evidentiate highly specific rule breaches in relation to the effects of the trading strategy itself (for example, of the Market Conduct sourcebook), shows the versatility of SYSC as a regulatory weapon.

Other enforcement outcomes with regulatory emphasis on senior management's role and compliance culture

There have been instances when, despite the fact that technically speaking breaches of the post-N2 SYSC regime have not been the grounds of enforcement action, nonetheless serious flaws in a firm's internal systems and controls have occurred. Many of these were under the pre-N2 regulatory regime and involved the firm's breach of what was previously Principle 9 (internal organisation and controls) such as the £1.35 million penalty on Royal and Sun Alliance Life & Pensions Ltd in respect of that firm's conduct and progression of the pensions review;[50] the £4 million penalty on Credit Suisse First Boston International (formerly Credit Suisse Financial Products) for conduct designed to mislead Japanese regulatory and tax authorities;[51] and the £1 million penalty for Abbey Life Assurance Company Ltd in respect of deficiencies in Abbey Life's compliance procedures and controls from 1995 to 1999 (inadequate record-keeping, inadequate communication of recommendations to customers, weaknesses in the firm's monitoring and supervising of advisers and failure to take adequate remedial steps in respect of all this), and failure to establish adequate procedures for mortgage

---

[50]FSA Final Notice Royal & Sun Alliance Life & Pensions Ltd, Royal & Sun Alliance Linked Insurances Ltd, and Sun Alliance and London Assurance Company Ltd (December 2002).
[51]FSA Final Notice Credit Suisse First Boston International (11 December 2002).

endowment sales to ensure suitability resulting in widespread misselling of these products.[52]

In the course of announcing the outcome of these enforcement actions the FSA has commented on the senior management of the firm and its role in setting the tone for that firm's controls, and the firm's more general culture of regulatory compliance. For example, in respect of the action against Royal & Sun Alliance, its senior management were castigated for their belief that the pensions review was progressing adequately when it was not in fact doing so. This led the FSA to conclude that management was insufficiently involved in the review. However, in the action against Credit Suisse the FSA laid great stress on changes in the firm's senior management and the greatly improved "compliance culture" (the FSA's words) which prevailed after extensive internal changes driven throughout the firm by that new senior management, and the very different relationship with regulators to which that new management had committed themselves.

Likewise, the conduct of the senior management of Abbey Life, following discovery of its regulatory contraventions in relation to deficiencies in compliance procedures, was described as "model". The firm was praised by the FSA as having

> fully recognised its moral, as well as legal and regulatory obligations, to its consumers. Where there has been any doubt or confusion about whether consumers may have been missold, Abbey Life has resolved this in favour of the customer

and having been

> open and co-operative with . . . the FSA. Its approach and, in particular, its proactivity in initiating the mortgage endowment review *represents a model of the type of senior management co-operation and acceptance of responsibility desired by the regulator and deserved by consumers.* . . . in the absence of such mitigating factors . . . the level of financial penalty would have been very significantly greater. [Emphasis added]

The two sides of the coin that senior management behaviour and attitudes can have on a firm's disciplinary outcomes was also shown by the contrasting approach by the FSA to actions taken by it against ABN

---

[52]FSA Final Notice Abbey Life Assurance Company (December 2002).

Amro Equities (UK) Ltd, and against Scottish Amicable plc in 2003.[53] During its commentary on the outcome of action taken against ABN Amro for breaches of (inter alia) SIB Principle 9 and SFA rules, the FSA castigated the absence of a strong and effective compliance environment and the unreasonable delay in a response by senior management after the firm's compliance officer had brought the relevant compliance contraventions to their attention. Whereas in relation to the action against Scottish Amicable for breaches of PIA rules and SIB Principles 2 and 9 arising from mortgage endowment sales and inadequate surrounding procedures, the FSA singled out what it saw as the initial poor reaction of senior management to the issue of the relevant regulatory guidance. However, it went on to commend (and also mitigate the level of financial penalty against the firm) what it termed the "responsible attitude" of senior management in addressing and remedying the failings once they had been discovered by PIA.

The strong and proactive leadership shown by Allied Dunbar Assurance plc's chief executive which showed that the firm intended to correct any defects in its procedures and to ensure fair customer treatment, mitigated a financial penalty imposed in respect of the firm's handling of mortgage endowment review.[54] And in the recent action against Citigroup under SYSC 3.1.1R and 3.2.6R referred to above, the FSA emphasised the mitigating effect of its senior management's, and CEO's in particular, response to the FSA's findings in relation to the firm's unacceptable trading strategy:

> The Chief Executive of Citigroup has personally emphasised to all staff the expectations of the bank as to the compliance standard required of all employees, and the need, in case of any doubt, to contact Compliance, Legal and Risk Management directly ... [the] FSA is satisfied that senior management within the bank have taken the matters raised by this trade, and the concerns raised by its regulators including the FSA, extremely seriously and have been fully engaged in seeking to resolve the matter and ensuring remedial actions are taken.[55]

---

[53] FSA Final Notice ABN Amro Ltd (April 2003) and FSA Final Notice (March 2003).
[54] FSA Final Notice Allied Dunbar Assurance plc (March 2004).
[55] FSA Final Notice Citigroup Capital Markets Ltd (28 June 2005), supra, n 49, para 9.5.

Regulatory expectations of individual managers: enforcement action since N2 taken directly against individual senior managers

As explained in the previous chapter, Part V of FSMA and the Approved Persons regime set up under it provide the "stick" to concentrate minds and actions on regulatory issues and objectives within the regulated firm. The recent research by Baldwin into the perceptions and effects of regulatory sanctioning of individuals, and indeed of what he terms "punitive" sanctioning of firms, provides some insight into whether or not senior management minds are being so concentrated.[56] Evidence emerged that the risk of individual sanction did indeed induce greater awareness of the need to manage regulatory risks within the firm, with one senior executive commenting "The threats are starting to get to people. When it's personal it's a different thing."[57]

Risk of loss of livelihood (through a prohibition order), reputational and personal financial damage (through public censure and/or fine of an approved person) demonstrate that regulatory "enrolment" of individual actors sometimes takes on a strong form. The legal bases of the ways in which individuals may be brought directly inside the regulatory tent, in particular those senior managers to whom the "Allocation and Oversight" and "Compliance Oversight" functions have been awarded and the way in which their realm of individual responsibility can include the firm's own compliance with SYSC, was explained in the previous chapter. The government minister responsible for steering Part V FSMA through the Commons Standing Committee described it as an extension of the previous system of individual registration that prevailed and its purpose as:

> [providing] powers for the FSA to exercise a degree of control over people employed by authorised persons. . . . The measures are an important part of the authority's armoury, which can ensure that it can regulate effectively.[58]

---

[56]R Baldwin, The New Punitive Regulation, *Modern Law Review*, 2004, 67(3), 351–383.
[57]R Baldwin, ibid at p 362.
[58]Mr Stephen Timms (Financial Secretary to HM Treasury), HC Standing Committee, A Financial Services and Markets Bill (HC Committee Papers 1998/1999), 26 October 1999 (Afternoon).

Such a metaphor of Part V powers as weapons in an armoury or as an "involuntary" mechanism, has some force. Of course in the broadest sense it could be argued that the decision to work in a regulated industry with an extensive individual regulatory subsystem connotes an implied consent to the risk of enforcement. Nonetheless, a desire to ensure mandatory application of these powers was implicit in the controversial decision by the FSA to prohibit authorised firms from making indemnity insurance arrangements to cover fines imposed by it. The FSA stated the justification for this restriction on firms' ability to shield and defend individuals from the impact of these weapons by contract as being that "the risk of a fine creates a significant incentive to comply . . . and [the prohibition on insurance against fines] will help to ensure greater compliance."[59]

This was in the face of the same concerns being expressed by industry as to the likely effect of these rule changes on the willingness of individuals to accept senior management appointments (especially non-executive directorships). Interestingly these concerns, and others in respect of aspects of Part V FSMA and individual responsibility for SYSC, are echoed throughout broader company law debates on issues such as the availability of directors and officers liability insurance; the appropriate standard of care and skill to be applied in judging directors' liability and the incentive effects (especially on non-executive directors) of setting that standard too low or too high; and the impact on risk-taking of the Directors' Disqualification regime and liability for wrongful trading under the Insolvency Act 1986. Parallels and differences between financial regulation of senior management and senior managers, and company law's shaping of standards and boundaries of behaviour for boards and their individual members are considered in more detail in the next chapter.

These FSA powers to proceed directly against individuals within regulated firms can be considered in the context of theoretical questions surrounding accountability and citizenship within complex organisations or "the problem of many hands within complex organisations"

---

[59] Para 3.3 FSA Policy Statement *The prohibition of insurance against financial penalties imposed by FSA* (December 2003), GEN 6 and ENF 13.1.3G. FSA Handbook.

considered by Bovens.[60] In Bovens' analysis of differing models of organisational accountability, he contrasts a model of "hierarchical accountability" with a model of "individual responsibility". The "one for all" characteristics of the former have a long pedigree in religious, public and military spheres whereby one person in de facto or de jure control or a small group of persons at the apex of a pyramidical structure are held to account before an external forum. Bovens describes this process:

> [t]he lower echelons can in their turn, however, be addressed by the leaders of the organisation regarding questions of internal accountability. In the case of hierarchical schemes, processes of calling to account thus happen along the strict lines of the "chain of command" and the middle managers are in turn both the persons addressed and the internal forum.[61]

Bovens admits this provides an attractively simple model but cites the long prevalent view within organisational theory of the "restricted capability of the higher levels to control the organisation".[62] In many ways the regulatory theorists' acknowledgements of the limitations and failures inherent in command and control regulation are a mirror image of the failures of top-down "command and control" models within organisations themselves, and the same difficulties that Bovens groups around "detecting" and "effecting", beset both the regulatory process and the apex of business organisations' pyramidical structures. Bovens describes a more subtle and intrusive model of individual accountability for a complex organisation's conduct whereby:

> [e]ach functionary is held liable in so far as, and according to the extent to which, he or she has personally contributed to the offending conduct on the part of the complex organisation. With this model, junior functionaries are not spared; the [accountability] forum does not need to restrict itself to the leading levels of the organisation, but can hold to account each functionary of whom it might be supposed that he or she was involved in the misconduct.[63]

---

[60]M Bovens supra, n 10.
[61]M Bovens, supra, n 10, Chapter 3 p 74.
[62]M Bovens, supra, n 10, Chapter 6 p 75.
[63]M Bovens, supra, n 10, p 106.

However, attractive as the potential for subtle calibration of responsibility against individuals' tasks, capacities, experience, etc. is, it too is not without extreme practical difficulties. As Bovens and others have pointed out, serious problems arise in unravelling causality and attributing blameworthiness, wherever "many hands" contribute to, and constitute, organisational conduct. However, both of these models of passive accountability, "command and control" and "task/role-specifc calibration", have characteristics in common with the Approved Persons regime under consideration here. Strictly speaking primary accountability for SYSC is that of the firm and hence an example of traditional accountability. Nonetheless its content is derived from a hierarchical business organisational model, despite the limitations thereof. The linkage of SYSC into the Approved Persons regime is achieved in such a way as to replicate characteristics of hierarchical accountability, that of the CEO (usually to whom the Allocation and Oversight function is allocated) and that individual in whom the Compliance Oversight function is placed. However, the Approved Persons regime, in its length and level of task demarcation detail, represents an attempt at construction of a more finely tuned model of individual accountability than Bovens describes as his prototype. The careful allocation and description of individual practice functions with Principles to guide individuals' conduct within firms, and Codes of Practice guidance as to how the tasks should be discharged, goes some way to countering practical problems of causality. There can be less argument about causal effect of A's conduct in contributing to the breach/offending behaviour by Firm X if the issue for determination by the accountability forum becomes, instead "[H]as A met the standards set for that conduct within the discharge of his regulatorily demarcated range of responsibility within Firm X?"

Likewise the element of individual "blameworthiness" that is, Bovens argues, a necessary component of accountability's legitimacy, is catered for by the regulator's stated commitment that evidence of "personal culpability on the part of [an] approved person" is necessary before it will take disciplinary action against such an individual. "Personal culpability" is defined as deliberate behaviour or behaviour where the approved person's standard of conduct was below what would be considered reasonable in the circumstances.[64] Assuming appropriate delegation has taken place and been appropriately monitored within a firm, the FSA has assured individuals that individual responsibility as an approved person is not the same thing as vicarious liability for the wrongs of the firm.[65]

Use of powers against individuals

The FSA has used its most stringent enforcement power over individuals, that of the prohibition order,[66] on several occasions since N2, and some of those on the receiving end of this power were previously in posts involving significant influence-controlled functions (senior positions), or that would have been so termed had the actions taken place after N2. In these cases the prohibition order power has deliberately been used in order to keep the individuals out of such positions in the future, and in others it has been used in an even wider manner to keep them out of any roles in the future (whether they would need approved person status or not).

The statutory power to fine and publicly censure under section 66 is exercisable over approved persons in respect of their "misconduct" (defined as a failure to comply with a Statement of Principle or being knowingly concerned in a contravention by a firm of a requirement imposed on that firm by or under FSMA), whereas the more nuclear option of a prohibition order is reserved for use in serious cases of lack of fitness and propriety.[67] However, the Court of Appeal in *R. v. FSA, ex p. Davies* has endorsed the FSA's view that this power is independent from other enforcement powers in the FSA's armoury, and can be used irrespective of whether the section 66 power to take disciplinary action against an individual could also be used in respect of the same conduct.

---

[64] ENF 11.5.4.
[65] ENF 11.5.6.
[66] Section 56 FSMA, see ENF 8 on guidance in relation to the prohibition of individuals.
[67] See FIT 2.1–2.3 for the fitness and propriety criteria to be applied to approved persons. ENF 8.5.1A.

It stated:

> Although there are different statutory criteria for invoking the procedures in s 56 and s 66, there is no clear and sharp punitive/preventive divide between them, the one looking only forwards to the prevention of future activities and the other looking only backwards to punishment of past misconduct. Both procedures are regulatory . . . Section 66 [which is subject to a limitation period of two years], is not the only provision in the 2000 Act available to the Authority in respect of past misconduct.[68]

Examples of use of section 56 FSMA Prohibition Order

Examples of the deployment of the section 56 power include the FSA's targeting of individuals within the previous management structure of Credit Suisse First Boston International (formerly Credit Suisse Financial Products "CSFP") who the FSA viewed as largely responsible for the conduct designed to mislead Japanese regulatory authorities in relation to the activities of the Tokyo branch from 1995 to 1998.[69] Neither of the two individuals concerned were approved persons under FSMA but had been, at the material time, in the case of Mr Blunden, compliance officer of CSFP and global head of compliance and company secretary (registered with the SFA, the previous regulator), and in the case of Mr Stevens, head of financial control at CSFP. The prohibition order against Mr Blunden barred him from fulfilling any future compliance function in connection with regulated activities, and Mr Stevens received a total prohibition from all regulated activities in the future.[70] In both instances the FSA carefully unpicked the demarcation of their areas of active responsibility within the firm, stressing their management responsibilities but also their lack of fitness and propriety, as shown by clear evidence of directing the misleading conduct.

However, Colin Gamwells, a former director and head of dealing at Brandeis Brokers Ltd, was targeted by the FSA with a prohibition order that went to his ability to perform management functions in the future

---

[68]*R v. FSA, ex parte Davies* [2003] 1 WLR 1284.
[69]FSA Final Notice Credit Suisse First Boston International (11 December 2002).
[70]FSA Final Notice Mr Anthony Blunden (10 November 2003); FSA Final Notice Mr Robert Stevens (10 November 2003).

as well as from investment adviser and customer trading functions.[71] The order encompassed Director, Compliance Oversight and Significant Management (Investment Business) functions and so removed him from senior management positions in any sector of the financial services industry beyond investment business alone. Action was taken against him by the FSA as a result of misuse of customer information within the firm, inadequacies in internal controls and systems (especially those designed to manage firm/customer conflicts of interest), mispricing of customer orders, and failure to ensure fair treatment for the firm's customers.

The FSA set out its justifications for its findings of lack of fitness and propriety in respect of both "competence and capability" and "honesty and integrity". With regard to "competence and capability" the FSA emphasised Mr Gamwells' failures to ensure the firm both treated customers fairly and that its trading was and remained compliant, as well as the lack of satisfactory systems of internal control. In the FSA's view these factors combined to give rise to a fundamental failure in the discharge of Mr Gamwells' managerial obligations. Even had there not been a lack of honesty and integrity, and this had "just" been a systems and controls failure (that went to managerial competence and capability alone), it is likely that the FSA would still have taken action vis-à-vis the senior management and significant influence functions and made those roles out of bounds to Mr Gamwells in the future. This would have had the effect of barring Gamwells from management functions but not from working in any capacity in the financial sector altogether.

Careful use of the prohibition order power thus provides the FSA with a significant "gatekeeping" role over the composition of the senior management tiers within the industry, a role that the DTI's Insolvency Unit and the courts in theory have over company boardrooms although the Company Directors Disqualification Act mechanism is often criticised for being unequal to the task.[72]

Again, the imposition by the FSA of an unlimited prohibition order under section 56 on Mr Barry Scott (formerly chief executive, director

---

[71] FSA Final Notice Colin Mark Gamwells (27 February 2004).
[72] See discussion in Chapter 5.

and controlling shareholder of Barum House Securities Ltd and previously SFA registered senior executive officer and SFA registered compliance officer) serves to demonstrate that a lack of probity, honesty and integrity (all present in his case) attracts the use of this individual banning order.[73] Although the conduct included inadequate supervision of an employee's unauthorised trading and lack of response to warning signs, it ranged far wider than that and included dishonesty and concealment. Hence the order was clearly overwhelmingly motivated by the lack of probity and honesty rather than more neutral "competence and capability" care and skill issues.

The FSA highlighted integrity again in its making of six prohibition orders under section 56 in respect of directors of Aioi Europe (a UK insurer) and Aioi Japan (a Japanese insurer).[74] The FSA referred specifically to a company director's general duties to that company, and imported these into its justification for the making of the regulatory prohibition orders, but clearly it had in mind the directors' general duty to act with honesty and integrity rather than their duty of care and skill. Three of the orders related to bans on the future performance of any function involving the exercise of management authority over any other person in relation to regulated activities carried on by any authorised persons. These three individuals were found by the FSA to have participated in conduct ranging from procuring the execution of improper policy, and refraining from revealing this conduct to Aioi Europe's directors, auditors, or to the FSA and also, in the case of one of the individuals, backdating his signature on a significant reinsurance policy without further enquiry or otherwise exercising his discretion. That latter type of conduct would be likely to be seen by many company lawyers as abnegation of discretion in breach of fiduciary office, as well as a breach of care and skill.[75]

However, what emerges from these considerations of instances where the enforcement power to eject individuals from earning a livelihood

---

[73]FSA Final Notice Barry Scott (6 March 2003).
[74]FSA Final Notices Messrs Yamazaki, Okazaki, McKibbin, Oda, Morota, Titterington (29 January 2004).
[75]Re D'Jan [1994] 1 BCLC 561.

in the financial services industry or certain tiers within it, tells us less about regulatory expectations in the more grey and indeterminate areas of SYSC and the extent of individual responsibility for organisational failures where that individual carries out a significant influence function. Really, it tells us little more than the FSA appears to be reserving its most drastic enforcement power to those cases where honesty and integrity are flagrantly absent, rather than managerial competence and capability per se.

Withdrawal of regulatory approval from individuals and power to levy financial penalties/censure individuals

The background to the FSA's decisions pursuant to section 63 to withdraw from individuals its approval to perform certain controlled functions, or to impose a financial penalty (or censure) for misconduct under section 66, provides some insight into the standards of conduct it expects from individuals discharging their various regulated responsibilities within regulated entities. The most serious consequence from an individual's point of view is the loss of approved person status, which entails a curtailment of earning ability. So far under FSMA 2000, as with the use of the prohibition order power, the use of this sanction has been confined to instances where the misconduct in question is flavoured with a lack of integrity. However, the whole concept of stripping away by force of law a person's right to earn a livelihood, clearly raises due process and human rights law issues which have, under the previous regulatory regime at least, been aired in court[76] and before the disciplinary system that operated under the Financial Services Act 1986.

The most notable example under the previous regime involved Mr Keith Percy, formerly global business head of the Asset Management Division of Deutsche Morgan Grenfell and former chief executive of Morgan Grenfell Asset Management Ltd at a time when serious irregularities in internal controls emerged within Morgan Grenfell

---

[76]R (on the application of Fleurose) v. Securities and Futures Authority Ltd [2001] EWCA Civ 2015, Court of Appeal.

managed unit trusts. These irregularities were revealed when problems arose within the trusts as a result of the fraudulent breaches committed by Peter Young, one of the unit trust managers within Morgan Grenfell, of allocation and investment rules which applied to collective investment schemes. IMRO took disciplinary action against both the companies involved with investment management and custodianship of the funds, and individual managers concerned with supervision and management of Mr Young's activities.

Of the individuals within Morgan Grenfell who were faced with revocation of their individual regulatory registrations it was only Mr Percy who escaped with a reprimand and costs penalties alone, having contested IMRO's disciplinary action on the grounds of its substantive and procedural fairness rather than immediately seeking to agree a settlement outcome. This almost undoubtedly resulted in a lesser penalty than might otherwise have been imposed on him by IMRO.[77] However, widespread sympathy at the time from many in the industry with Mr Percy's cause; the difficulties he faced in funding and sustaining legal challenge to IMRO's action against him; and the UK commencement of the Human Rights Act 1998, all combined to raise the profile of human rights law-based challenges to financial regulatory discipline. Indeed these human rights issues surrounding discipline and enforcement against individuals under FSMA were indeed considered in some depth by the pre-legislative Joint Parliamentary Committee in 1999 and are not the subject of further discussion in this book but will undoubtedly surface for UK and Strasbourg judicial consideration at some point.[78]

---

[77] IMRO Press Release 001/99, IMRO Reprimands Keith Percy, Former Chief Executive of Morgan Grenfell (6 January 1999).

[78] The June 1999 Second Report of the Joint Committee on Financial Services and Markets Bill (HL Paper 66, HC 465) provides an interesting starting point for analysis of the relationship between regulatory discipline and human rights law. Also see "Discipline, Enforcement and Human Rights: Regulatory Discipline and the European Convention on Human Rights – a Reality Check", D F Waters and M Hopper, in E Ferran and C Goodhart (eds) *Regulating Financial Services and Markets in the 21st Century* (Hart Publishing: 2001).

In light of the greater prominence now of such concerns it is interesting that faint echoes of procedural justice concerns can be heard on a careful reading of a recent decision of the Financial Services and Markets Tribunal (*Hoodless & Blackwell v. FSA*) concerning challenges to the decisions to withdraw approvals of two individuals' Investment Adviser controlled functions.[79] The Tribunal, in asserting jurisdiction to hear the challenges even when the individuals' employer had already terminated the relevant employment arrangements under pressure from the FSA, commented that while it did not consider the FSA's action improper "it would be very unsatisfactory if FSA's action meant that the applicants were effectively deprived of the opportunity to challenge FSA's Decisions."[80]

The factual background to the withdrawal of approval decisions that gave rise to the Tribunal reference in *Hoodless & Blackwell v. FSA* lay in a placing of shares on the Alternative Investment Market by a stock broking firm, Hoodless, Brennan and Partners plc, in which Mr Hoodless and Mr Blackwell were at the relevant time directors and shareholders. Both performed the controlled function of investment adviser, and Mr Hoodless also performed the controlled function of investment management. They had approval from the FSA under Part V FSMA 2000 and it was their fitness and propriety for such approved person status that was in issue before the FSA and the Tribunal. Interestingly they had also performed the Significant Influence controlled functions of director and Apportionment and Oversight and Mr Hoodless had also been approved to perform the Chief Executive controlled function. These management-level functions had been terminated by the firm itself when the FSA's investigations into the firm were coming to a conclusion. With regard to this termination the Tribunal commented that it had happened "due to pressure from FSA".

This shows the increased and often informal influence that has resulted from regulatory penetration of the firm, "informal" in the sense

---

[79] Decision of Financial Services and Markets Tribunal, *Geoffrey Alan Hoodless and Sean Michael Blackwell v. FSA* (3 October 2003).
[80] Ibid., para 8.

that public challenges to decisions may never be made and hence it is hard to gauge the level of this influence. Although not the subject of reference before the Tribunal, the quality of discharge of those management functions was, nonetheless, factually relevant to the applicants' fitness to hold the operational-level approvals. Briefly, an error in a placing agreement had resulted in Hoodless, Brennan and Partners (HBP) being party to an unintended obligation to underwrite the placing to the extent to which it was undersubscribed. An inaccurate market announcement was made which stated the placing was complete, and shares were admitted to AIM trading as fully paid up on 5 April 2000 by which time signed placing letters had been received for only £1.475 million worth of the shares.

Both the error in the placing agreement and the shortfall had been discovered by 11 April 2000 but a substantial quantity of the shares remained unplaced.

HBP notified the client company and its nominated adviser but not the compliance department, legal advisers, or the AIM team at the London Stock Exchange, or the SFA (its then regulator). Neither was a corrective announcement made. The FSA contended that this constituted a breach of SFA Principles 1 (integrity and fair dealing), 2 (skill, care and diligence) and 3 (market conduct).

In the period between the errors and shortfall being discovered and the placing being finally completed, which lasted nearly two months, Mr Hoodless and Mr Blackwell took a series of steps and decisions. These included Mr Blackwell contacting business associates to persuade them to take and, it was alleged, "hold" some of the stock, and the investment of some £150 000 in the shares by a fund managed by HBP (Mr Hoodless being a manager of that fund) pursuant to a discretionary investment management agreement. Also £170 000 worth of the shares were placed through HBP's retail broking operation. The FSA argued that these retail sales were made in the interests of HBP rather than its retail clients, and that such clients had then been treated unfairly as full disclosure of HBP's principal position in the stock had not been made.

An SFA routine inspection team visit which took place later in 2000 was not told of problems with the placing but began its own probing and investigation. It was alleged by the FSA that replies given to SFA by the applicants during investigations and conversations between Mr Hoodless and the client company's chairman prior to being interviewed by SFA were indicative of dishonesty on the part of the first applicant and, the FSA contended, of a general failure on the part of both applicants to be open and candid in their dealings with regulators in breach of Principle 10. It was further alleged the second applicant was in breach of Principle 1 (integrity) in his conduct in response to investigators.

On 20 December 2002 the FSA (now the relevant regulator) served decision notices on both Mr Hoodless and Mr Blackwell to withdraw approval for their performance of controlled functions on the grounds that they were not fit and proper. The grounds for taking this action were (1) the applicants' failure to notify the AIM team dealing with the placement, or to seek guidance, breached the then applicable SFA Principles 1 and 3 (integrity and fair dealing, and market conduct) in that it demonstrated a lack of due skill, care and diligence; (2) Mr Blackwell's attempt to support the company's share price through his conversations with business associates relating to the possibility of the associate taking and holding onto the shares was in breach of SFA Principles 1 and 3; (3) they had both failed to deal openly and cooperate with regulators in breach of SFA Principle 10; and (4) their conduct operated to the detriment of consumers and to confidence in the financial system (two of the four key objectives of the FSA).

However, having considered detailed transcripts of interviews, series of events and conversations and the possible interpretations of their content in the light of its preferred standards of dishonesty and integrity, the Tribunal ruled that the FSA's Decision Notices went "substantially beyond what was justified by the evidence we have heard". It reached a rather different conclusion as to whether the decisions to withdraw approval in the first place had been correct, and where the withdrawal of approval was appropriate, whether the reasons given by FSA for those decisions were correct. It ruled that Mr Hoodless' conduct did not operate to the detriment of consumers and confidence in the financial system and he *was* fit and proper to perform the controlled functions of investment adviser and investment management. Whereas, with respect to Mr Blackwell's attempted share price support (termed by the Tribunal "half hearted and ineffectual"), this was improper and in breach of SFA Principles 1 (integrity) and 3 (market conduct) so that he was *not* fit and proper to perform the controlled function of investment adviser. The Tribunal also commented that both the applicants' failure to cooperate with the regulator was in limited respects only and not a generalised failure as alleged by the FSA, and that the lack of due skill, care and diligence shown by the applicants in their failing to notify AIM and SFA as to the shortfall and the error in the market announcement and to seek guidance, did not constitute a breach of either SFA Principle 1 (integrity and fair dealing) or Principle 3 (market conduct). They ruled that the failure of skill, care and diligence (SFA Principle 2) revealed by these events and conduct merited only a private warning and not the further action of withdrawals of approval broadly based on pejorative reasoning. Mr Hoodless then, according to the Tribunal, should have escaped any form of public censure and discipline.

It is interesting to note what weight the Tribunal attributed to the way in which Mr Hoodless discharged his management responsibilities, and failed to exercise adequate supervision of the manager with day-to-day responsibility for the placing, or to exercise day-to-day control during the placing. It saw this as a case of being "in too deep" in terms of his job, in the sense that he was bearing onerous responsibilities that exceeded his abilities and, viewed like this, his abdication of supervisory management responsibilities was appropriate in light of his capabilities. The Tribunal is clearly attempting here to show that it will, and hence the FSA must, consider individual responsibilities and fitness and pro-priety to perform very different levels and types of controlled functions, discretely and on a task-by-task basis. If such a finely tuned regulatory model of individual accountability is to work well and have legitimacy (a key requirement of an effective regulatory "enrolment" strategy one would have thought), then it must be seen to be operating on a highly individualised basis. What Ayres and Braithwaite might term, although not admittedly in the discussion of UK FSMA controlled functions, "different selves".[81]

---

[81] I Ayres and J Braithwaite, *Responsive Regulation: Transcending the Deregulation Debate* (OUP: Oxford, 1992), p 31.

One other aspect of the Tribunal's decision of note here is its view on the way in which the FSA used the concept of integrity to justify its enforcement actions. The Tribunal saw a qualitative distinction in levels of culpability as between shortcomings in due skill, care and diligence on the one hand, and shortcomings in integrity on the other. It thought that the FSA was inferring a lack of integrity in instances where, on the Tribunal's view of the appropriate meaning of "integrity", such inferences were unjustified. Importing the standard of dishonesty used in civil law, which requires conduct to be both dishonest by the ordinary standards of reasonable and honest people and appreciated as such by the person engaged in the conduct,[82] the Tribunal stated that "integrity" was a more objective concept than dishonesty and that it:

> involves the application of objective ethical standards [and] . . . connotes moral soundness, rectitude and steady adherence to an ethical code. A person lacks integrity if unable to appreciate the distinction between what is honest or dishonest by ordinary standards. (This presupposes . . . circumstances where ordinary standards are clear. Where there are genuinely grey areas, a finding of lack of integrity would not be appropriate.)[83]

What the Tribunal is saying here is that it will make allowances where it suspects conversations occur in delicate circumstances. It acknowledges that patterns of behaviour which are out of the ordinary are open to more than one interpretation, some more innocent than others, and so it will lean against finding dishonesty in such circumstances. But if an individual acts in such a way to show disregard or complete ignorance of the standards of honesty applied by others so as to amount almost to a lack of an "ethical or moral compass", then such an inability to consider the ethical angle (whatever its origins and cause) will show a lack of integrity. This point should be borne in mind in the context of the discussion of compliance and ethical organisational culture in the concluding chapter.

---

[82] *Twinsectra Ltd v. Yardley* [2002] 2 All ER 377 accepted as the appropriate standard of dishonesty to employ when questioning honesty in regulatory enforcement.
[83] Supra, n 79, para 19.

Further examples of fine-tuning and calibrating individual regulatory responsibility

Application of the Part V regime allows for a degree of fine-tuning and calibration of capacity to task. The differing capacities and capabilities of individuals have been acknowledged by the FSA in the exercise of its enforcement jurisdiction under Part V. It has exercised its power to make a prohibition order under section 56 in such a way so as to prohibit individuals from exercising "Significant Influence" controlled functions yet leaves open the future possibility of exercising other controlled functions which do not carry management or oversight responsibilities on several occasions subsequent to the Tribunal's decision in *Hoodless &* *Blackwell.*[84] On careful reading of the way in which the FSA presents the factual background to, and reasons for, each of these enforcement outcomes it is possible to detect due regulatory castigation of the individuals' various breaches of expectations, accompanied at the same time by a degree of implicit acknowledgement that the individuals concerned were overwhelmed by the responsibilities laid upon them by the more senior controlled functions they were charged with.

The enforcement action taken against Mr Michael Ackers, an employee of ABN Amro (Equities) UK Ltd (ABN), in April 2003 by the FSA provides another example of an attempt to operate the individualised regulatory system in Part V FSMA with a degree of subtlety.[85] The action was taken for misconduct under SFA rules for the part he played in the firm's breaches of the FSA's former Principle 3 (market conduct) and regulatory guidance on market conduct. He accepted dealing instructions in relation to a company's shares in circumstances where he had strong reasons to suspect a price manipulation strategy was in motion vis-à-vis those shares, he effected the trades knowing they were or were likely to have a price effect, and delayed reporting them to the London Stock Exchange so the final trade was posted at an artificially

---

[84]FSA Final Notice Redvers David Evans (13 December 2004), FSA Final Notice Jonathan Paul Elms (29 July 2005), and FSA Final Notice Idris Nagaty (14 September 2005).

[85]FSA Final Notice Michael Ackers (15 April 2003).

inflated price. He failed to report these instructions either to senior management or to ABN's compliance department. In imposing a financial penalty of £70 000 under section 66 FSMA the FSA pointed out that it had considered withdrawing Mr Ackers' approved person status under section 63 and that under the previous regime a temporary suspension of his trader status had been agreed between his director and the SFA.

No such "interim" power being available under Part V FSMA a financial penalty was considered appropriate since a withdrawal of approved person status would be too punitive for a number of reasons. Interestingly, one of these reasons was that despite being a senior trader, he was "unsupported" by ABN "insofar as there was an inadequate presence of compliance [and] [h]e was denied the ability readily to plead compliance in aid of a refusal to accept the improper instructions".[86]

Again, this appears that at least in terms of exercise of discretion as to appropriate individual sanctions, the FSA will, in considering the degree of "passive" responsibility, examine the practical capacity for an individual's exercise of active individual responsibility. Quite what the FSA means by an "inadequate presence of compliance", however, is unclear and in some ways might be open to criticism of engaging in the same "compartmentalisation" of compliance issues and compliance functions that it has expended so much energy exhorting firms and senior management not to engage in.

Finally, on practical examples of individual discipline, the FSA's action against Mr Christopher Goekjian, former CEO of Credit Suisse First Boston International (at the relevant time Credit Suisse Financial Products "CSFP"), also demonstrated efforts to apply individual discipline in a way that reflects the reality of the reasons why that individual's conduct fell short of expected standards. The FSA imposed a financial penalty of £150 000 on Mr Goekjian rather than withdrawing his approval. The conduct in respect of which the action was brought involved Mr Goekjian's role in the firm's attempt to mislead the Japanese tax authorities during an audit of the extent of activities being carried

---

[86]Ibid., para 6.2(c).

out in Japan. This was also the subject of action against the firm considered above. Mr Goekjian's conduct in his failure to read documents, inform others of his system of managing documents, detect and investigate warning signals arising during the audit and properly supervise and monitor the firm's response to the authorities all amounted to breaches of the FSA's former Principles 2 (due skill, care and diligence) and 9 (internal organisation and controls). This was so in light of both his positions as CEO and SFA designated senior executive officer (the pre-FSMA forerunner of the current individual responsibility regime) and the personal responsibility he further assumed as a result of his instruction to be kept personally informed as to how the audit was progressing. However, a sizeable financial penalty, rather than withdrawal of current approved person status, was enough, the FSA stated. The reasons for this it gave as being (inter alia) the width of responsibilities that Mr Goekjian had while CEO at CSFP, the fact that matters relating to CSFP's responses on the tax audit had in fact been delegated to other senior management (recognising the fact that appropriate delegation can serve as an exonerating factor for senior managers), and the fact that his role in relation to which his then current approved person status was with a company far smaller in size and structure than CSFP.

This provides further evidence of regulatory awareness of the need to deter through mechanisms of individual accountability and yet retain a degree of enrolment and commitment to regulatory objectives by those actors charged with cognisance of them and whose roles and responsibilities are defined to include the furtherance of such objectives. The FSA must keep an element of "buy-in" in the minds of firms and individuals to the whole regulatory enterprise. One way it can do this is through showing a willingness, in the context of disciplinary action against an individual approved person, to look at issues such as that individual's capacity to act responsibly or irresponsibly, both at the time the breaches occurred, and at the time of their being held to public account.

Another CEO, Keith Rutter, while suffering a financial penalty of £20 000 levied under section 66 FSMA, escaped more severe consequences (this time in relation to the amount rather than type of penalty) because of his responsible actions and his cooperation with the FSA investigation into the issues within his company.[87] The firm (Underwriter Insurance Company Ltd) itself was closed to new insurance business, having been in run-off since July 2003, prior to which time it had been subject to premium income limits imposed by the FSA in the preceding four years. It too was publicly censured by FSA at the same time that the FSA took enforcement action against its CEO, Mr Rutter, under the Approved Persons regime. Mr Rutter had, since N2, been approved for the performance of CEO, Director and Apportionment and Oversight controlled functions. Therefore the FSA saw him as ultimately responsible, despite the involvement of others within the company, for the firm's restructuring of its insurance contracts in such a way as to enable it to evade the premium income limits that had been imposed by the FSA. While the FSA accepted that he had not knowingly contravened its Principles, nonetheless his position as CEO, along with his involvement in the business decision that triggered the contravention, was enough to vest him with clear and ultimate responsibility for the firm's own breaches of its Principles. This was so despite the fact that he had not been solely responsible for the relevant strategic decision.

Evidence from firms on early impact of SYSC and individual approval requirements

Valuable, empirically reliable data was gathered by the Financial Services Practitioner Panel (FSPP) in the form of large-scale, quantitative and qualitative surveys into regulated firms' views of the effectiveness of regulatory performance in 1999, in 2002, six months after N2, and again in 2004.[88] The 2002 survey, undertaken six months after N2, did reveal many areas where those questioned either had no experience of the issues under investigation, or felt it was too early to give a reliable opinion. Nonetheless where answers were given by both chief

---

[87]FSA Final Notice Keith John Rutter (29 November 2004).
[88]Financial Services Practitioner Panel Survey of Membership 1999, Survey of the FSA's Regulatory Performance Report 2002 (November 2002), Third Survey of the FSA's Regulatory Performance 2004 (December 2004) available at www.fs-pp.org.uk.

executives and heads of compliance (the two groups received slightly different questionnaires) then those answers provide some insight into the changes brought about by N2 on the upper tiers of management within the firm and on the internal organisation of the firm.

The 2002 survey was "outward" looking in nature since the questions asked were directed to firms' perceptions of the FSA's regulatory performance in the six months since N2. Therefore it did not shed a great deal of light on firms' own assessment of the efficacy or legitimacy of the increased direct regulatory penetration downwards into the firm that SYSC and Part V FSMA introduced at N2. However, certain of the responses given and some of the comments made in the qualitative part of the survey appear consistent with the broad hypotheses that (1) the FSA's regulation post-N2 has engaged senior management within the firm more than the previous regulatory system did, yet (2) from the perspective of the FSA's attempt to enrol a wider number of actors within the firm into its regulatory processes, there may be a degree of mismatch of expectation between regulated and regulator as to respective responsibilities within those processes.

The first hypothesis was borne out by the survey's conclusions comparing experience of the post-N2 regulatory framework to previous expectations of it (as measured in the 1999 survey). Chief executives and heads of compliance had experienced more change in the regulation of their businesses than their counterparts had been expecting when asked by the 1999 survey.[89] The fact that the transition to N2 and beyond involved a lot of senior management and compliance department time (the diversion of senior management time and the impact on a firm's business plan being two illustrative responses given in the qualitative study), along with the fact that only 13% of CEOs expected "a lot of change" in 1999 from N2 compared to those 46% who reported their experience at this level of change in 2002,[90] tends to support the notion that the changes in financial regulation introduced at N2 succeeded in greater engagement of senior management and CEOs in regulatory issues.

---

[89] FSPP Survey of FSA's Regulatory Performance Report 2002 ibid at pp 4, 95–100.
[90] Ibid., Chart 8.1, p 96.

Some support for the second hypothesis is provided by the largely enthusiastic welcome given throughout the 2002 survey for the FSA's risk-based approach to supervision, 60% of respondents reporting they found a willingness on the part of the FSA to "hold a dialogue with them on compliance issues".[91] Many of the specific responses given in the qualitative survey to questions directed at firms' opinions as to what are desirable requirements from a regulator, echo the language of regulatory enrolment and co-regulation rather than command and control. For example, "The principles they are following should make it lighter than before, less dictatorial and dogmatic ... To create a framework *which we all operate together*" (emphasis added).[92] and "It's [the FSA's role is] more of a promotional role, promoting good practice ... To make sure that the commercial aspects of those decisions are properly balanced with the risks, controls ... Making sure there are proper people in the right place to do things, as opposed to getting to the next level of detail."[93]

There was much high-level support for the more general principles-based approach to regulation along with risk-based supervision. As one head of compliance put it "Put the emphasis on firms to put their own house in order, concentrate on where are the risk areas, on themes that have manifested themselves and rely on management to get on with it."[94] Interestingly, the results of the 2004 survey reveal the same enthusiasm among firms surveyed for the whole concept of risk-based supervision, and support the survey's tentative conclusion that a greater number of firms expressed an increase in overall satisfaction with the FSA after a decrease in 2002.[95]

Another respondent to the 2002 survey identified emphasis on senior management responsibility as an example of what the FSA is "doing right".[96]

---

[91] Ibid., pp 9 and 6.

[92] Response given to questions on requirements from a regulator by CEO of a firm of brokers, ibid., p 24.

[93] Response given by bank head of compliance.

[94] Head of compliance asset management firm, ibid., p 37.

[95] FSPP Third Survey of FSA's Regulatory Performance (December 2004) at p 19, www.fs-pp.org.uk.

[96] Head of compliance of asset management firm, ibid., p 40.

However, responses given in 2002 by both heads of compliance and chief executives on areas of weakness of the FSA's performance revealed that one of the two weakest areas in their view was a failure to "provide reliable guidance when needed" (the other being the FSA's administrative efficiency). That aspect of the FSA's performance saw the greatest quantitative decline in mean score in the quantitative survey since the 1999 survey. The Survey Report identifies this as a particular source of concern to the Practitioner Panel's constituency since provision of reliable guidance was rated by respondents as the most important of the 15 criteria for evaluating the FSA's performance. In 2004 surveyed firms' unhappiness with the willingness to give and effectiveness of guidance given by the FSA was even more marked, suggesting that, despite stated support for risk-based, principles-oriented regulation, its implementation was becoming a source of concern and frustration for firms.

The two worst performing areas for the FSA shown up by the 2004 survey were its understanding of firms' businesses, and problems with the obtaining and giving of guidance. The first of these concerns found expression in comments and responses about mismatch of "culture" between regulator and firms as well as regulatory failure to appreciate the broader environment in which firms must operate. Although it is easy to say that these are criticisms made of every regulator the world over by their regulated constituencies, the point remains that the reasons for this require more sustained exploration since they may, if brought into the foreground, become less intractable. The discussion in Chapters 5 and 7 aims to contribute to that process.

The second of those concerns is a more practical manifestation of the first, and reflects the real frustrations and tensions that arise when regulatory enrolment techniques are used to seek to move responsibility downwards to firms and within firms. Concerns about guidance are a code for the tussle between various levels of regulation and actors within regulation who seek to pass responsibility like a baton to and fro between themselves. The comments made by firms' representatives have an especially plaintive ring when heard in the context of the discussion in the concluding chapter of this book about the fairness and acceptability of devolving and obfuscating responsibility for uncertainty: "you tend to get a 'do whatever you think is right,' which I find deeply unhelpful."[97] "There is no such thing as informal guidance. There is no one at the FSA who is willing to give you informal guidance. They put it back to you. That's the rule, you interpret it as you want."[98] And, perhaps most tellingly in the light of the discussion on political responsibility and regulatory responsibility in the concluding chapter, "They're not allowed to be open. They are frightened of their own shadows."[99]

It might be argued that this mismatch between key firm actors' expectations and regulatory willingness and/or capacity to give specific direction or meaning to regulatory standards (and hence regulatory view of risk and uncertainty) in specific practical circumstances reveals a more fundamental mismatch in views of the two constituencies over the exact meaning of regulatory enrolment. It may well be that on the one hand regulated firms are still at the stage of saying to the regulator "Look – we accept and indeed applaud your new outcome-oriented approach to rule making, risk-based approach to supervision and reliance on our internal controls and management commitment and capabilities to make standards work, and indeed we are now willing to accept and acknowledge the individual responsibilities that accompany that ... BUT ... we cannot always work out for ourselves what rules, standards and regulatory objectives mean in your eyes (for it is, as Chapter 2 showed, *your* view of risk to *your* statutory objectives that matters at the end of the day ...). So we need a steer in the form of guidance from yourselves, and that, after all, is how the two way 'co-regulatory' processes that enrolment of the regulated by the regulator ought to work and hence demand."

On the other hand it could well be that the FSA has very different expectations as to how the greater enrolment of the firm and its actors should work and very different concerns as to how much individual handholding it should properly be doing by way of issuing specific guidance that firms can "rely" on. It might argue that it has already set the

---

[97] Bank CEO's response to 2004 survey question on effectiveness of guidance from FSPP Survey Report, December 2004, supra, n 88, p 68.
[98] 2004 response from head of compliance at IFA Network, supra, n 88, p 69.
[99] 2004 response from building society CEO, supra, n 88, p 68.

framework within which firms should construct and disseminate their own regulatory and compliance expertise: it has spelt out its views of risk to its objectives and developed detailed standards and rules geared to the achievement of those objectives and the minimisation of relevant risks in consultation with firms. It is therefore now up to the firms themselves to develop and promote familiarity with the FSA's standards and objectives on a far wider scale than simply within their compliance department. This, the FSA might argue, is what it means by, and why it places continuing emphasis on, the development and promotion of a compliance and regulatory risk-oriented culture. After all, any regulator could be forgiven for fighting shy of putting itself in a position whereby it responds to specific requests from firms as to the application of its rules and principles in specific commercial situations.

Quite apart from the need to preserve scarce regulatory resource, it could involve the FSA in operational issues of commercial sensitivity that pose a risk of contagion to its other areas of work. It also would presumably wish to develop both the confidence and maturity within firms' own decision-making and judgement formulation processes to increase the purchase and grip that the highest-level ethical standards and regulatory themes (for example, fair treatment of customers) have within firms. Were firms to be better enrolled in this way then, perhaps, what were previously seen by firms as "just" commercial decisions and accompanied by a request for guidance to the regulator, would instead be transformed into a more holistic decision taken within the firm that would be informed by a mixture of commercial factors and also broader ethical regulatory factors. Instead of asking the question "Can we do this and be safe from a regulatory perspective?" firms would instead ask "*Should* we do this in light of possible risk to any regulatory objectives?" Firms would, hopefully, have internalised those regulatory objectives and accepted their own role in pursuing them as the necessary price of a lighter touch and mature relationship with the FSA.

In many ways the parent–child/adult–adult relationship axis is an appropriate metaphor. Transition from the former to the latter level presupposes a degree of independence in decision-making, and absorption and action upon a set of reasonably shared values. The mismatch in expectations between regulator and industry in relation to levels of guidance forthcoming from the FSA might be seen as that same transitional tension surfacing in the new regulatory framework where "enrolment" places responsibilities for independent decision-making within firms as part of the attempt to "grow" a greater compliance and ethical culture within them. That is one view of the trend evident in the Practitioner Panel survey results. However, as the discussion in the concluding chapter will show, this tension may be evidence of a far more fundamental problem in the way that society and its institutions deal with risk and uncertainty.

A smaller and more homogeneous group of firms was surveyed in 2003 with the British Bankers Association survey of its own membership. It revealed a broad level of satisfaction with both the functioning of the Approved Persons regime in Part V FSMA (with 94% replying that there were no aspects of the Approved Persons regime causing material difficulties to their business) and with the clarity of the obligations incumbent upon senior management in circumstances in which disciplinary action could result (with again 94% respondents reporting that they found them either fairly or very clear).[100]

Finally, the authors themselves conducted a small questionnaire-based survey in 2003 into a randomly chosen sample of 100 investment management firms, insurers and private client securities broking firms; the response rate produced being 8%, it proved of limited and anecdotal value only. However, questions were put to heads of compliance (to whom the questionnaires were sent) on the implementation of the FSA's rules on senior management responsibilities and also on the understanding within and evaluation by firms of the concept of "compliance culture". In relation to the impact of the FSA Handbook's requirements on senior management responsibilities only one respondent felt that its own senior management had not been fully prepared for the changes introduced by SYSC at N2. However, opinion was more evenly divided over to what extent the introduction of SYSC had had a real effect in

---

[100]BBA Membership Survey on FSA Regulatory Framework (December 2003).

terms of the FSA's stated objective for SYSC:

> to encourage firms' directors and senior executives to take appropriate practical responsibility for their firms' directors and senior executives to take appropriate practical responsibility for their firms' arrangements on matters likely to be of interest to FSA.[101]

Unsurprisingly the one firm reporting unpreparedness responded "Totally!" to whether or not that objective had been enhanced by SYSC. One question asked for specific examples of organisational change wrought internally by the introduction of SYSC. To this one firm responded that it would like to see more detailed guidance from the FSA on the need for supervision within the firm given to those to whom business functions had been delegated pursuant to SYSC. Another respondent thought that the introduction of SYSC had in practice enhanced the taking of individual responsibility for firms' arrangements and it reported generally increased awareness among holders of significant influence functions of regulatory issues. That same firm gave a specific practical example of how the risk of disciplinary action under Principle 4 of the Approved Persons Code of Practice (an individual must deal openly and cooperatively with the regulator) meant that the firm's parallel obligation under the FSA Principles of Business 11 was now taken more seriously by individuals within that firm. As the respondent put it "Our APs are very aware of this [linkage between the two parallel principles – the one incumbent on the firm, the other on them] and how it should guide decisions on disclosure to FSA."[102]

Another firm, a small compliance training consultancy in the Life Office/IFA sector, responded to this general question on overall effect of SYSC that, while there might have been some slight positive enhancement of individual responsibility within regulated firms due to the introduction of SYSC, "most senior management in this industry have no idea of complaints, compliance or customers and they continue to demonstrate this".

---

[101] SYSC Guidance G1.2.1(1).

[102] Anonymised response to Strathclyde University Survey 2003, UK Director of Risk and Compliance (General Insurer).

Nevertheless the majority of responses (which were also from firms that placed themselves in the largest 20% in their business sector) reported that the introduction of SYSC had wrought no significant practical changes internally, since reporting lines were already clearly defined and internal controls had already been strong and robust prior to N2 as the result of either the need to comply with other external regulatory regimes (general corporate governance arrangements) or in order to enhance internal management responsibility for the operation of the business itself.

In light of the growing trend for general corporate governance requirements to extend downwards through the corporate veil to fix directors and board committees with responsibility, it is of course no surprise that the intrusion of SYSC represented nothing new in itself to larger firms. This was despite the fact that its requirements were generated from a different policy angle and with a different set of interests to that of general company law and corporate governance. However, for those smaller and unlisted firms that do not have as much experience of devising, maintaining and operating formal governance structures, then SYSC does indeed represent a departure from the previous approach of a limited degree of key individual registration, and responsibility for firms' compliance still largely being perceived as an area for "the compliance department".

In addition, even the larger firms may need to consider in more depth that, although the similarities may be obvious between what they were already used to in terms of corporate governance and internal controls and SYSC and the Approved Persons regime, there are also dissimilarities. These may result from the differing policy remit of financial regulation to that of company law and corporate governance. This could raise awkward questions for both boards of directors and individual directors when faced with a decision that might involve a conflict between the objectives of both regimes. It is this type of question, the similarities between SYSC and the Approved Persons regime and other types of "in-firm" or "in-company" regulatory and legal frameworks that much of the next chapter now turns.

5

The wider regulatory and legal context for senior management

This chapter positions the FSA's regime of regulatory senior management responsibilities against both the existing duties owed in company law by the board of directors of a company and by individual members of it, as well as against broader corporate governance trends.[1] It charts how the increasing intrusiveness of regulatory law shown by SYSC and the Approved Persons regime can be seen throughout a wider sharpening of corporate law mechanisms of individual accountability such as the Company Directors Disqualification Act 1986 and the UK Listing regime.

---

[1] In particular the *Higgs Review of the Role and Effectiveness of Non-Executive Directors* (January 2003) which led to the reformulation in November 2003 of the *Combined Code on Corporate Governance* and, in the USA, the introduction of the Sarbanes-Oxley Act 2002.

SYSC and the Approved Persons regime compared with board and individual director responsibilities under "general" company law

Any industry-specific regulatory regime does not operate in a vacuum but rather in an extremely crowded and noisy business environment throughout which are layered all manner of other individual regulatory regimes (data protection, competition, tax, etc). Added to these are the overarching responsibilities and obligations imposed by company and insolvency laws, as well as the need to comply with the Listing regime and the Combined Code on Corporate Governance where applicable. This raises both theoretical and practical concerns. On a practical level, when considering a course of action on behalf of the firm such as signing off the marketing of a new product or service line, declaring annual bonuses for policyholders, or reviewing delegation and organisational structures within a particular area of the business, to take but a few examples, boards and individual directors of FSMA-regulated firms facing these decisions must consider not just how the firm and they as individual approved persons will be seen to measure up against the standards of SYSC and the Approved Persons regime as a result of their discharge of their management responsibilities. They must also consider what bearing the fiduciary and common law duties and statutory obligations owed by a director to her company should have on their decision-making, as well as the need to avoid wrongful trading under the Insolvency legislation,[2] and the expectations of the standards of conduct for individual company directors developed by the courts in actions brought against directors under the Company Directors Disqualification Act 1986. That is without even beginning to consider the expectations of the Listing regime and Combined Code on Corporate Governance as far as both board action and individual directors are concerned, or whether the position a director may hold as a non-executive member of the board

---

[2] Section 214 Insolvency Act 1986.

ought to distinguish in some way her decision-making from her executive peers and, if so, how?

Each of the aforementioned legal and regulatory regimes has a different pedigree, enforcement jurisprudence and emphasis to SYSC and Part V FSMA. Each one is concerned with differing policy interests and the protection of different stakeholders, yet each operates on the same actors in relation to the same commercial decisions. The possibility of conflict in the objectives and desired outcomes between these different regimes should be obvious and has been explored on a theoretical (and empirical) level by Haines and Gurney.[3] They assert that much regulatory scholarship suffers from a tendency to view regulatory regimes in isolation and hence ignores the ideological conflicts played out at the interface of discrete legal and regulatory regimes which may actually have fundamentally different expectations of what should constitute "ideal behaviour and proper responsibility" in the same factual context.

Bamford discusses an interesting and intensely practical example of such conflict in the context of the interaction of a director's fiduciary duties under general company law with her responsibilities as an approved person under Part V FSMA 2000.[4] In posing the question whether the Approved Persons regime might have different expectations to the course of conduct required of an individual in a given situation to the expectations that general company law would have of that same individual in the exact same situation he foresees "[T]ension between the two because they spring from different roots and serve different purposes. One regulates behaviour so as to safeguard the interests of the public, while the other protects private property rights."[5]

---

[3] F Haines and D Gurney, The Shadow of the Law: Contemporary Approaches to Regulation and the Problem of Regulatory Conflict, *Law & Policy*, October 2003, Vol 25, No 4.

[4] C Bamford, "Directors' Fiduciary Duties and the Approved Persons Regime" in E Ferran and C Goodhart (eds) Chapter 6, *Regulating Financial Services and Markets in the 21st Century* (Hart Publishing: Oxford, 2001).

[5] Ibid p 76.

At the time of writing UK company law on directors' duties (and indeed many other aspects of company law) is still under review.[6] The manner in which it articulates both the fiduciary and common law duties is set to change to take the form of a statutory statement[7] rather than being gleaned primarily from case law built up over the years.[8] However, what will *not* change, as Bamford points out, is that company law's primary concern in imposing directors' duties remains *how* a director should carry out her function as director rather than prescribing *what* she should do, since those duties, although owed to the company, are ultimately concerned with the protection of private property being that of the shareholders and they are seen by the law as the best judges of how their property should be applied by the directors rather than the courts.

Company law has evolved directors' duties that are largely aligned to the economic incentives of safeguarding and maximising invested capital. Despite calls for a wider more "public" interest basis for company

---

[6]An extensive DTI consultation on and review of the framework for UK company law began in 1998 and has led to the publication of two DTI White Papers containing proposals for draft legislation *Modernising Company Law*, Cm 5553 (July 2002: DTI) and *Company Law Reform*, Cm 6456 (March 2005: DTI), the latter contains the current erosion of the Draft Company Law Reform Bill. Although DTI has published further draft clauses in July and September 2005 none of these relate to directors' duties.

[7]The most recent proposals in relation to directors' duties can be found in the Draft Clauses in Part B Draft Company Law Reform Bill 2005 – Part B (Chapters 1–3), DTI White Paper *Company Law Reform* (March 2005), Cm 6456 along with accompanying explanatory text at para 3.3, pp 20–24 of the March 2005 White Paper.

[8]Cases such as *Aberdeen Railways v. Blaikie Bros* (1854) 1 Macq 461, *Regal (Hastings) Ltd v. Gulliver* [1967] 2 AC 134 and *Industrial Developments Consultants Ltd v. Cooley* [1972] 1 WLR 443 provide examples of the courts' formulation of a director's fiduciary duty while decisions such as *Re D'Jan* [1994] 1 BCLC 561 and *Norman v. Theodore Goddard* [1992] BCLC 1028 provide good examples of the courts' articulation of a director's common law duty of care and skill. See Chapter 16, Gower and Davies, *Principles of Modern Company Law*, 7th edition (Sweet & Maxwell: 2003) for further discussions of directors' duties.

law[9] it looks set to continue with its basis rooted firmly in shareholder value. What has emerged from the company law reform process as the proper scope of company law (and hence *raison d'être* of companies) is described as "enlightened shareholder value".[10] It is presented as something qualitatively different from a crude focus on maximisation of shareholder value alone without regard to how this might be achieved by taking cognisance of the interests of a wider group of stakeholders in the company. Nevertheless, it still falls far short of any enshrinement in law of the need for company decision-making to be genuinely open and plural in the sense of not privileging shareholder value over other broader public and stakeholder interests.

Shareholder value, albeit viewed and measured through a more contextually aware and enlightened prism, still remains the dominant driver for boards' decision-making in company law. The task of protecting and advancing other interests such as creditor protection, employee safety, environmental quality, social and community cohesion, financial citizenship, and depositor and investor protection will continue to be left primarily to other bespoke regulatory regimes.[11] Before considering examples of tensions and dissonance between the requirements of general

---

[9] See, for example, discussion in J Parkinson, *Corporate Power and Responsibility: Issues in the Theory of Company Law* (OUP: Oxford, 1993) at Chapters 9–11. A useful exposition of the arguments in favour of a wider, stakeholder-oriented basis to company law and corporate governance is provided by C Mallin, *Corporate Governance* (OUP: Oxford, 2003), Chapters 1 and 4.

[10] See discussion in paras 5.1.13–5.1.16, Chapter 5. Modern Company Law for a Competitive Economy: The Strategic Framework, DTI Consultation Document (February 1999) URN 99/654.

[11] There was considerable discussion in the *Company Law Review* of the merits and demerits of a more pluralist "socially responsible" approach to the scope of company law before this approach was rejected in favour of an "enlightened shareholder value" approach. Chapter 5, *Modern Company Law for a Competitive Economy: The Strategic Framework*; DTI Consultation Document (February 1999) URN 99/654 and Chapters 2, 3 and 4, *Modern Company Law for a Competitive Economy: Developing the Framework*, DTI Consultation Document (March 2000) URN 00/656, Chapter 3; DTI White Paper, *Modernising Company Law* (July 2002), Cm 5553, para 3.3; Chapter 3, DTI White Paper, *Company Law Reform* (March 2005), Cm 6456.

company law and an approved person's responsibilities under the FSMA regime the discussion will consider briefly what those general company law requirements are at present and how they look set to evolve.

Existing and proposed directors' duties under general company law

Company law texts provide numerous accounts and discussions of the nature and scope of a director's duties under common law and statute.[12] It is not proposed to provide anything even approaching an exhaustive account here for this work's interest in directors' duties is from the perspective of how they cut across a director's additional responsibilities as an approved person under Part V FSMA 2000. However, a director's fiduciary duty can be briefly formulated as a duty of loyalty to the company, which translates into a duty to act in good faith for the benefit of the company. Well-worn manifestations of the practical meaning of such a duty include a director's obligation not to profit from his position as director and to avoid conflicts between personal interests and those of the company.[13] Disclosure to and ratification by the company of a director's breach of fiduciary duty can, in certain circumstances, permit a director to commit to a course of action that would otherwise be an actionable breach. Part X Companies Act 1985 entitled "Enforcement of Fair Dealing" has further buttressed the application of this duty of loyalty by singling out various specific potential abuses ranging from corporate loans to directors to long-term service contracts for either absolute prohibition, or prohibition subject to disclosure and consent.

A director's common law duty requires her to act with the skill, care and diligence which, so long as she acts honestly, has been interpreted by the courts not as a duty to take absolute care but rather to take

---

[12]Chapter 16, Gower and Davies, *Principles of Modern Company Law* 7th edition (Sweet & Maxwell: 2003), Part III, B Hannigan, *Company Law*, (Butterworths: London, 2003).
[13]*Abberdeen Railway Co v. Blaikie Bros* (1854) 1 Macq 461, *Regal (Hastings) Ltd v. Gulliver* [1967] 2 AC 134 and *Industrial Developments Consultants Ltd v. Cooley* [1972] 1 WLR 443, *Cook v. Deeks* [1916] AC 554 PC, *Guinness plc v. Saunders* [1990] 2 AC 663.

"reasonable" care and she need not exhibit any greater skill than may be reasonably expected of someone with her knowledge and experience, she is not bound to give continuous attention to the company's business and may delegate functions to another where the business demands delegation and the company's constitution permits it.[14] More recently the courts have imported into the common law standard of skill and care the standard used by insolvency legislation in judging liability for "wrongful trading", namely whether a director should be required to contribute personally to an insolvent company's assets in circumstances where she knew or ought to have concluded there was no reasonable prospect of the company being able to avoid insolvency.[15]

Faced with a misfeasance action by the company's liquidator against its managing director who had made an erroneous statement in the company's insurance proposal form, hence invalidating the insurance cover which resulted in loss when the company's assets were destroyed by fire, Hoffmann J. had to decide if the director had been negligent in not reading the proposal before he signed it. He stated that the duty of care owed by a director at common law was exactly coterminous with the degree of diligence necessary to avoid liability for wrongful trading, namely the conduct of

> a reasonably diligent person having both – (a) the general knowledge, skill and experience that may reasonably be expected of a person carrying out the same functions as are carried out by that director in relation to the company, and (b) the general knowledge, skill and experience that that director has.[16]

Although he acknowledged that company law would not expect a busy director to read the whole of every document she ever signed, in this instance signature of a wholly unread yet simple and crucially important form showed a lack of the degree of reasonable diligence expected by the law.

---

[14]*Re City Equitable Fire Insurance Co* [1925] Ch 407.

[15]Section 214 Insolvency Act 1986. For a useful review of the wrongful trading case law see *Re Continental Assurance plc* 2 All ER (D) 229.

[16]Sections 214(4) Insolvency Act 1986 cited by Hoffmann J in *Re D'Jan* [1994] 1 BCLC 561.

As for likely future formulations by company law of directors' duties following the conclusions of the Company Law Review, the most recent version of the Draft Company Law Reform Bill promises to introduce a statutory statement of directors' duties intended to make the scope and content of a director's general law responsibilities clearer and more accessible than do the existing common law and equitable rules it is set to replace.[17] The combined effect of the introduction of this reformulated statutory statement of directors' duties, along with the new more outward looking and "stakeholder-oriented" board reporting requirements introduced for quoted companies in the 2005 Operating and Financial Review Regulations[18] should, in the government's view, reflect and promote "enlightened shareholder value" as the life force of corporate decision-making.[19]

The statutory statement provides that directors' duties continue to be owed to the company, that directors must act within their powers and that their duty is "to promote the success of the company for the benefit of its members".[20] Within the confines of that overall objective they should shape their decision-making in an "enlightened" fashion by taking account of:

where relevant and so far as reasonably practicable ...

(a) the likely consequences of any decision in both the long term and the short term,

(b) any need of the company – (i) to have regard to the interests of its employees, (ii) to foster its business relationships with suppliers, customers and others, (iii) to consider the impact of its operations on the community and the environment, and (iv) to maintain a reputation for high standards of business conduct, and

(c) the need to act fairly between members of the company who have different interests.[21]

---

[17] Draft Clauses B1–B55 in Part B, Directors Draft Company Law Reform Bill, DTI White Paper, *Company Law Reform* (March 2005), Cm 6456.

[18] Operating and Financial Review and Directors' Report Regulations SI 2005/1001 which took effect 22 March 2005.

[19] Para 3.3, p 20, *Company Law Reform*, March 2005, DTI White Paper, Cm 6456.

[20] Draft Clause B3, Part B, Draft Company Law Reform Bill, Part 7, White Paper, supra, n 19.

[21] Draft Clause B3(3).

The government takes the view that such a formulation reflects "modern business needs and wider expectations of responsible corporate behaviour".[22] However, it remains the directors' own bona fide measure of what they consider most likely to promote the success of the company for the benefit of the members as a whole that matters, and even then only when relevant *and* reasonably practicable so to take account. This leaves boards with considerable autonomy in their decision-making.

Nonetheless the attempt to place directors' decision-making in a broader context has parallels with the FSA Handbook's more explicit basing of regulatory obligations and requirements for firms and individuals against the backdrop of the four key regulatory objectives (protection of consumers, market confidence, prevention of financial crime and promotion of public awareness of the financial system[23]). The statutory statement of principles for directors provides that directors should maintain independence of judgement in relation to exercise of their powers. The degree of care, skill and diligence a director is to be expected to exercise is to remain objectively expressed and to be measured against the knowledge, skill and experience which may reasonably be expected of a director in her position *and* any additional knowledge, skill and experience she may have. Thus any subjective enquiry into what that director *actually* knew or what was within and without her *actual* competence and skill can only be undertaken with a view to asking if she had higher levels of skill and experience which ought to expose her to a higher standard of liability against which to be measured. The subjective enquiry will only be relevant to condemn rather than to excuse a director for inexperience or limited competence.

---

[22] Supra, n 19.

[23] These four statutory objectives laid down in s 2 FSMA 2000 with which the FSA is tasked form the four corners of UK financial regulation and, as explained in Chapter 2, underlie the FSA's operating framework of risk-related regulation. They are recurrent explanatory themes running throughout the FSA's rule-making process and hence the Handbook, the FSA's enforcement and disciplinary process as well as and increasingly feature as reference points in both Tribunal and judicial decision-making of issues arising under FSMA 2000.

One company law commentator, Riley, has argued that while an objective standard for the "diligence" component of a director's duty of care is justifiable in economic terms (i.e. how a director approaches her tasks and functions), it is less easy to see a clear justification for an objective standard of the "skill" element (i.e. the outcome of the exercise of her functions – what she achieves or does not achieve).[24] He argues that since no one individual can possibly exceed the boundaries of their competence at any given time, however hard they may try to do so, then the imposition of an objective standard for measuring a director's skill is as unrealistic and deterrent in effect as is an absolute liability standard. Indeed, he argues, an objective standard for *skill* (as opposed to *care*) may lead to inefficient outcomes in that the director knowing that she is still at risk of liability even if she performs with all the competence and skill she can muster, may demand remuneration at a level to compensate her for this risk which she cannot herself minimise so that company law's attempts to impose higher standards of skill and competence through an objective standard of skill will simply lead to mispricing of the directors' services as overly high compensation packages are demanded. Although this argument has not found its way into the standard of care, skill and diligence in the proposed statutory statement of directors' duties under general law it is still possible to discern traces of a willingness to consider the actual boundaries of a director's competence in some respects throughout the case law dealing with disqualification under Company Directors Disqualification Act 1986 considered below.

The individual regulatory and disciplinary regime that forms the Approved Persons regime bears more resemblance to the supposedly protective and prophylactic regime for directors disqualification than it does to the general duties of company directors so it is argued below that there are strong arguments for the FSA's disciplinary process applying this same distinction within Approved Persons regime enforcement decisions.

---

[24]C Riley, The Company Director's Duty of Care and Skill: The Case for an Onerous but Subjective Standard, *Modern Law Review*, 1999, Vol 62.

As for the fiduciary duty hitherto owed in general law by an individual company director, the relevant general principles in the proposed statutory statement of duties which are designed to play the role played to date by the general fiduciary standard are grouped under three headings: "Duty to avoid conflicts of interest", "Duty to declare interest in proposed transaction with the company" and "Duty not to accept benefits from third parties". These principles impose prohibitions on certain conduct and transactions by directors subject to strict conditions and are designed to provide clearer and more succinct guidance to directors than has been possible to discern from the sometimes conflicting morass of case law on fiduciary conduct in a corporate context, on exactly what they can and cannot do, and in what circumstances they may do something that would usually be impermissible. Interestingly the word "fiduciary" is nowhere to be found in the proposed statutory statement of directors' duties.

As Birds has argued in his critique of the reformulation of directors' duties beget by the Company Law Review, the word "fiduciary" is not just any old term of legal jargon to be lightly swept aside by modernising zeal. For what is inherent in this particular term is one of the most enduring, successful and adaptive of behavioural standards devised by private law.[25] Its success is partly attributable to its widely understood moral content and hence moral force and to remove it as a defining element of the general duties of a company director is to lose something important from the very core of the legal framework of governance of business enterprise. This omission may be driven by an attempt to emphasise the facilitative nature of general company law to play up its role as a framework for a more entrepreneurial UK corporate sector, implicit in the stated objectives of the CLR.[26] However, it is somewhat ironic that, at a time of increasing realisation of the importance of strengthening corporate ethical cultures as a means of combating

[25] Birds *Reform of Company Law*, De Lacey (ed) (Cavendish: 2002).
[26] See discussion of Objectives of Company Law Review and Reform Process, Chapter 2, DTI White Paper *Company Law Reform* (March 2005, Cm 6456).

corporate fraud and wrongdoing,[27] perhaps the strongest moral descriptor in private law looks set to be stripped out of UK company law. The same charge cannot be levelled at UK financial regulation. As the last chapter showed, considerable disciplinary force has been given by the FSA to the requirement that approved persons act with integrity when carrying out controlled functions.

Tensions and dissonances

A company director pulled one way by general law and another by regulation

Bamford posits two hypothetical examples, from the retail and wholesale financial services sectors, of potential conflict between a company director's obligations under the Approved Persons regime and under general company law.[28] These examples provide neat practical illustrations of the problem of regulatory conflict identified by Haines and Gurney.[29] Bamford uses the by now all too well-known example of pensions misselling where an industry-wide systemic review of the need for compensation to individual investors had been ordained by the FSA. This review imposed compliance obligations on firms, and therefore on individual approved persons in a senior management position of a pensions provider, to ensure that such reviews were properly carried out and due compensation paid.[30] Insofar as that individual's responsibilities under the approved persons regime go (concerned as it is with investor protection and public confidence in the financial system) her obligations

---

[27]For example, s 406 Sarbanes-Oxley Act 2002 empowers the SEC to require corporate issuers to disclose their adoption of codes of ethics for their senior financial officers.

[28]Supra, n 4.

[29]See text to n 3, supra.

[30]For a more extensive discussion of the legal basis to this review see *R v SIB, ex parte IFAA and LIBM Ltd* [1995] 2 BCLC 76, *R v. PIA, ex p Lucas-Fettes* (Unreported: Queen's Bench Division High Court: 10 July 1995) and Black and Nobles, Personal Pensions Misselling: The Causes and Lessons of Regulatory Failure, *Modern Law Review* 1998, 61, 789. Now under the FSMA regime such reviews would take place pursuant to s 404 FSMA 2000 – see J Gray, The Legislative Basis of Systemic Review and Compensation for the Mis-Selling Of Retail Financial Services and Products, *Statute Law Review*, 2004, 25(3), 196–208.

are clear, she must take all reasonable steps to ensure that her firm co-operates with the pensions review and effects it in a compliant manner. That will most likely entail the payment to individual investors of large amounts of compensation, something that is not necessarily in the best interests of the company's shareholders, such interest being what she is first and foremost bound to consider in her position as a director of the company. Although an argument could be made that it is in the long-term interests of the company's shareholders to maintain a "clean" regulatory reputation this is tenuous at best and would be irrelevant, Bamford points out, to the case of an insurance company that is closed to new business and is in run-off.

Although there have been no challenges based on breaches of directors' duties to the large amounts of compensation payments paid out in the last few years of retail financial services companies' funds in relation to personal pension, mortgage endowment and, most recently, spilt-capital investment trust business, Bamford argues that individually approved persons who are also company directors would be in less jeopardy from such challenges if company law provided a specific safe harbour from suit for breach of duty for actions taken by a director in compliance with obligations under the Financial Services and Markets Act 2000.

Such a safe harbour would also protect the directors in the second hypothetical example he gives of a large banking group where the directors of the holding company are also directors of three subsidiaries, a deposit-taking company (Company A), a futures trading company (Company B) and a fund management company (Company C). Company B has made disastrous speculative losses and is technically insolvent; it owes £350 million to Company A which in turn has net liabilities of an equivalent amount to UK retail depositors. Company C is uninvolved with its sister companies and has a small net worth and an excellent business reputation hitherto. Now that the facts have emerged the directors of the holding company have received a valuable offer for the share capital and business of Company C. What are the directors of the holding company to do? For they are also directors of each of the three subsidiaries since the group has a matrix management structure and their responsibilities as approved persons fulfilling significant influence senior management functions are clear. They are to unwind the mess the group is in as a whole as it is currently constituted, and they are to do so by giving priority to the achievement of the regulatory objectives of FSMA, which of course include protection of the UK depositors at risk (in Company A) and broader systemic confidence in the financial system.

Such a course of action would point them in the direction of selling Company C on condition that the buyer inject sufficient funds into Company A to meet the shortfall in liabilities to depositors. However, as directors of the holding company their obligations are to its shareholders to realise the holding company's assets (i.e. Company C) and to leave the depositors in Company A to their fate. If their obligations under the Approved Persons regime are in fact to have the practical effect of this kind of veil piercing in situations such as this then, Bamford argues, it should specifically state that in any conflict between an approved person's obligations (which are considered by the FSA in the context of the broader regulatory responsibilities of the group as a whole) and her duties as a director of an individual company (which are considered by company law in the context of duties owed to that company's shareholders and to no other interests), that compliance with the Approved Persons regime under FSMA is to preclude any action for breach of a director's duty in company law.

In a previous formulation the Draft Statutory Statement of Directors' Duties had provided that none of the general principles by which directors are to be bound "authorises the contravention by a director of any prohibition or enactment imposed on him by or under any other enactment or rule of law".[31] That was a long way short of being even an implied safe harbour of the type that Bamford would like to see made explicit and has in any event been removed from the latest version of the Draft Statement. The latest version simply states that the general duties incumbent on company directors are to have effect in place of certain common law rules and equitable principles governing directors but shall be interpreted in the same way, and applied with regard to those rules

---

[31] Clause 19(3) Draft Companies Bill, DTI White Paper (July 2002), Cm 5553.

and principles.[32] But what happens when regulatory rules and preferred regulatory outcomes cross over and conflict with these general duties?

Black has provided some perspective to this question in her recent examination of the potential for what she terms "collisions" between regulatory rules and common law or equitable principles and uses several examples drawn from a financial services and markets context.[33] She reminds us that the Law Commission did examine one such problematic collision in its 1995 report on "Fiduciary Duties and Regulatory Rules"[34] in which it examined the ways in which courts might resolve such juristic overlap and potential conflict. The Commission preferred a "hybrid model" of conflict resolution. Under this model the courts would allow for some degree of recognition by common law (rooted as it is in efficacy and certainty of private ordering, the traditional concerns of private law) of regulatory rules' very different genesis and concerns and would seek to adapt common law rules in light of these. Black likens this to the familiar devices through which common law has always reached out to and imported from other norms of ordering. For example, contract law's easy facility over the years with market practices and trade customs, or the shaping of common law rules on confidentiality by regulatory requirements on Chinese walls.[35]

Recent comments from the Court of Appeal on the significance to their common law responsibilities in making statements to bidders in the context of an acquisition of a target company directors' compliance with regulatory obligations (such as those imposed by the Takeover Code and Listing Rules) lend some support to this "creative collision" thesis.[36] She is reasonably optimistic as to the prospect of mutual collisions between common law and regulation being creative and resulting in "mutual learning". However, sometimes collisions will occur that require stark

---

[32]Draft Clause B10(1) and (2) Draft Company Law Reform Bill 2005 (March 2005), Part 7, DTI, White Paper, Cm 6456.
[33]J Black, Law and Regulation: The Case of Finance, in C Parker, C Scott, N Lacey and J Braithwaite (eds) Regulating Law (Oxford University Press: Oxford, 2004), pp 33–59.
[34]Law Com No 236 (London: Law Commission, 1995).
[35]J Black, supra, n 33, pp 46–47.
[36]Partco Group Ltd and Another v. Wragg and Scott [2002] 2 Lloyd's Rep 343, per LJ Potter at p 354.

and difficult choices between private interests and public regulatory ones and the uncertainty of how to call these decisions creates real legal risk for those company directors who are faced with these choices ex ante. Interestingly, she points out that recent consultation by the FSA on the issue of conflicts of interest in investment research is silent on the effects of common law or equitable principles, leading one to conclude tentatively that Bamford's points remain live ones.

It is of course both politically and juridically easier to leave open to the courts and the Financial Services and Markets Tribunal the question of how the legal system should rank the public law broader protections of the FSMA regime alongside the continuing private law focus of company law on shareholder value (albeit now to be more "enlightened" in nature). However, it sends an unfortunate message to those in senior positions in the UK financial services industry that government and the FSA are happy to devolve upon them compliance responsibilities for the achievement of these broader policy objectives through the introduction of SYSC and the Approved Persons regime but is not willing to offer concomitant clarity on how these responsibilities sit alongside their pervasive responsibilities in company law. Indeed Haines and Gurney highlight this "devolution of political tension" that often comes about by the delegation of responsibility of all risks onto the regulated.[37]

Insurability of risks attendant to senior management positions

Another anomaly as between the position of a director under general company law and of that same director in her capacity as an approved person under FSMA 2000 has arisen from the recent relaxation by sections 19–20 Companies (Audit, Investigations and Community Enterprise) Act 2004 of the prohibition on companies' protecting their directors by way of indemnity or exemption from liability arising in respect of any negligence, default or breach of duty of trust owed the company.[38] The new law permits companies to indemnify directors

---

[37]Supra, n 3.
[38]Section 310 Companies Act 1985.

against both legal and financial costs in respect of proceedings brought against them by third parties, but specifically excludes from the scope of such permissible indemnities any "sum payable to a regulatory authority by way of a penalty in respect of non-compliance with any requirement of a regulatory nature".[39] It also permits them to indemnify directors against the costs of defending any legal proceedings as they are incurred, even if brought by the company itself subject to their repayment to the company if its claim against a director were to succeed.[40] However, in 2004 the FSA changed its general requirements which apply to all authorised firms so as to prohibit firms from taking out any insurance arrangements which would indemnify any person (including an approved person) against all or part of a financial penalty imposed by it under FSMA 2000.[41] So companies regulated by the FSA may not easily provide comfort against the personal risk of large financial penalties to their senior (and indeed other) staff who are subject to individual disciplinary and enforcement action in their capacity as approved persons.

It is interesting to note that in the government's justifications for the amendment to the prohibition in general company law on companies providing directors with indemnities it couched its arguments in terms of incentives and the need to avoid the risk of personal financial liability acting as a deterrent to well-qualified individuals accepting board positions, particularly as non-executive directors.[42] These same arguments were put by industry respondents to the FSA's consultation on its prohibition of firms' arrangement of insurance against individual financial

---

[39] Section 309B(3) Companies Act 1985 added by s 19 Companies (Audit, Investigations and Community Enterprise) Act 2004.

[40] Section 337A Companies Act 1985 inserted by s 20 Companies (Audit, Investigations and Community Enterprise) Act 2004.

[41] GEN 6 FSA Handbook, *Insurance Against Financial Penalties*, this rule change was the subject of FSA Consultation Paper 191, July 2003.

[42] Parliamentary Statements by Patricia Hewitt, Secretary of State at the Department for Trade and Industry (DTI), 7 September 2004, *Hansard*, and Jacqui Smith, DTI Minister on 14 September 2004, *Hansard*, and see Commentary at p 23 in DTI White Paper *Company Law Reform* (March 2005: Cm 6456).

penalties payable by directors.[43] They met with less of a sympathetic response in that context.

Position of non-executive directors in company law and under FSMA regime

As just noted, the relaxation in company law's prohibition on indemnities for directors made by the Companies (Audit, Investigations and Community Enterprise) Act 2004 underwent Parliamentary scrutiny and debate that was couched firmly in terms of the need to maintain a balance around the incentives to undertake non-executive directorships of UK companies. For example, Jacqui Smith, the DTI Minister responsible for the legislation, quoted the responses received to the DTI's Consultation on the question of whether or not the recruitment of non-executive directors (hereafter "NEDS") was being affected by growing focus on their liability:

> Two thirds of the responses to the [DTI] consultation accepted... that issues relating to potential liability might affect the recruitment of able non-executive directors. The Institute of Directors suggested that there is a particular problem in sectors such as financial services and that concerns are especially acute where companies face difficulties.[44]

Indeed Baldwin's recent research into the effects of the growing climate of regulatory and legal risk for individual senior managers reveals that these concerns about the incentive effects on individuals willing to serve as NEDs are not misplaced.[45] There has been much discussion within general company law and corporate governance over the past few years on the proper role and responsibilities of non-executive directors. Some commentators argue that to obtain a true contemporary understanding of the ambit of legal duties owed by NEDs it behoves us to look less to general law standards developed by the common law over

---

[43]FSA Policy Statement, December 2003.
[44]Standing Committee on Companies (Audit, Exemption and Community Enterprise) Bill debate, 14 September 2004 (Morning), *Hansard*.
[45]R Baldwin, The New Punitive Regulation, *Modern Law Review*, 2004, 67(3), 351–383 at 362.

the years and increasingly to how courts develop behavioural standards for directors under legislative regimes such as the Company Directors Disqualification Act 1986,[46] or the statutory jurisdiction in section 459 Companies Act 1985 to grant relief where the company's affairs are being conducted in such a way as to result in unfair prejudice to a minority shareholder or minority group of shareholders.[47]

Important proceedings in respect of breach of the extent of the common law duty of care and skill owed by NEDs are ongoing at the time of writing, having been brought by the Equitable Life Assurance Society against a number of its former non-executive directors. Those proceedings have given this debate a particularly sharp focus in the regulated financial services sector.[48] The question arises therefore as to whether general company law and, for UK listed companies, the Combined Code on Corporate Governance impose expectations on NEDs that are different in either substance or emphasis to the behaviour expected of NEDs by the FSA as evidenced in both SYSC and the Approved Persons regime?

The principle of the UK board of directors as a unitary board has long been dear to UK company law and is a distinctive feature of the Anglo-American corporate governance model. *Dorchester Finance v. Stebbing* established that as a matter of general principle company law does not distinguish between executive and non-executive directors in its application of the standards of skill and care it expects[49] and continues

---

[46]D Arsalidou, The Liability of Non-Executive Directors for Negligent Omissions: A New Approach under Legislation, *Company Lawyer*, 2002, 23(4), 107–114.

[47]D Arsalidou, ibid., quotes a comment of Professor Sealy *"today's law on directors' duties is being shaped on the one hand by the non-legal codes of good practice which are obligatory for listed companies and on the other hand . . . by the myriad of disqualification and section 459 cases"* (from a paper on *"Directors' Duties Re-examined"* presented at Institute of Advanced Legal Studies, 26 June, 2000).

[48]*Equitable Life Assurance Society v. Bowley and others* [2003] EWHC 2263 Queen's Bench Division Commercial Court, 17 October 2003, at which the directors' interlocutory application for summary judgement awarding them relief under s 727 Companies Act 1985 against the company's claim was dismissed. At the time of writing actions against some of the directors have settled but remain live against a number of the non-executives.

[49][1989] BCLC 498.

to find expression in the expectations as to skill and care of a NED in the Combined Code on Corporate Governance applicable to listed companies.[50] In the *Dorchester Finance* case two non-executive directors who were also accountants were held to have been negligent in signing blank company cheques and leaving them in the hands of the sole executive director. However, this does not mean that the law lays different nuances on what is expected of executive and non-executive company directors in terms of imposing an expectation on NEDs that they will act as a guarantor against executive incompetence or fraud.

For example, Mr Justice Park in *Re Continental Assurance plc* commented, in the course of his dismissal of the liquidator's claims against six non-executive directors of the insolvent insurer for redress for wrongful trading and misfeasance based on breaches of the duty of care and skill based on the NEDs' alleged failure to challenge the executive finance director's assertion that the company was still solvent when problematic accounting systems and polices masked its true financial positions, that

> one of the duties of non-executive directors is to monitor the performance of the executive directors. I accept that the managing director of a company... has a general responsibility to oversee the activities of the company, which presumably includes its accounting operations. But I do not think that those responsibilities can go so far as to require the non-executive directors to overrule the specialist directors, like the finance director in their specialist fields. The duty is not to ensure that the company gets everything right.[51]

He cited with approval the Australian authority of *AWA Ltd v. Daniels*[52] which indicated that NEDs in particular were entitled to rely on the accuracy of audited company accounts and indeed in that same litigation the Australian Court of Appeal went on to apply the same standard of skill and care to executive and non-executive directors' monitoring of certain transactions in a way so as to exculpate the latter but hold the former liable.[53]

---

[50]Schedule B *Combined Code on Corporate Governance*.

[51]*Re Continental Assurance Co of London plc*, 27 April 2001, Chancery Division [2001] BPIR 733.

[52](1992) 7 ACSR 759.

[53]*Daniels v. Anderson* (1995) 6 ACSR 607.

Elsewhere in his judgement he described the liquidator's claim under section 214 Companies Act 1985 as "infested with hindsight" and expressed the same concerns which had arisen throughout Parliamentary scrutiny of the Companies (Audit, Investigations and Community Enterprise) Act 2004, that the law on directors' liability for wrongful trading did not come to operate in such a way so as to deter potential NEDs from the role.

However, Davies points out the importance, as companies grow in size, numbers of management layers and complexity, of the oversight as opposed to management role of the board and especially of the role of NEDs in monitoring oversight of executive directors' conflicts of interest as opposed to expecting a diffuse and often relatively powerless body of shareholders to perform this role alone.[54] He comments that general company law in the traditional form of statute and case law might look positively patchy on issues of the proper functions of the members of the board were it not for the fact that the broader framework of accountability and control developed by the various corporate governance initiatives for listed companies had addressed these issues, at least for the most economically significant UK companies (those with a UK listing).[55] It is to the way in which the UK corporate governance standards for listed companies has developed in the past decade or so that the discussion must now turn.

Development of corporate governance of listed companies in the UK

Of all the fields of corporate law scholarship it is perhaps corporate governance that has attracted the most attention in the UK and elsewhere. This has been stimulated partly by a growing litany of corporate governance malfunctions in the past 20 years from Polly Peck plc, Guinness plc, Enron, Worldcom, Tyco, Shell and Parmalat. These have all

---

[54]*Principles of Modern Company Law* (Gower and P Davies 2003), Chapter 16 at pp 441–442.
[55]Ibid.

stimulated interest in the nature and exercise of corporate power, as well as lower-level concerns and unease about issues such as executive remuneration, quality of business risk management practice and board structures and accountability. The official response in the UK to growing concerns about corporate governance has been marked by a welter of quasi-official and industry-driven initiatives that began with the Cadbury Committee Report of 1992 which ushered in a Code of Best Practice for UK companies through to, most recently, the Higgs Review of the role and effectiveness of NEDs.[56] It is not the purpose of this work to present any comprehensive account or critique of UK corporate governance arrangements for such work abounds elsewhere[57] and the focus of this work's interest in UK corporate governance is to what extent it operates within companies in such a way as to either mirror or conflict with the FSA's framework of intra-firm regulation that is SYSC and the approved persons requirements for senior managers.

How then are NEDs defined in terms of their role, function and responsibilities by the Combined Code on Corporate Governance on the one hand and by SYSC and the Approved Persons regime on the other hand? Are there any points of resonance and dissonance between the two regimes?

There has been a steadily growing awareness of the potential for conflict between "management" and "monitoring" roles inherent in the position of a NED as a member of a unitary board of directors and the extent to which this weakens their effectiveness as monitors of executive managerial performance.[58] This led the DTI to commission a wide-ranging review of the role and effectiveness of NEDs in the UK under the chairmanship of Sir Derek Higgs.[59] The Higgs Review recommended

---

[56] DTI, January 2003.

[57] Riley, Juridification of Corporate Governance, in De Lacey (ed) *The Reform of UK Company Law* (Cavendish, 2002) provides a good stock of references to such accounts.

[58] M Ezzamel and R Watson, Wearing Two Hats: The Conflicting Control and Management Roles of Non-Executive Directors, in Keasey, Thompson and Wright *Corporate Governance: Economic, Management and Financial Issues* (OUP: Oxford, 1997); J Parkinson, Evolution and Policy in Company Law: The Non-Executive Director, Chapter 10 *Political Economy of the Company* (OUP: Oxford, 2000).

[59] *Higgs Review of the Role and Effectiveness of NEDs* (DTI, January 2003).

that a lack of both clarity and guidance surrounding the role of a NED had a deleterious impact on the role's potential for effectiveness. Hence it was time for a description of the role of the non-executive director to be incorporated into the Combined Code on Corporate Governance.[60] In response to his recommendations the Combined Code on Corporate Governance, with which UK listed companies must either comply or explain any non-compliance, was amended in November 2003 in a number of respects all designed to stiffen the rigour of and improve the transparency and degree with which the role of the NED is thought through, reviewed and performed. The fundamental principle of a unitary board is reaffirmed at the outset of the Code as it sets out the main principle that

> Every company should be headed by an effective Board which is collectively responsible for the success of the company.[61]

This in turn is supported by principles which apply to all directors (executive and non-executive) which state the board's role as being to:

> provide entrepreneurial leadership of the company within a framework of prudent and effective controls which enables risk to be assessed and managed ... [to] set the company's strategic aims, [to] ensure that the necessary financial and human resources are in place for the company to meet its objectives and review management performance ... [to] set the company's values and standards and ensure that its obligations to its shareholders and others are understood and met.

It is worth noting here that the phrase "obligations to its shareholders and others" at this level of the Code must surely broaden the remit of the governance standards in the Code to potentially include the achievement not just of general company law standards of performance expected of directors (being owed by the company to shareholders) but also different forms of regulatory compliance and performance of regulatory objectives as well. For the phrase "obligations owed by the company ... to others" is easily broad enough to encompass the firm's compliance with the FSA's codes and expectations as well as those applying in respect of other regulatory regimes. Thus the language of the

---

[60] Ibid., paras 6.1–6.8.
[61] Main Principle A.1.

Combined Code itself uses the language of enrolment analysis discussed earlier in its shaping of expectations of boards. It is silent, however, on how a board is to resolve the potential for practical conflicts between legal codes which set obligations primarily to shareholders and those which set obligations primarily to "others" – the dilemma that meta regulation leaves firmly in the boardroom. In its additional articulation of the role that is specific to NEDs the language of the Code is strongly redolent of issues dealt with in a financial regulatory context by SYSC:

> As part of their role as members of a unitary board, non-executive directors should constructively challenge and help develop proposals on strategy. Non-executive directors should scrutinise the performance of management in meeting agreed goals and objectives and monitor the reporting of performance. They should satisfy themselves on the integrity of financial information and that financial controls and systems of risk management are robust and defensible. They are responsible for determining appropriate levels of remuneration of executive directors and have a prime role in appointing, and where necessary removing, executive directors, and in succession planning.[62]

Other changes to the Combined Code as a result of the Higgs Review include: a requirement that at least half the board consist of independent NEDs (other than in smaller companies),[63] the need for a senior independent NED to be identified who has a special role as a channel of communication with shareholders,[64] and a series of factors in the form of guidance which go to the crux of whether or not a NED has discharged her duty of skill, care and diligence owed to the company.[65] The factors that comprise that guidance, although expressed to be in support of the general proposition that non-executive directors and executive directors have the same legal duties and objectives, nonetheless list specific expectations of NEDs that the Code sees as being enquiries a court would make in any determination of liability for breach of the duty of care, skill and diligence. Thus NEDs are expected by the Code

---

[62] Supporting Principles to Main Principle A.1 (The Board).
[63] Supporting Principles to Main Principle A.3 (Board Balance and Independence).
[64] Code Provision A.3.3.
[65] Guidance on liability of NEDs: care, skill and diligence, Schedule B to Combined Code (July 2003).

to take it upon themselves to:

> undertake appropriate induction and regularly update and refresh their skills, knowledge and familiarity with the company; seek appropriate clarification or amplification of information and, where necessary, take and follow appropriate professional advice; where they have concerns about the running of the company or a proposed action, ensure that these are addressed by the board and, to the extent that they are not resolved, ensure that they are recorded in the board minutes; and give a statement to the board if they have such unresolved concerns on resignation.[66]

Likewise the expected appropriate behaviours of NEDs are amplified further by the Combined Code's annexation of the Higgs Review's Good Practice Suggestions and their implicit inclusion as Code guidance. Examples of these suggestions include guidance to NEDs on their role, a sample letter of appointment for NEDs, and induction checklists (induction being something that the liability guidance expects NEDs to insist upon). These suggestions all combine to form a quasi-code that it is inevitable that NEDs will increasingly look to for guidance as to exactly how they should go about performing their role in a way that insulates them as far as possible from legal risk. All things being equal, courts are highly likely to look to how a NED's conduct measured up in terms of compliance with these detailed expectations of the Code in any future actions against NEDs in respect of their duty of skill and care. To what extent would a court interpret the Code's general expectations of a NED to encompass any special responsibilities for monitoring and review of the firm's regulatory compliance where that NED is on the board of a company regulated by the FSA? This is obviously an issue of the utmost concern to NEDs in the financial sector. The meta-regulatory language of the Combined Code's statement about "obligations to shareholders *and others*" (emphasis added) may reach out to visit NEDs in particular with responsibilities for the attainment of regulatory objectives imposed by regimes other than general company law.

Turning to the FSA's definition and characterisation of the proper role of NEDs, it is possible to discern that the FSA was concerned not to

---

[66]Schedule B, para 2(ii) Combined Code.

layer a separate and potentially conflicting model of the appropriate role of NEDs than prevails more broadly in corporate governance practice. During consultation on earlier drafts of regulatory standards that would govern its definition and expectations of the role and conduct of non-executive directors in the context of both SYSC and the arrangements for the Approved Persons regime, the FSA was at pains to emphasise that it was not attempting to prescribe any standardised role for NEDs and that it fully recognised that the functions they fulfilled and responsibilities they had would vary from company to company and indeed from NED to NED.[67] It was *not* the intention of the interaction between Approved Persons regime and SYSC to act in such a way so as to:

burden non-executives with any duties or responsibilities in addition to those which they would generally be expected to perform . . . the personal regulatory obligations of non-executives under the Principles and Code of Practice for Approved Persons will mirror their conventional responsibilities . . . [so that] the role taken on by a non-executive will set the limits to his or her responsibilities as an Approved Person.[68]

Despite these assurances, suspicion must inevitably linger that NEDs might be expected by both regulator and courts to take a stand and perspective on matters within the firm is more akin to a compliance/systems monitoring and oversight role. Again Baldwin's research provides some fascinating insights here as he reports reasons put forward to him for the diminished attractions of the non-executive board appointment as including, not just greater individual legal and regulatory risk but also that "[t[here [is] a tendency to cast the post-Enron [NED] in a compliance monitoring and quite negative role...Here was a change that made the job less interesting and more onerous as well as more risk-laden."[69]

The FSA defines a NED as a director without executive responsibilities, i.e. one who *"has no responsibility for implementing the decisions*

---

[67]FSA Consultation Paper 35, *Senior Management Arrangements, Systems and Controls* (December 1999), Chapter 4.
[68]Ibid., Chapter 4, paras 4.2–4.3.
[69]R Baldwin, supra, n 45 p 363.

of the policies of the governing body of a firm"[70] and the NED controlled function is defined in such a way so as to avoid a one-size fits all view of what a NED's role and responsibilities are. Examples of responsibilities of a non-executive director may include:

(1) *playing his part, by providing an independent perspective to the overall running of the business, in setting and monitoring the firm's strategy;*
(2) *scrutinising the approach of executive management, the firm's performance and its standards of conduct; and*
(3) *carrying out other responsibilities as assigned by the firm: for example, as a member of a board committee on audit or remuneration or as a member of a committee having the purpose of a With-profits Committee.*[71]

However, since what the FSA termed those "conventional responsibilities" of a NED have been refined, amplified and expanded by the Higgs Review-inspired reworking of the Combined Code explained above, so too must the potential ambit of regulatory individual risk for those NEDs of companies regulated by the FSA.

Hence the emphasis on pluralism and variety in the FSA's view of NEDs' role and responsibilities as expressed in, for example, SYSC guidance[72] and in consultative comment [73] must be revisited for listed companies against the recent changes in the Combined Code's expectations of NEDs consequent upon the Higgs Review. For those changes have carved out the NED's role more sharply and the Code provisions and guidance considered above have added detail to what the FSA has

---

[70] Glossary and SUP 10.6.10G.
[71] SUP 10.6.9G.
[72] SYSC 2.1.2G which provides "The role undertaken by a non-executive director will vary from one firm to another. For example, the role of a non-executive director in a friendly society may be more extensive than in other firms. Where a non-executive director is an approved person, for example where the firm is a body corporate, his responsibility and therefore liability will be limited by the role that he undertakes. Provided that he has personally taken due care in his role, a non-executive director would not be held disciplinarily liable either for the failings of the firm or for those of individuals within the firm."
[73] FSA Policy Statement, *High Level Standards for Firms and Individuals: Issues Arising Out of CP 35 and CP 26* (June 2000), para 2.23.

termed the "conventional responsibilities" of NEDs. Of course, SYSC and APER also contain their own expectations of NEDs for the purposes of the FSMA regime and it is quite possible that the two parallel, separate yet overlapping regulatory systems of the Combined Code on the one hand, and of the FSA's Handbook on the other, may well cross over in accountability contexts and each might import from the other that system's view of the role and appropriate liability standard for NEDs. So a court in a future case concerning whether a NED of a listed company that is regulated by the FSA had shown the required degree of skill, care and diligence, might look not just to the Combined Code standards of guidance, but might also look to the standards expected of her by SYSC and APER and whether or not she had met those. The converse too might occur so that, in the context of disciplinary action by the FSA, the relevant decision-maker in relation to alleged breaches by a NED of the Statements of Principle for Approved Persons would look across to how well she had complied with the Combined Code's expectations as to skill and care of a NED. But, as already argued, there is no guarantee that such cross-fertilisation between financial regulation and more general corporate law and governance standards will occur.

To some extent guidance given in SYSC and APER does recognise that in some companies NEDs will have specific responsibilities such as membership of board committees (audit committees, for example) which in turn have responsibility for areas within the purview of the Apportionment and Oversight function (which, as seen, is normally to be placed on the CEO).[74] In such an instance then, allocation of responsibility for the firm's own apportionment of responsibilities and responsibility for the firm's systems and controls in compliance with SYSC must reflect where those responsibilities properly lie and if corporate governance requirements applicable to a firm mean that the chief executive ought not to be concerned with some aspect or aspects of the firm's governance (such as in the audit committee or remuneration committee examples) then guidance to Rules 2.1.3 and 2.1.4 SYSC envisage flexibility in a shared allocation with the relevant NEDs.[75]

---

[74]SYSC 2.1.4R.

[75]See SYSC 2.1.6G (especially Question 14 in the table of frequently asked questions).

SYSC has undoubtedly been written and devised against the reality of the broader backdrop of the Combined Code requirements and language used by the FSA's senior officers implies acknowledgement of the need to "look across" to the Combined Code's standards in shaping financial regulatory expectations of NEDs.[76] However, against this must be weighed the risk that the two parallel yet overlapping systems of corporate law and governance and financial regulation limit the extent to which each will allow a NED, or indeed any other holder of a governing body controlled function, to rely on her compliance with the Combined Code to excuse a regulatory breach alleged under Part V, or compliance with the Statements of Principle for Approved Persons and spirit of SYSC to excuse an action for breach of duty of skill and care against a NED (or indeed an executive director) in which non-compliance with Combined Code standards is pleaded. The discussion in the next section addresses this point in the broader context of the relationship between the FSA's Handbook and the Combined Code on Corporate Governance.

Other aspects of the interrelationship between Combined Code on Corporate Governance and the FSA's Handbook expectations of boards and governance arrangements

It is possible to take issue with the FSA's insistence in consultation on this point that *"there are few requirements that are the same in both the Combined Code and the FSA's rules"*.[77] As already shown the Code

---

[76]See, for example, speech by Philip Robinson, Director Deposit-takers Division of the FSA (17 July 2003) to the Building Societies Association, when he gave a number of examples of matters the FSA saw as peculiarly within the remit of NEDs of building societies all clearly derived from the Combined Code: "First, we think non-executives should play their part by providing an independent perspective to the overall running of the business, in setting and monitoring the society's strategy. Second, they should scrutinise the approach of executive management, the society's performance and its standards of conduct . . . [T]hird . . . they should carry out other responsibilities as assigned by the society, for example as a member of a board committee on audit or remuneration."
[77]Supra at n 73, para 2.20.

contains quite specific expectations about appropriate behaviours of NEDs and these must inevitably flavour and inform how any NED who is also an approved person performs the NED controlled function and thus assesses her own compliance with the FSA's regulatory framework. Simply because legal and regulatory requirements are not literally the same is far from meaning that, viewed from the perspective of their impact and how they are embedded and received in those subject to them, they are not intrinsically entwined. Combined Code Principle D.2 (Internal Control) provides the most striking area of similarity between the Combined Code and the FSA's SYSC regulation:

> The board should maintain a sound system of internal control to safeguard shareholders' investment and the company's assets

The similarities become obvious when this is read in conjunction with the Turnbull guidelines annexed to the Combined Code which amplify that main principle by way of guidance on internal controls and risk management processes.[78] Both the Turnbull guidelines and SYSC requirements emphasise the need for firms to embed required control systems as *part of* the core business processes rather than seeing "the business" and "risk management" (in the case of Turnbull) and "responsibility for regulatory compliance" (in the case of SYSC) as separate processes. So Turnbull's introductory words to the 1999 report strongly echo more recent rhetoric from the FSA on the centrality of regulatory compliance to the very core of the business as the objectives

---

[78]The Turnbull Report issued by the Institute of Chartered Accountants of England and Wales in 1999 was little commented upon by academic lawyers at the time but in fact represents a real advance in the degree of penetration and intrusion into companies' internal affairs and organisation, far more so than the other main policy initiatives that wrought changes to the Combined Code, Cadbury Report in 1992, (*Report of the Committee on the Financial Aspects of Corporate Governance*, Gee: London, 1992); Greenbury Report on Executive Remuneration 1995, and the *Committee on Corporate Governance* (commonly referred to as the Hampel Committee) in 1998. These reports were concerned primarily with board structure, composition and responsibility issues (Cadbury), executive remuneration (Greenbury) and the drafting and the juridical/regulatory basis of arrangements for corporate governance (Hampel).

of the guidelines are described as being to:

- reflect sound business practice whereby internal control is embedded in the business processes by which a company pursues its objectives;
- remain relevant over time in the continually evolving business environment; and
- enable each company to apply it in a manner which takes account of its particular circumstances...

...[and being] based on the adoption by a company's board of a risk-based approach to establishing a sound system of internal control and reviewing its effectiveness. The company within its normal management and governance processes should incorporate this. It should not be treated as a separate exercise undertaken to meet regulatory requirements.[79]

Indeed the Turnbull guidelines specifically refer to the improved regulatory compliance effect that should follow from their implementation when they state that sound internal controls should "help ensure compliance with applicable laws and regulations, and also with internal policies with respect to the conduct of business". So to what extent then may a firm regulated by the FSA safely rely on those systems and processes of internal control and risk management implemented to comply with Turnbull guidelines as also being good compliance with SYSC Rule 3.1.1 "A firm must take reasonable care to establish and maintain such systems and controls as are appropriate to its business"?

From the perspective of the subjects of these differing yet overlapping systems of intra-firm regulation the practical question arises to what extent will the FSA recognise and give credit for compliance with the Combined Code's requirements on firms and management in any determination of either the firm's responsibility for breaches of SYSC rules (such as SYSC 3.1.1R extracted above) or of an individual director's responsibility for breach of Statements of Principle applying to holders of significant influence functions under the Approved Persons regime? The FSA stated in consultation on its high-level standards for firms and individuals, that when considering compliance of firms regulated by it which are also subject to the Combined Code's guidance on internal controls (the Turnbull guidance), it would "give due credit for following

---

[79]Turnbull Report, Introduction (ICAEW, 1999).

corresponding provisions in the Code and related guidance" and that position is now reflected in its Handbook.[80] In relation to an individual's position under the Approved Persons regime the same "due credit" approach is employed "In forming an opinion whether approved persons have complied with its requirements, the FSA will give due credit for their following corresponding provisions in the Combined Code and related guidance".[81]

The FSA had been pressed in consultation by those potentially subject to the overlapping regimes to be more specific about the likely practical meaning of "due credit" and to strengthen the protection offered to offer a "safe harbour" of compliance with the Code. However, the FSA rejected this approach while emphasising that its policy of giving "due credit" was

> intended to minimise the burden of complying with the FSA's rules where firms already comply with the Combined Code. Firms will not be expected to duplicate procedures or documents which they have created in order to meet the requirements of the Combined Code where these also meet the requirements of the FSA's rules and guidance.[82]

The FSA based its objection to the "safe harbour" effect of Code compliance on the ground that few requirements of the Code and the FSA are the same. That admission itself rather obviates the utility of its assurances about "due credit" and avoidance of duplication. In addition, the FSA failed to address how firms themselves are to address the meta-regulatory conflict that several industry respondents pointed out to it as being "between the Code's emphasis on board responsibility and protection of and accountability to shareholders and the focus on individual responsibility and the protection of consumers in the FSA's requirements".[83]

There are real areas of similarity between the general tenor and some of the governance and control standards contained in the Combined

---

[80]SYSC 3.1.3G and FSA CP 35, p 9.
[81]APER 3.1.9.
[82]Supra, n 73 para 2.20.
[83]Supra, n 73 para 2.18.

Code with the FSA's own regulatory code for senior management contained in SYSC and APER. This is no accident as the two areas of regulatory concern cover the same territory, albeit from differing policy motivations. Both regulatory codes expect firms subject to them to position each code's respective compliance processes centrally into the firm's business processes, yet the problem remains, as identified by both Haines and Gurney and Bamford as discussed earlier, that compliance with each may entail something rather different in exactly the same commercial situation. The board and/or senior manager are "enrolled" by both the FSA's regulatory framework and the Combined Code into, respectively, FSMA regulatory objectives and shareholder value creation and accountability to shareholders. Which (very different) policy agenda is to motivate real commercial decisions?

Individual responsibility of directors for compliance with the listing regime

Individual responsibility of directors of listed companies for breaches of the listing rules provides another example of possible overlap and conflict. Firms and individual directors subject to the FSA's regulatory requirements as to senior management responsibility may also be subject to parallel and potentially conflicting firm and individual obligations under the listing regime. Part VI FSMA conferred competence on the FSA as "competent authority" for the purposes of the relevant EU capital market directives,[84] a role previously performed by the London Stock Exchange, and empowered it to promulgate and enforce the rules

---

[84]EU securities markets directives have been undergoing considerable review and revision in consequence of the adoption of the 1999 Financial Services Action Plan by the EU Council of Ministers. The regime introduced by the Consolidated Admission and Reporting Directive 2001/34/EC ("CARD") and implemented in the UK by FSMA 2000 (Official Listing of Securities) Regulations 2001/2956 is, at the time of writing, undergoing significant change. Of particular relevance has been the implementation in the UK in July 2005 of the Prospectus Directive 2003/71/EC and the forthcoming further reform to CARD to be made on implementation in 2006 of the Transparency Obligations Directive 2004/109/EC.

governing admission and trading of securities to the Official List. With the adoption and implementation of a new EU capital markets regime the distinction between securities being admitted to and trading on a regulated market and those admitted to and trading on the Official List has now gone at EU level[85] but not at UK level so Part VI FSMA has been amended recently to reflect the fact that the FSA will continue to make and enforce listing rules for issuers whose securities are to be admitted and traded under a super-equivalent UK regime, and "disclosure rules" for issuers whose securities are admitted and traded on a regulated market.[86]

What has not changed, however, is the original extension to the competent authority's (i.e. the FSA's) powers to sanction breaches of the listing rules. When FSMA was first introduced what was then referred to as the "Official Listing" regime in Part VI was largely carried over from Part IV Financial Services Act 1986. However, one important amendment, of central concern to this work, was the extension of regulatory power to make the listing rules "bite". Section 91 FSMA contained what was then a wholly new power for the FSA acting as competent authority to impose a penalty (in the form of either a public statement of censure or a financial penalty) where an issuer or applicant for listing was in breach of the listing rules not just on the issuer or applicant, but also on any person who was a director at the material time and whom the FSA believed was "knowingly concerned" in the contravention. The original justification given for this extension of disciplinary reach into the firm was to better target the effect of sanction for any breach to those at fault, not necessarily always shareholders of the issuer concerned but rather the culprits were to be found in the issuer's boardroom. Lord MacIntosh of Haringey, introducing this new power to the House of Lords on the passage of the legislation, put it thus:

---

[85]Prospectus Directive 2003/71/EC and Transparency Obligations Directive 2004/109/EC.
[86]Section 73A inserted into FSMA by the Prospectus Regulations, SI 2005/1433, implementing the Prospectus Directive requirements in the UK.

> By allowing the competent authority to impose penalties on directors who are knowingly concerned in a contravention of the listing rules, it can get at the right people.[87]

The same power to reach inside an issuer of securities and sanction culpable directors for breaches of the new rules governing issuers of securities traded on regulated markets survives into the amendment of section 91 made in July 2005 which implemented the new EU securities market regulatory regime.[88] In fact, adopting as it does the language of the relevant EU law implementing measure[89] the power is now expressed in a way so as to reach tiers of senior management of the issuer *other* than directors "knowingly concerned" in an issuer's contravention but *also* potentially may encompass, in relation to issuers of financial instruments traded on a regulated market who have contravened the rules made by the FSA under Part VI applicable to such issuers (i.e. those whose securities are publicly traded but not on the UK Official List), "a person discharging managerial responsibilities within such an issuer".[90]

Complex as this revised legal basis for breaches of the new regime applicable to admission of and trading of publicly traded securities is, the point made here is simple, we witness yet another extension of veil-piercing regulation – this time of the FSA's powers under Part VI FSMA aimed at implementing the EU securities market regulatory regime. The potential subjects of this enhanced regulatory reach, namely directors and managers of issuers of publicly tradeable securities, although closely advised in corporate finance matters by firms regulated by the FSA, are not themselves necessarily already within the FSA's regulatory net. They may just as easily be directors and managers of Midlands-based widget manufacturers (should any remain), they are not approved persons, they are not necessarily familiar with regulatory techniques and culture yet they are, through their decision to seek access to regulated capital

---

[87]Lord MacIntosh of Haringey, 21 March 2000, HL *Hansard*.
[88]Section 91 FSMA 2000 as amended by Prospectus Regulations 2005, SI 2005/1433.
[89]Prospectus Directive (2003/71/EC).
[90]Section 91(1) (b)(ii) added to FSMA by SI 2005/381.

markets, also harnessed and enrolled into the objectives of capital market regulation. They are given the sharp incentive of personal financial and/or reputational responsibility to ensure their company complies with and remains compliant with the rules that govern its access to capital and investors.

The FSA has had to review its listing regime in light of the implementation of the latest wave of EU securities markets directives. The previous version of what was known as the UKLA Sourcebook was replaced on 1 July 2005 with the Listing, Prospectus and Disclosure Block of the FSA Handbook of Rules and Guidance. The Listing Rules have been revised and reformulated, and now include a set of seven high-level Listing Principles, and have been joined by the new Prospectus Rules.[91] However, the emphasis on the need for directors of listed companies to take individual responsibility to ensure their companies' compliance with various aspects of the new version of the Listing Rules is, if anything, even more apparent now.

Where the FSA has made use of the power in section 91 FSMA 2000 to date to sanction individual directors it regards as culpable in breaches of Listing Rules it has done so in both instances in order to levy financial penalties on the CEOs of the companies concerned.[92] In both cases it highlighted the effect of what was then Listing Rule 16.2 which visited responsibility for the company's compliance firmly on its directors collectively *and* individually. However, it took some care in giving reasons for these decisions to emphasise that it was the fact that in each situation the individuals concerned did carry primary responsibility for the companies' breaches (which consisted of a misleading trading statement in one case and a delay in a significant announcement to the market in the other contrary to the rules on continuing obligations[93]), they had not delegated it to any other board member.

---

[91] These Rule changes are detailed in FSA Handbook Notice 45 (20 June 2005).

[92] FSA Final Notice, 29 March 2004 – Sportsworld Media Group plc and John Geoffrey Brown; FSA Final Notice, 19 May 2004 – Universal Salvage plc and Martin Christopher Hynes.

[93] Rule 9.2 in the case of Sportsworld and Rule 9.1 in the case of Universal Salvage plc. (pre-July 2005 version of the Listing Rules).

In the case of Mr Brown, then CEO of Sportsworld plc, the FSA considered that as CEO of the company he bore a responsibility to put before its board the information as to trading performance and profitability for the period in which what transpired to be an overly optimistic trading announcement had been made and he should have put this information before the full board without delay in order to consider making the required corrective announcement. His failure to do so constituted being knowingly concerned, the FSA considered, in the company's primary breach and earned him a financial penalty of £45 000.[94]

In the case of Mr Hynes, then CEO of Universal Salvage plc, the non-renewal of a valuable contract which comprised a significant portion of the company's business was not announced publicly without delay as required by what was then Listing Rule 9.2. Again, the FSA was at pains to stress that Mr Hynes was not being targeted purely because he was CEO but rather he had actually been personally involved in events leading up to the non-renewal, and had appreciated the need to consult the company's advisers as to the significance of this but had let several days elapse before he did so, which the FSA termed a lack of appropriate urgency. Of course it is the inclusion of the word "knowingly" in section 91's conferral of power to levy sanctions on directors knowingly concerned in issuer's breaches that imposes the discipline on the FSA to forge this link of real factual responsibility between the director (no matter how senior) and the breach itself.

However, it is possible to speculate that the care it has taken to draw these causal links between individual action/inaction and the breach itself in the reported instances of section 91's use against individual directors and the limited use of that power it has made up until now suggest that it perhaps appreciates that levels of awareness of the risk of individual responsibility for breaches of listing rules may not be as high among the boardrooms of the general corporate sector as are levels of awareness of the risk of individual responsibility under Part V FSMA of senior management of firms regulated by the FSA. The level of fine at

---

[94]See Final Notice, supra, n 92.

£10 000 reflected that the FSA took into account factors such as it did not regard this as a deliberate attempt to mislead the market, and that it received full cooperation from the company and Mr Hynes.

Just as in the context of the disciplinary actions considered in the previous chapter so too here, in exercise of its Part VI FSMA competence, does the FSA seek to deploy its power to hold individuals accountable for their firm's breaches in such a way as to further their enrolment in the regulatory enterprise by showing a willingness to sanction less harshly when individuals are receptive to that enterprise.

Company Directors Disqualification Act 1986

The individual regulatory and disciplinary regime that forms the Approved Persons regime has more immediate resemblance to the regime for the disqualification of unfit company directors contained in the Company Directors Disqualification Act 1986 (CDDA), designed as it is to be protective and prophylactic in effect, than it does to the general duties of company directors. The problem that the CDDA sets out to counteract is that of controlling and curbing the activities of what are often colloquially termed "rogue directors" in recognition of the need for some degree of ex ante protection against the losses and costs that can be imposed on those dealing with companies run by unsatisfactory directors as well as society at large. Company law and insolvency law contain a number of ex post compensatory mechanisms for recovery of losses where such directors have, through their mismanagement of the company, caused loss.[95] But since no prior approval or minimum "fit and proper" qualifications are applied generally to those serving as company directors in the UK some evidence-based mechanism must also exist for the selection out of those directors whose conduct and business stewardship falls short of some minimal standard of propriety and/or competence, as well as for the prevention of such individuals acting as company directors in the future. The need for such a

---

[95]Such as ss 212–214 Insolvency Act 1986 (liability for misfeasance in the running of the company, fraudulent or wrongful trading).

mechanism was identified in the UK as long ago as 1962 and now takes the form of the CDDA 1986.

The objective of this regime is protective of those at risk from trading with companies run by unfit directors, it is thus designed to raise the general standard of stewardship of companies. However, it can also be characterised in terms of its effects as deterrent, often punitive and sometimes "penal"[96] and that characterisation contains strong echoes of arguments that have been made elsewhere as to the quasi-criminal/penal nature of the loss of livelihood effects of the making of a prohibition order or the levying of a financial penalty against an approved person under section 56 or section 66 FSMA.[97]

Under the CDDA the court may order that a director of an insolvent company be prohibited from acting as a director or having any direct or indirect involvement with the formation, promotion, or management of a company without leave of court for a finite period. A disqualification order may be made on a number of grounds but, for the purposes of what lessons this regime can provide of relevance to the Approved Persons regime, the most significant ground is that of "unfitness" contained in section 6. That provision provides that the court is under a duty to disqualify unfit directors of insolvent companies where satisfied that:

> He is or has been a director of a company which has at any time become insolvent (whether while he was a director or subsequently). That his conduct as a director of that company (either taken alone or taken together with conduct as a director of any other company(ies)) makes him unfit to be concerned with the management of a company[98]

Unfitness falls to be judged with reference to a number of criteria including the extent to which the director has engaged in any

---

[96]J Dine, Punishing Directors, *Journal of Business Law* , 1994, July, 325–337.
[97]*R (on the application of Fleurose) v. Securities and Futures Authority Ltd* [2001] EWCA Civ 2015, Court of Appeal, D F Waters and Martyn Hopper, Discipline, Enforcement and Human Rights: Regulatory Discipline and the European Convention on Human Rights – A Reality Check, in E Ferran and C Goodhart (eds) *Regulating Financial Services and Markets in the 21st Century* (Hart Publishing: Oxford, 2001.)
[98]Section 6 CDDA 1986.

misfeasance/breach of fiduciary or other duty, misapplication/retention of company property, or any other conduct giving rise to liability to account, responsibility for transactions that offend the insolvency legislation, any responsibility for various statutory defaults such as accounting, maintenance of proper registers, record-keeping, filing and disclosure requirements, etc.[99] Also to be considered are the extent of the director's responsibility for causes of the company's insolvency, the extent of responsibility for any failure by the company to supply prepaid goods/services and the extent of responsibility for the company's giving of any insolvency preferences (namely transactions contrary to insolvency legislation which give unfair preference to creditors).

Thus although motivated by a quite different policy agenda (safeguarding the standard of stewardship of the incorporated business sector generally) and concerned with countering different risks (protection of creditors) to the FSMA Approved Persons regime the list of factors and techniques used to define "unfitness" does sound a resonant chord when viewed against the FSA's Statements of Principle and Code of Conduct applicable to Approved Persons. The same concerns are there – *integrity* above all, but also a degree of care and skill, and regulatory compliance requirements (in the case of the CDDA a director must show regard to compliance with Companies Act requirements). In the development of this "unfitness" standard in the case law under section 6 CDDA the courts have resorted to a broad standard of "commercial morality". Examples of what they mean by this have included a failure to introduce any working capital into a persistently loss-making company and thus flagrantly trading at the risk of suppliers, bankers and the Crown (in the form of unpaid Crown debts),[100] yet unfitness can encompass less obviously morally culpable conduct too:

> The public is entitled to be protected, not only against the activities of those guilty of the more obvious breaches of commercial morality, but also against someone who has shown in the conduct of more than one company... a failure

---

[99] Schedule 1 CDDA 1986.
[100] *Re Ipcon Fashions Ltd* [1989] BCC 773.

to appreciate or observe the duties attendant on the privilege of conducting business with the protection of limited liability.[101]

There is a clear parallel here with the way in which the ability of the FSA to prohibit an individual approved person from a particular controlled function or set of controlled functions (such as the significant influence controlled functions which broadly equate to holding senior management responsibility) can be used in the instance of an individual approved person who, while not exhibiting any lack of integrity, has nonetheless exhibited a lack of appreciation of the importance of and urgency of the firm's compliance with regulatory requirements which it would normally be incumbent upon someone in their position to appreciate. Such an individual approved person may not merit any outright prohibition from working in any capacity in the regulated financial sector but may thus be prevented from occupying a senior management role and indeed examples where both the FSA and the Financial Services and Markets Tribunal adopted such a course of action have been considered in the previous chapter.[102]

How have the courts in the development of their expected standards for directors under section 6 CDDA viewed the whole question of responsibility of individual directors for breakdowns caused by malfunction in internal systems of control within the company, or the failure of a delegated function to be performed properly? After all such internal organisational issues are ultimately the responsibility of the board as a whole so how does individual responsibility emerge from that collective responsibility? These questions are of course also central to the way in

---

[101] Vinelott J in *Re Stanford Services Ltd* [1987].

[102] See discussion in Chapter 4 text to nn 81 to 86 of the FSA's use of s 56 FSMA 2000 and discussion of the Financial Services and Markets Tribunal decision in *FSA v. Hoodless & Blackwell*. It was implicit in the Tribunal's approval of Mr Hoodless' voluntary relinquishing of any future supervisory management role in its decision in Hoodless and Blackwell which it exonerated him from showing any lack of integrity under the FSA's Statements of Principle for Approved Persons but had shown a lack of care and skill and had not been equal to his management responsibilities for, among other things, notifying as required by someone in his position AIM and SFA of misleading market announcements made.

which the Approved Persons regime of individual responsibility links up with the organisation and control requirements of SYSC to give them "bite". They were also central to the series of hearings before the courts in which the Secretary of State sought disqualification orders on the grounds of unfitness against members of the board of Barings plc in the wake of the banking group's collapse caused in part by the failure to properly supervise and hence detect Leeson's unauthorised overtrading of derivatives contracts on behalf of a Barings Singapore subsidiary, his falsification of trading accounts to conceal the scale of losses incurred, and the fundamental internal organisational flaw which had left Leeson in charge of both dealing and settlement operations and hence in a position to engage in these activities. Much of the language used by the courts in the Barings series of cases could, with only the slightest of refinements, have been employed by the FSA in justifying the need to forge links between individual responsibility for senior managers under the Approved Persons regime with the firm's own compliance with SYSC. For example, Sir Richard Scott V-C said, in justifying a disqualification order against one director he described as a senior group director:

> That particular description of his role in the group is, in my view, important for the purpose of considering the degree of culpability that attaches to him in regard to the matters that brought about the collapse and insolvency of the Group. [Counsel for the director concerned] has rightly drawn attention to the need in any large organisation for senior members of management to delegate functions to others, to subordinates . . . and made the point that if an efficient system is in place, or if the individual in question has good reason for believing there to be an efficient system in place, the delegation within the system of functions to be discharged in accordance with the system by others cannot be the subject of serious criticism if, in the event, the persons to whom the responsibilities are delegated fail properly to discharge their duties. That may be so up to a point in theory, but the higher the office within an organisation that is held by an individual, the greater the responsibilities that fall upon him. It is right that that should be so, because status within an organisation carries with it commensurate rewards. These rewards are matched by the weight of the responsibilities that the office carries with it, and those responsibilities require diligent attention from time to time to the question whether the system that has been put in place and over which the individual is presiding is operating efficiently, and whether individuals to whom duties, in accordance with the system, have been delegated are discharging those duties efficiently. It plainly becomes individuals holding

high office to be responsive to warning signs that indicate some failure in the system, or in the discharge by individuals within the system of their respective responsibilities.[103]

The Court of Appeal examined the Barings directors' responsibility for the acts and omissions of their delegates.[104] It approved the distinction drawn by the lower Court between the delegation of the discharge of a particular function, and the overall responsibility for the establishment of that delegation itself and for the subsequent review and monitoring of its efficacy. FSA's Code of Conduct for Approved Persons which addresses the issue of the effect of delegation on an individual approved person's responsibility under Statements of Principle 5 and 6 draws the same distinction.[105] Namely, the delegation of the function is not delegation of the responsibility for it, a residual responsibility for supervision and control is maintained, and that distinction lies at the heart of much of the SYSC rules and guidance. Directors of companies regulated by the FSA are subject to the parallel behaviour shaping constraints of the CDDA at the same time as being subject to the FSA's regulatory framework for senior management responsibilities, and the courts continually have to examine the degree of individual responsibility of directors for the efficacy of internal systems and controls and set liability standards for disqualification purposes. It would therefore seem perfectly open, where individual approved persons are faced with disciplinary action under the Approved Persons regime in respect of their failure to ensure the firm's compliance with SYSC (or indeed any other regulatory requirements), for the Financial Services and Markets Tribunal to import arguments and reasoning that have been employed under the CDDA. As Financial Services and Markets Tribunal jurisprudence develops further around the making of section 56 FSMA orders against senior managers, then more crossover between the two regimes may emerge. As Arsalidou has argued persuasively, citing comments by Professor Sealy "it is judgments in cases such as Barings rather than Re D'Jan that are the real driving

---

[103] *Re Barings plc* [1998] BCC 583.
[104] *Re Barings plc and others (No 5)* [2000] 1 BCLC 523.
[105] See discussion in Chapter 3 text accompanying in 49–53.

force in the development of the contemporary law governing the duties of directors".[106]

When alleged dereliction of responsibility under the Approved Persons regime is under scrutiny then any director concerned would do well to plead that his or her action was shaped and constrained just as much by the general law of directors' duties, the risks under CDDA, the expectations of the Combined Code on Corporate Governance (if applicable) and indeed any other overlapping regulatory or legal regime that coloured his or her and the company's actions as it was shaped by the FSA's regulatory standards and conduct exclusively. The inherent intellectual dishonesty and commercial uncertainty of applying complex legal and regulatory regimes as if they existed in isolation that the critics of meta-regulatory strategies such as Haines and Gurney have exposed could be brought into sharper focus if lawyers were to look outside immediately applicable legal standards and across to others which are similar in tenor yet not quite identical. The extent to which the voguish concepts of "compliance culture" and "compliance ethos" are useful aids to achieving that more holistic (and commercially workable) understanding of overlap between regulatory expectations is considered further in the final chapter.

---

[106]D Arsalidou, supra, n 46.

6

Regulation and the emergence of the financial citizen

This chapter returns to the discussion in Chapter 2 of the redrawing of the boundary between collective and personal responsibility in the context of the political desire to shift downwards the responsibility for longer-term financial security from the government to the individual citizen. This goal has been most recently reflected in various government initiatives including the introduction of the "Sandler suite" of longer-term savings products, the government's Informed Choice strategy[1] and the recent pensions reforms, designed to incentivise citizens to invest in markets. This downward shifting is also implicitly reflected in the FSA's statutory objectives of "public awareness" and "protection of the consumers" and in the supporting principles of "good regulation" contained in section 2(3), including "caveat emptor".

The FSA has in turn responded by focusing on regulating processes, including imposing information disclosure rules on the industry and improving citizen financial awareness and literacy. Such initiatives are designed to enable "consumers" (specifically the individual citizen) to

---

[1] See the Department for Work and Pensions Green Paper, *Simplicity, Security and Choice: Working and Saving for Retirement*, Cm 5677, December 2002.

make more informed and knowledgeable investment choices about the suitability of various investment products and to compare between various products and providers – in other words to foster the development of the "financial citizen" as a knowledgeable, competent, confident, self-reliant and willing market participant. The purpose of this chapter is to look more closely at the alignment between government policy and FSA regulatory strategy, and to critically assess the process-based regulation implemented by the FSA, particularly the information disclosure regime for retail packaged products, in the light of the literature on decision-making and consumer behaviour. It will consider the implications of this regulatory strategy for citizens increasingly expected to take responsibility for their own longer-term financial security.

The growth of the consumer market for financial services

Since the 1980s there has been an explosion in the number of retail products designed by both industry and government for the private citizen investor. These range from endowment policies and TESSAs in the 1980s, to PEPs, ISAs, various forms of collective investment schemes, personal pensions, CAT standard products, stakeholder pensions and the like, and, latterly, the more specialised retail products such as spilt capital trusts, equity reversion schemes, precipice bonds, etc. Some of these have been supported by various tax concessions designed to enhance their attractiveness to this market. There are now apparently some 30 000 retail investment products available, including over 1600 unit trusts or OEICs.[2]

Closely aligned to this development of mass market retail finance is the desire and need for successive UK governments (and indeed most governments with developed financial economies) to structure their public finances in order to reduce or withdraw from welfare provision, including meeting the cost of retirement and long-term care. In the case

---

[2]Sandler Review: *UK Medium and Long-Term Retail Savings in the UK*, HM Treasury (HMT, July 2002).

of politically conservative governments this has been underpinned by an ideology that markets represented the optimum form of economic organisation while collective social welfarism led to inefficiency, dependency and stagnation.[3] In the case of the UK's New Labour on the other hand this continued support for the development of private markets has reflected its particular view about the role of government and the role of individuals in society. It believes that fundamental economic and social changes, including globalisation and technological transformations such as information technology, have resulted in a period of "institutional individualism" in which citizens, freed from the old restraints of poverty as well as class and tradition, have much greater opportunities and choice. But at the same time these changes have resulted in a "society too complex, fluid and diverse to be managed by a central state".[4]

No longer concerned with community and social solidarity as expressed through universal welfare, according to Shaw, New Labour has invoked a new concept of community "detached from social solidarity and collective protection against risk". Instead, this concept is based on a commitment to a set of shared values and norms, including those of mutual responsibility and duty, coupled with a concept of citizenship based around personal responsibility.[5] Hence, it believes the role of government is no longer about automatically providing a welfare safety net. Rather is about creating in individuals the capacity to make effective use of the opportunities and choices presented in late modern society (including the negotiation of risk). At the same time and like neo-liberal governments before it, the concept of the citizen as entrepreneur is central to its vision of the good society.

It is also true that rather than necessarily reflecting any political ideology, this downward shifting can be understood as a worldwide

---

[3]See, e.g., S Hall and M Jacques (eds) *The Politics of Thatcherism* (Lawrence and Wishart in association with *Marxism Today*: London, 1983); C Gray, Suburban Subjects: Financial Services and the New Right, in D Knights and T Tinker (eds) *Financial Institutions and Social Transformation* (Macmillan Press: 1997).
[4]A Finlayson, Third Way Theory, *Political Quarterly*, 1999, 271–279.
[5]E Shaw, Britain: Left Abandoned? New Labour in Power, *Parliamentary Affairs*, 2003, Vol 56, 6–23.

phenomenon and a function of the international macro-economic environment in which governments reformulate public spending and fiscal rules to shift spending off government balance sheets – in other words, as a product of the macro-economic climate and the competitive discipline of global capital markets to which governments are exposed as much as any other economic actor. Minns in his book *The Cold War in Welfare* on the other hand argues that the withdrawal of the state from welfare provision and the privatisation of pensions in particular is primarily about the extension and growth of stock markets and liberalised financial markets, markets which play a significant role in UK GDP. In other words, the privatisation of welfare and in particular pensions is more about promoting stock markets than controlling deficits, or promoting citizen welfare.[6]

As Hamilton and Wisniewski have observed,[7] for whatever reason, Labour ideology is much more positive about markets than earlier social democratic governments had been in the past. Markets are not just seen as engines of wealth creation, they also provide individuals with a variety of opportunities for action.[8] This ideology has been identified as located somewhere between liberalism, conservatism and socialism. It encompasses the socio-economic practices associated with liberalism, including the consumer and managerial efficiencies that flow from a mixed economy and from competition, together with an emphasis on human well-being pursued in part by the welfare state (especially in areas such as health and education) and, in part, by the exercise of

---

[6]R Minns, *The Cold War in Welfare: Stock Markets versus Pensions* (Verso: London, 2001). Minns further questions the evidence for claims that the stockmarket system will improve rates of returns; that state pensions are more expensive than private pensions, or that privatisation will increase savings and support productive investment.

[7]J Hamilton and M Wisniewski, Economic Appraisals of Rule Making in the New Society: Why, How, and What Does it Mean?, in the Challenge for the Consumer, C Rickett and T Telfer (eds) pp. 196–230, *International Perspectives on Consumer's Access to Justice* (Cambridge University Press: Cambridge, 2003), reproduced with permission.

[8]R Mullender, Theorizing the Third Way: Qualified Consequentialism, the Proportionality Principle and the New Social Democracy, *Journal of Law and Society*, 2000, 27, p 413.

personal responsibility.[9] Moreover Hamilton and Wisniewski observe that all of these various strands of Labour ideology run through the Financial Services and Markets Act 2000 (hereafter "FSMA") as indicated in the statutory objectives listed in section 2(2).[10] The communitarian objective of "well-being" is reflected in the statutory objective of "consumer protection", while personal responsibility is underscored by the proviso to the consumer protection objective that consumers must accept personal responsibility for decision-making.[11] Empowering consumers is reflected in the "public awareness" objective, while the potential of markets as an instrument of wealth generation is reflected in the objective of "market confidence". All of these objectives are underpinned, in turn, by the requirement that the regulator consider the need for innovation and competition and for cost-effective regulation in carrying out its general functions.[12]

But even if it is accepted that the downward shifting of responsibility for longer-term financial security has been primarily as a response to macro-economic conditions, it is nevertheless the case that the government had a choice as to how that could be done. The same policy could, for example, have been implemented by the introduction of compulsory methods of saving, as in Australia.[13] Instead, it is clear that not only is there a desire for citizens to assume voluntarily more responsibility for their long-term financial security, but to do so through direct engagement with the market.[14] One implication of this is that the citizen is being encouraged to invest in the financial markets (either directly through equity ownership or indirectly through packaged retail products), as the primary mechanism for securing their longer-term

---

[9] M Freeden, The Ideology of New Labour, *Political Quarterly*, 1999, 70, p 42.

[10] J Hamilton and M Wisniewski, supra, p 198, n 7.

[11] Section 5(2)(d).

[12] The principles of "good regulation" are set out in section 2(3).

[13] A list of countries with compulsory savings schemes is provided in the Pension Commission First Report, *Pensions: Challenges and Choices*, 12 October 2004, at p 252.

[14] Though it is clear that greater compulsion has not been ruled out – see the Pension Commission First Report ibid; interview with Adair Turner, Pensions Guru who Believes People must be Forced to Save, *The Independent*, Saturday, 28 May 2005, Business Section, p 48.

financial security. In 1998 the government stated that that it wanted to reverse the current ratio of 60% state provision of pensioner income and 40% private provider provision.[15]

The FSMA and the financial citizen

The language of the FSMA is particularly telling in respect of the political ambition to entice citizens into the markets. Whereas the previous legislation introduced by the Conservative government (the Financial Services Act 1986) used the term "investor", the FSMA instead uses the term "consumer", a term significant in the context of the broader political objective of constructing a retail market. The term "consumer" is not a neutral term but conveys a particular set of values: consumers are individualistic and acquisitive participants in a market exchange looking after their own interests, and taking responsibility for their choices. At the same time, "consuming" in modern society has become an everyday event. In fact, so powerful has become the image of the citizen as a consumer that Gabriel and Lang suggest that "we have gradually learned to talk and think of each other and ourselves less as workers, citizens, parents or teachers and more as consumers".[16] The term "consumer" rather than "investor" in the legislation suggests a vision of the citizen as an active market participant, and where rights, powers and responsibilities derive from markets, rather than deriving from the state (or earlier civic association form such as guild, clan or feudal structure).

As Dean has commented, consumerism has emerged as a distinguishing feature of late modern society and must be seen against "the reconfiguration of the social as a set of quasi-markets in services and expertise at the end of the 20c, of the governed as customers or consumers of such services and expertise".[17] In the context of financial services this

---

[15]Department of Social Security, *A New Challenge for Welfare: Partnership in Pensions*, 1998. The Pensions Act 2004 and the Finance Act 2004 introduce new measures to simplify private pension provision in the UK and are intended to make it easier for employers to offer company pension schemes.

[16]Y Gabriel and T Lang, *The Unmanageable Consumer* (Sage: London, 1995) p 1.

[17]M Dean, *Governmentality and Rule in Modern Society* (Sage: London, 1999), at p 6.

is nowhere more evident than in relation to long-term financial security. Financial provision for old age is increasingly a product to be bought individually in the market. Pensions, for example, have become commoditised (they are "products"): they are no longer a public (social) benefit provided by the state, they are a private consumption "good" to be obtained in the market. The terms "consumer" and "product" have a normalising power, we are all consumers in one form or another in our everyday lives, and their use suggests that the acquisition of financial products is no more different or difficult than the consumption of other goods or services. Investment is no longer the preserve of a few wealthy individuals but is to be part of commonplace life for the ordinary citizen.

In introducing the FSMA the public reason most often given by the Labour government was the need to "protect the consumer". There was a perception that the previous regulators had been captured by the industries they were regulating to the detriment of the consumer and hence consumer protection was to be placed at the heart of the reformed regime. Various "scandals" (including that of personal pensions misselling) had dented consumer confidence in the industry, and without adequate protection individuals would not remain in, or enter, the marketplace. Given the public rhetoric surrounding the reforms one would expect consumer interests to be at the heart of the new structure. An obvious means of meeting this expectation was to introduce a specific statutory objective to this effect and this has been done by requiring the FSA to "secur[e] the appropriate protection of consumers".[18] Significantly, however, this is only one of four statutory objectives, the other three being "maintaining market confidence", "promoting public understanding of the financial system", and "reduction of financial crime".[19] Further, the consumer protection objective is qualified by the principle that consumers should take responsibility for their decisions[20] as well as the need for the FSA to have regard to the differing degrees of risk involved in different kinds of transactions; the differing levels of

---

[18]FSMA 2000, s 5.
[19]FSMA 2000, s 2(2).
[20]FSMA 2000, s 5(2)(d).

experience and expertise of different types of consumers; and the needs of consumers for advice and information.[21]

The seven guiding principles of "good regulation" underpinning the FSA's general duties contained in section 2(3) make no reference to consumer protection. Instead, their emphasis is upon the importance of innovation and competition in the market and the need for cost-effective regulation. Consumer protection therefore is to be balanced against other market-based goals of innovation, competition and efficiency; a balancing act made more sensitive by the statutory obligation of the OFT to keep the FSA rules and practices under competition scrutiny.[22] While the reform of the financial services regulatory structure introduced in 2000 was premised upon the need to protect the consumer, the regulatory objectives and underlying principles revealed a strong commitment to markets as wealth creators, to competition and innovation and to the concept of the individual as a "responsibilised citizen".

The FSA, regulation and the financial citizen

The way in which the FSA interprets its objectives acquires a particular significance given that citizens are being increasingly expected to assume greater personal responsibility for their longer-term financial security, through their participation in financial markets. In implementing a consumer protection objective it would seem that a financial regulator has (at least) two choices: to regulate products or to regulate processes. Regulating products has the advantage that it has the potential to both reduce unnecessary complexity in product features (that complexity itself being a feature commented upon repeatedly by the FSA and in various reports into the retail investment industry[23]), and to reduce consumer search costs. However, product regulation has the disadvantage

---

[21]FSMA 2000, s 5(2)(a),(b),(c).

[22]FSMA 2000, s 160.

[23]See, e.g., FSA Consultation Paper 28, *Comparative Information for Financial Services*, October 1999; FSA Response Paper 28, *Response to CP 28*, June 2000; Sandler Review, supra, n 2.

that it restricts firms' abilities to innovate and hence compete. Process regulation on the other hand is more consistent with neo-liberalism and welfare economics: intervention is only justified where there is market failure but otherwise market forces, and in particular consumer sovereignty, should reign supreme.

The FSMA 2000 framework has been carefully constructed to attempt to ensure that the FSA is independent of government in the way in which it operationalises its objectives. Nevertheless, the existence of the four statutory objectives and underlying principles with their strong commitment to the market, to competition, innovation and to consumer sovereignty, provide a powerful intellectual constraint on the ability of the regulator to adopt any strategy other than a 'process-based' regulatory strategy (even should it be minded to). The FSA made clear very early on its commitment to an economic-based rational for regulation: regulation is "only justified in the presence of substantial market imperfection, and only where the crisis is worse than the disease".[24] Consistent with this market failure -based rationale for regulation, a major focus of FSA activity under its "consumer protection" and "public awareness" objectives has been on overcoming information asymmetries between firms and consumers through developing information disclosure requirements, and on "consumer education".

Regulating processes provides a framework of ground rules for the operation of the retail market but at the same time avoids direct interference with the ability of product providers to innovate and compete in terms of the products they offer, and of consumers to choose. Armed with the information and skills needed to enable them to make effective and informed choices that reflect their individual needs, the consumer is sovereign in that consumer interests are presumed to drive firms' behaviour through competitive market forces. Developing information disclosure and consumer education regimes in order to strengthen

---

[24]H Davies, *Why Regulate*, speech of 4 November 1998, available at www.fsa.gov.uk/pubs/speeches/sp19.html. Typical examples of market failure include barriers to market entry; imperfect or asymmetric information; the presence of transaction costs: see FSA, *Reasonable Expectations; Regulation in a Non-zero World*, September 2003, Chapter 4; FSA Occasional Paper 1, *The Economic Rationale for Financial Regulation*, April 1999.

consumer decision-making therefore becomes crucial, not just for the individual consumer, but because it is believed that informed consumer demand promotes competition and leads to great market efficiency and this in turn leads to even greater consumer benefit.

While the regulator is constrained by statutory objectives and principles of good regulation, the government is not. The government has become increasingly concerned at the perceived shortfall in the level of household savings, particularly in long-term savings for retirement finance. A number of forces and factors have combined to fuel concern over a savings gap.[25] These include the reduction in the coverage and levels of state welfare provision, as well as changes in the basis of occupational pension schemes from defined benefit to defined contribution, falling equity markets and lower investment returns, together with increased consumer mistrust of the markets as the result of various misselling scandals. Anxious to encourage low and middle income earners in particular to enter the market, the government has introduced "stakeholder" retail products whose features are tightly regulated and which are designed to appeal to low and middle income earners who do not have any current form of private investment. The specific purpose behind their introduction is to entice citizens into the market.[26]

Government policy favours markets as wealth creators and sees consumers as tools of economic development. It is clear that this policy, along with the desire to shift responsibility for long-term financial security downwards, and the FSA's approach to the implementation of its

---

[25]See, for example, the Pensions Commission First Report, October 2004, supra n 13, which reports that 12 million people aren't saving enough for their pensions, and 75% of people saving into a defined contributions pension plan aren't saving enough. The existence of a savings gap is not universally accepted, see, e.g., T Congdon, The Pensions Commission: Is Adair Turner Irrational or Confused?, *Economic Affairs*, March 2005, 25(1).

[26]Certain changes to the regulatory regime were announced by the government in November 2004 in order to "encourage the increased uptake of personal pensions and stakeholder pensions." HMT *FSMA 2 Year Review: Changes to Secondary Legislation, Government Response*, November 2004, para 2.1. See also J Gray, Sandler Review of Medium and Long-term Savings in the UK: Dilemmas for Financial Regulation, *Journal of Financial Regulation and Compliance*, 2002, 10(4), pp 385–392.

consumer protection and public awareness objectives, have all become intertwined. The government is encouraging citizens towards private retail investments. "[R]ather than tell people how much they should save, the Government instead believes it should enable people to make informed choices about retirement income, so individuals can plan to save in accordance with their preferences and circumstances."[27] The FSA, in turn, through its information disclosure and consumer education regimes, is seeking to arm citizens with the knowledge and skills to participate more effectively so that they

> will be better equipped to exercise a stronger influence in these markets; to take greater responsibility for their own actions; and to protect themselves through less mis-buying and being less susceptible to mis-selling.[28]

Although it is not the role of the FSA to be concerned with "savings gaps" it is nonetheless, through its interpretation of its consumer protection and public awareness objectives, creating a particular model of citizen that conforms with government policy and ideology.[29] In the sense that the FSA is attempting to shape behaviour it is not merely a regulator of the industry, it is also a regulator of the citizen, seeking to mould the consumer into an active, informed and responsible market participant, looking after their own longer-term financial security. In the light of this regulatory goal it becomes important to consider the effectiveness of the regulatory tools adopted in order to achieve it, as well as the implications for the citizen of "regulatory failure" – where the citizen fails to conform to the desired model.

Information disclosure as a regulatory tool

Information disclosure regimes have been a significant part of consumer protection strategy since at least the 1960s and are evident in a number

---

[27] Treasury Committee Report: *Restoring Confidence in Longer Term Savings*, Vol 1, HC 71-1, July 2004, p 9.
[28] C Briault, speech, 7 December 2004, *The Lending Landscape post October 31*, available at http://www.fsa.gov.uk/Pages/Library/Communication/Speeches/2004/SP217.shtml.
[29] See also the DTI consultation paper on consumer strategy, *Extending Competitive Markets*, DTI, July 2004.

of contexts: product labelling, consumer credit, advertising, and securities legislation to name just a few. The purpose has generally (but not
always[30]) been expressed in terms of directly benefiting consumers by
enabling them to make more informed choices about the goods or services they buy, without restricting their choices. This strategy is evident
not only at UK level but also at European level where the concept of
the "informed consumer" has been central to EU policymaking since
1975 and is reflected in various financial sector directives such as the
Distance Marketing of Financial Services Directive[31] and the Market
in Financial Instruments Directive.[32] This is so despite the suggestion
that information disclosure reflects a political compromise as it is less
controversial than other more interventionist measures and therefore
less likely to attract member state resistance.[33]

As has been noted elsewhere,[34] information disclosure regimes as a
regulatory technique fit well with neo-liberal economic theory, itself a
dominant force since the 1970s. Information disclosure regimes can be
seen as augmenting the pre-conditions of a competitive marketplace and
of enhancing consumer sovereignty, in turn promoting competitiveness
and market efficiency. Similarly, such regimes don't restrict or impede
consumer choice, or impede producer/supplier flexibility and are therefore consistent with notions of market freedom and the superior ability
of the markets to distribute the greatest good to society through producer

---

[30] Its purpose can also be to facilitate discovery of breaches of regulations – S Breyer,
Regulation and its Reform (Harvard University Press: 1982), or to facilitate delibera-
tive democracy – C Sunstein, Information Regulation and Informational Standing,
University of Pennsylvania Law Review, 1998–1999, 147, 613.

[31] Directive 2002/65/EC.

[32] Directive 2004/39/EC.

[33] S Weatherill, The Role of the Informed Consumer in EC Law and Policy, *Consumer
Law Journal*, 1994, 49.

[34] J Hamilton and L Gillies, The Impact of E-commerce Developments on Consumer
Welfare – Information Disclosure Regimes. *Journal of Financial Regulation and Compliance*, 2003, 11(4), 329–348, reproduced with permission of Emerald Group Publishing
Ltd, http://www.emeraldinsight.com/jrfc.htm. See also A Ogus, *Regulation: Legal Form
and Economic Theory* (Clarendon: Oxford, 1994) for further discussion of the justifications for mandatory disclosure; and London Economics, *Consumer Detriment under
Conditions if Imperfect Information*, OFT Research Paper 11 (OFT: 1997).

competition. Consumer advocates have also championed information disclosure, primarily on the basis of redressing the inequality of bargaining power between consumers and producers/suppliers that prevents consumers obtaining better quality or more cost-effective products or services.[35]

Extending this information strategy into financial services is consistent with long-standing policy in other consumer markets. The assumption is that consumers make poor decisions because they lack sufficient, or adequate, information about the products on offer. Poor decisions result in consumers not entering the market at all (i.e. not purchasing any product) or entering the market but not buying the right type of product, or buying the right type but the wrong quality, leading in turn to consumer detriment and market inefficiency. An answer to this problem, it is generally believed, lies in ensuring that consumers receive adequate and sufficient information. Information thus becomes synonymous with knowledge, and knowledge with power. As Tsoukas notes: we live in a society where the wealth of information available

> seems to fulfil the modern dream of the knowledgeable actor who, freed from the shackles of ignorance, can think for himself/herself and can undertake informed responsible action. Indeed a society in which information has become the most valuable resource holds out the promise, or so it seems, for the realisation of one of the most cherished values in the western tradition, the making of a transparent, self regulated society.[36]

Information disclosure and retail packaged products

Information disclosure regimes in the retail financial services sector are not new. The Personal Investment Authority (a former regulator under the Financial Services Act 1986) introduced information disclosure

---

[35]The Consumer Association's *Which? Magazine* is premised on the need to provide consumers with better information about products and services. See also Consumer Association, *Disclosure: Protecting Consumers*, Policy Paper (CA: 1998).

[36]H Tsoukas, The Tyranny of Light, *Futures*, 1997, 29(9), 827–843.

requirements for the retail investment industry in 1988. The current regime is largely based on the disclosure regime it subsequently introduced in 1995 for life and pension products and extended in 1997 to unit trusts, OEICs, investment trusts and trust savings schemes (these together comprising the major retail investment vehicles for private retail investors).

This current information disclosure regime sits within a broader regulatory framework governing information and disclosure, including the requirement that financial promotions be clear, fair and not misleading.[37] The focus of this discussion, however, is specifically upon the information disclosure measures introduced to overcome information asymmetries operating to the detriment of citizens looking to invest in retail "packaged products", that is, those mainstream mid- to longer-term investment products designed to provide private investors with indirect access to equity markets.[38]

There are four principal groups of information that firms are required to supply to private consumers prior to the point of sale. Those groups are information about: the firm, the firm's status (in the case of advisers), charges, remuneration and commission, and finally, of course, the product offered.[39] The core provision in relation to product information is the requirement that the consumer be provided with a 'Key Features Document' ("KFD") that contains information about the aims of the product, the risks involved, the charges, and the commitment the consumer is making (the detailed information requirements varying

---

[37]FSA Discussion Paper 4, *Informing Consumers: A review of Product Information at the Point of Sale*, November 2000.

[38]Namely life and pension products, unit trusts, OEICs, ISAs and Investment Trust savings accounts (including those packaged products that are also stakeholder products). See FSA Handbook, COB 6.5.

[39]With depolarisation (the removal of the requirement that financial advisers either be tied to one product provider and able to advise on its products only, or be fully independent), from 1 December 2004 new rules require firms to inform consumers about the range of products it offers advice on (through an "Initial Disclosure Document") as well as about the costs of the advice service including the different ways of paying for that advice (the "menu" document). See FSA Policy Statement 04/27, *Reforming Polarisation*, November 2004.

depending on the type of product).[40] This document must be supplied to the consumer at the latest at the point of sale. The introduction of the product disclosure regime had two main purposes. First, it was designed to help consumers shop around by providing information that enabled comparison between products. Second, it was intended to give consumers the key information they needed to make informed decisions about whether to invest or not.[41]

The content of the disclosure regime has been the site of tensions between the regulator, the industry and the government since the inception of that regime. Between the regulator and the industry these tensions have centred around matters such as the extent to which the regulator should prescribe the detailed content of the disclosure regime, compliance issues, and industry concerns over competition and access to adviser outlets. Tensions between the regulator on the one hand and the government (primarily through the Office of Fair Trading and Department of Trade and Industry) on the other have centred around perceptions of the "informed consumer". The OFT and DTI have subscribed more strongly to the economists' model of the consumer as disciplining the market and driving competition through rational decision-making. The regulator has been more concerned with consumer information overload and with issues around the comprehensibility of the information disclosed.[42]

In 2000 the FSA announced a review of the product disclosure regime. The FSA acknowledged in its discussion paper introducing the review that its market research had revealed that "most consumers do not use KFDs for shopping around. Many consumers do not read KFDs,

---

[40]With the inclusions of general insurance and mortgages as regulated activities the requirement has been subsequently extended to these products through the requirement that consumers be supplied with a "Key Facts" document.

[41]FSA Discussion Paper 4, supra, n 37.

[42]For a discussion of these perceptions, and tensions, see further J Black, *Rules and Regulators* (Clarendon Press: Oxford, 1997), p 163. For a more recent discussion of OFT perspective on the role of the consumer see also the speech of J Vickers, Chairman, OFT, *Economics for Consumer Policy*, 29 October 2003, available at http://www.oft.gov.uk/News/Speeches+and+articles/2003/spe04-03.htm.

or only skim them; and those who do read KFDs often have difficulty understanding the material and in some cases misunderstand it."[43] The FSA also suggested a review was needed in the light of significant industry and regulatory developments, including the availability of new regulatory tools such as the publication by the FSA of comparative tables, and the FSA consumer education programme. As a result of this review the FSA announced reform of the regime. The KFD is to be replaced with a "Quick Guide/Key Facts" document.[44] The FSA intend this document will use plain language, no jargon and a question and answer format, as well as a generic checklist to act as a step-by-step guide to decision-making process and to signpost more detailed information.[45] Depending on the product,[46] it will also include a personal example in the form of a shorter and clearer personal illustration of projected outcomes based on assumed growth rates. The FSA is also exploring the viability of including a standardised consumer friendly risk rating system in the Quick Guide/Key Facts document (at the behest of the House of Commons Treasury Committee Report into longer-term savings,[47] the likely effectiveness of which we have already commented on in Chapter 2).[48]

---

[43]FSA Discussion Paper, supra, para 5 n 37. The FSA cannot be criticised for paying too little attention to the information disclosure regime. But the sheer volume of consultation papers, discussion papers, occasional papers and consumer research papers that touch on (directly or indirectly) this issue pose difficulties for external parties (including, no doubt, the industry) attempting to track particular themes or issues.

[44]FSA Consultation Paper 170, *Informing Consumers: Product Disclosure at the Point of Sale*, February 2003, and see also Consultation Paper 05/12, *Investment Product Disclosure: Proposals for a Quick Guide at the Point of Sale*. (The disclosure regime may yet require further revision in the light of the Markets in Financial Instruments Directive, to come into force for firms on 30 April 2007.)

[45]In the case of unit trusts and OEICs, the EU UCITS III Directive will require the "Key Facts" to contain some different information, see FSA Discussion Paper 05/03, *Wider Range Retail Investment Products*, June 2005.

[46]FSA Consultation Paper 170, supra, paras 1.6 and 5.64, n 44.

[47]Supra, para 29, n 27.

[48]And see Annex 2 of Consultation Paper 05/12 for a mock-up of a "quick guide", including information on risk.

The purpose of information disclosure

The FSA suggested in its discussion paper announcing the review that, while the objective of providing consumers with information they needed to make informed decisions remained valid, the first objective of the original disclosure regime (facilitating comparison between products) might no longer be so relevant. This was as a result of the publication by the FSA of its comparative tables[49] (although, as the Miles Review reported, when comparative tables for mortgages were introduced the website containing them received 7000 visitors, dropping to 1000, despite new mortgages running at between 200 000 and 300 000 per month[50]).

The objective of the KFD (or Quick Guide/Key Facts, once implemented) is specifically to enable consumers to make "informed" decisions about the proposed investment.[51] But what is actually meant by an "informed decision"? Informed about what? Presumably (although not expressly stated by the FSA) a decision is informed if it is made on the basis of a consideration of the quality of the investment offered. But the meaning of the term quality in relation to services is particularly elusive[52] for it implies a value judgement, but against what values is the quality of a financial product to be judged prior to its purchase? The essence of retail investment "products" such as pensions, unit trusts, equity ISAs' etc., either directly or indirectly, is performance (both by the fund managers and by the investee companies selected). As Paul Myners (author of the HM Treasury report into "Institutional Investment in the UK: a Review"[53]) said in his evidence to the Treasury Select Committee inquiry into restoring confidence in long-term savings, "this

---

[49]Supra, para 48, n 37 (but see subsequent Consultation Paper 05/12 supra, para 1.2, n 44 in which the FSA states the comparison objective remains valid).

[50]D Miles, *The UK Mortgage Market: Taking a Longer Term View*, HMT, March 2004, available at www.hm-treasury.gov.uk/consultations_and_legislation/miles_review/consult_miles_index.cfm.

[51]Supra, paras 1.1 and 2.2, n 44.

[52]See M Gabbott and G Hogg, *Consumers and Services* (John Wiley & Sons Ltd: Chichester, 1998).

[53]HM Treasury, P Myners, *Institutional Investment in the UK: A Review* (HMT: 2001), available at http://www.hm-treasury.gov.uk/media/2F9/02/31.pdf.

industry sells trust-based products, it sells a hope, it sells an expectations – it rarely sells a product".[54] This performance occurs only after
the purchase and will be influenced by the participants themselves and
other more extraneous influences such as market conditions, effects of
other market actors and the circumstances in which performance is to
take place. But performance by its very nature cannot be standardised
across all providers or assessed in advance. Pre-contractual information
about price and terms is therefore limited in its ability to provide the
basis of any judgement about quality. Investors are unlikely, for example,
to know about, let alone be able to evaluate, the financial risks taken
by fund managers, the asset allocations, the care taken in managing the
fund and processing transactions, or the likelihood of misappropriation
of funds.

Because of the difficulty in pre-assessing the quality of services generally there has been a trend, not only in financial services but in other
service industries and in the provision of public services, to use other,
quantifiable, information as proxies for information about quality (this
trend is evidenced in, for example, education where pass rates are used
as proxy measures for assessing quality of teaching, and in surgery where
death rates provide a proxy measure for surgeon skill). In relation to
packaged products, proxies for quality are provided by information about
aims, charges, commitment, and risk.[55] While this information may be
useful simply in terms of confirming for the consumer the terms of the
commitment they are making, it is questionable to what extent this
information is, and can in the future be, effective proxies for quality,
or the basis for effective competitive pressure on retail markets, particularly as these products are unlikely to be repeat purchases. Rather,
this disclosure is only likely to provide competitive pressure from consumers[56] in relation to those factors disclosed, (which may or may not

---

[54]Transcript of oral evidence taken before the House of Commons Treasury Committee, Thursday, 22 January 2004, available at http://www.parliament.the-stationery-
office.co.uk/pa/cm200304/cmselect/cmtreasy/71/4012203.htm.
[55]See FSA Consultation Paper 05/12, supra, Annex 2, n 44, for exemplars of the proposed Quick Guide using these proxies.
[56]Although, as the FSA have pointed out, suppliers may improve the competitiveness
of their products in response to the *potential* for consumers to shop around, even if they
do not in fact do so – see FSA Discussion Paper 4, Supra, para 27, n 37.

bear any relationship to the ultimate performance of that product), and only then to the extent that the factors disclosed are considered to be significant when choosing an investment. If those factors are not considered significant they will be ignored by consumers and will not form the basis of competitive pressure.

The risk for the regulator is that it may provide or mandate disclosure of information that it believes consumers need, but actually consumers don't want and so won't use, or worse will use wrongly. Or a regulator may mandate disclosure of information consumers are interested in, but which has little impact on their decision-making. The risk for the "consumer" is that they are held responsible, in the absence of fraud or misrepresentation, for decisions made in the face of information disclosed which the regulator believes should form the basis for rational decision-making, but which doesn't in fact form that basis. This could be because the information is not understood, or because the investment decision is based on factors other than provided in that information (such as "reputation" or "trust").

Information and consumer decision-making

As part of its review into the effectiveness of the product disclosure regime in 2000, the FSA commissioned various pieces of research into how consumers use KFDs.[57] That research revealed interesting information about consumer decision-making behaviour. It found that the disclosure regime has had little effect in meeting its objectives of facilitating product comparisons or of enabling consumers to make more informed decisions. It posited a number of reasons for the regime's ineffectiveness. These included the timing of disclosure, the language used in the document and its format, and the fact that the KFD did not always provide information that consumers regarded as key. Such information would include information as to return (the amount of money consumers may receive on maturity), commitment (whether or not the

---

[57]The research findings are synthesised in FSA Consumer Research 5: *Informed Decisions? How Consumers use Key Features*, November 2000 (a companion document to FSA Discussion Paper 4, supra, n 37).

consumer could afford the premiums), and what would happen to the money if the consumer died during the term of the investment.[58]

In addition, the research suggested that consumers tended to read the "risk" information in the KFD as simply a disclaimer, rather than as information to guide their decision-making.[59] Consumers might well be justified in taking this view when even the chair of the Investment Management Association has admitted, "a lot of [savings] products which have been designed have just been too complicated for people to understand the risk within them, or even for the providers to fully understand the risks that are implicit within them".[60] Overall, the research showed that KFDs appeared to have little impact on consumer decision-making behaviour. The information supplied was not the information that consumers wanted, but even more significantly, the research reported that the very peripheral value of KFDs led to the consumer respondents having little to say with respect to possible improvements in the document.[61] In other words, irrespective of its clarity and content, the KFD was not seen by the consumer respondents to be a key component of their decision-making process, so much so that they apparently saw reform as largely irrelevant.

The FSA has responded by redesigning the KFD to reduce its length and to place a greater emphasis on product suitability, by encouraging the use of plain language, and by using a question and answer format for delivering information, as well as revising the charges information.[62] Product information disclosure is not to be abandoned, it is to be adjusted, despite the scepticism expressed by consumers over its value. The FSA's response would appear to be that if the disclosure

---

[58]FSA Discussion Paper 4, supra, para 28, n 37; FSA Consumer research 5, ibid., para 3.26.

[59]Consumer Research 5, supra, para 3.34, n 57.

[60]Supra, para 25, n 27.

[61]Consumer Research 5, supra, para 4.4, n 57.

[62]FSA Consultation Paper 170, supra, paras 5.17 and 5.51, n 44. Other proposed reforms include focusing on core product information and allowing firms greater discretion as to the treatment of other disclosable information and the use of a question and answer format for delivering general information.

regime hasn't worked so far, it is because the information has not been sufficiently transparent. Alternative interpretations might be that investors have not yet learned to properly perform the role of "consumers" because of relative inexperience, or that private investors are in some way "irrational" or financially illiterate (and arguably both of these interpretations are reflected in the FSA's financial capability and consumer education work). Another alternative interpretation, and one that proponents of the market failure rationale for regulating find more difficult, is that investors may make decisions on a different basis to that assumed by the model of the rational, autonomous, evaluative and goal-driven cognitive criteria comprised in the model of the rational consumer that (implicitly) underpins most information disclosure regimes.

Understanding decision-making behaviour has provided a rich seam of research within a number of disciplines including economics, cognitive psychology, sociology and marketing. This research has challenged the assumptions of the rational choice actor so prevalent in economics (and reflected in law). Many of the insights provided by cognitive psychology are now familiar, and form the basis of much of the work of behaviour economists that in turn have become influential in legal scholarship.[63] These insights include that: all decision-makers are subject to bounded rationality and will search only until a satisfactory rather than the best alternative is found;[64] how information is framed affects decisions (in particular whether the information is presented as resulting in a loss or a gain for the decision-maker); heuristics (shortcuts) are used to facilitate decision-making; oral communication is more influential than written communication[65] (acknowledged by the FSA when

---

[63]See, e.g., G Howells, The Potential and Limits of Consumer Empowerment, *Journal of Law and Society*, 2005, Vol 32/3, 349–370; I Ramsay, From Truth in Lending to Responsible Lending, in G Howells, A Janssen and R Schulze (eds) *Information Rights and Obligations* (Ashgate: Aldershot, 2005).

[64]See H Simon, *Administrative Behaviour* (Macmillan: New York, 1947). But see G Ingham, Critical Survey: Some Recent Changes in the Relationship between Economics and Sociology, *Cambridge Journal of Economics*, 1996, 20, 243–275 who argues that rationality is not bounded but is socially constructed – at 263.

[65]D Langevoort, Selling Hope, Selling Risk, *California Law Review*, 1996, 84, 637–701.

it raised the possibility of requiring, where possible, that the KFD be delivered orally, to increase its impact[66]).

The tendency to overconfidence is a well-documented psychological "error" and impairs the ability to rationally reassess decisions once they have been made. This suggests that much disclosure after the point of decision is ineffective,[67] while "confirmation bias" results in information which confirms an existing view being overweighted, while conflicting information is underweighted. "Anchoring" is the term used to describe the need in the face of uncertainty to find a basis for decision-making, and can explain why, despite the warning about relying on past performance of investments as a guide to future performance, investors continue to rely on these figures to guide decision-making, in the absence of any other hard "anchors".[68]

All of this research suggests that designing effective information disclosure strategies in order to improve consumer decision-making is extremely difficult, a fact the FSA is aware of as it carries out market research into various models of the new product disclosure format. Information overload (and the KFD is but one document investors receive among the promotion material supplied by the firm), limited ability for information processing, preferences for oral communications, overconfidence, confirmation bias and anchoring will, it seems, inevitably impact on decision-makers' abilities to perform as rational utility maximisers.

Other research within the cognitive psychology field draws attention to the need for a better understanding of communication processes associated with information disclosure. As Jacoby discusses,[69] it is generally assumed that the effect produced by information on an individual

---

[66]FSA Discussion Paper 4, supra para 63, n 37.

[67]D Langevourt, supra, n 65.

[68]See further the collection of essays in C Sunstein (ed) *Behavioural Law and Economics* (Cambridge University Press: Cambridge, 2000); J Montier, *Behavioural Finance* (John Wiley & Sons: Chichester, 2002).

[69]J Jacoby, *Is it Rational to Assume Consumer rationality? Some Consumer Psychological Perspectives on Rational Choice Theory*, 2001–2002, 6 Roger Williams UL Rev 81–161. For a summary of trends in consumer research, see I Simonson, Z Carmon, R Dhar, A Drolet and S Nowlis, Consumer Research: In Search of Identity, *Annual Review of Psychology*, 2001, Vol 52, 249–276.

occurs in a sequential and hierarchical fashion (the "hierarchy of effects" model). This model suggests that in order to produce action by the receiver of the information the following must occur (in sequence): exposure, attention, comprehension, evaluation, integration, intention retention, action (purchase, or rejection). He suggests that the focus of much cognitive psychology and behavioural economics has been directed at the evaluation and decision-making phase, (where, for example, biases and heuristics manifest themselves), and too little attention has been paid to the earlier information acquisition and processing stages. Studying these earlier stages reveals, for example, that a receiver's evaluation of message content may vary considerably depending on the order in which the message components are supplied.[70]

Although cognitive psychology and behavioural economics research has focused on identifying barriers to rational decision-making, it does not challenge the underlying model of the rational decision-maker. In other words, it assumes that decision-makers would be rational, but for the presence of cognitive barriers. Research from within other disciplines, particularly marketing but also sociology, however, highlights the role that non-cognitive factors may play in decision-making or at least certain types of decision-making and, in so doing, challenges the validity of this underlying model. Typically, the model of the rational consumer assumes decisions are "purposive choices made by informed, disinterested, and calculating actors working with a clear set of individual or organisational goals".[71] Optimum decisions are rational decisions, emotions should play no part. It is well accepted however, that financial service products are high in what marketeers call "experience" or "credence" qualities, such that their quality can only be assessed after purchase, if at all.[72] Because of the difficulty in evaluating the "products", and because consumers are exposing themselves to certain risks in purchasing them, the evidence suggests that emotions such as trust and confidence are significant influences on decision-making. This to a

---

[70]The FSA is consulting on introducing a requirement that the Quick Guide be placed on the top of the product marketing pack, see Consultation Paper 05/12, para 2.10–2.12.
[71]K Hawkins, *The Uses of Discretion* (Clarendon Press: Oxford, 1992), p 21.
[72]M Gabbot and G Hogg, supra n 52.

certain extent echoes the shift in contract theory towards recognition of relational contracting, where concepts such as trust and cooperation can play a more fundamental role in characterising the relationship between the parties than does the formal contract itself.[73]

The FSA's own consumer research identified four factors as important in consumer financial decision-making: company name/reputation; adviser recommendation; existing relationship; and charges (but interestingly, not risk).[74] Similarly, the FSA's research into the context in which individuals about to buy an investment product approach product disclosure and pricing information,[75] found that older individuals tended towards what it labels as the "rational" end of the approach spectrum (shopping around, etc.), while younger individuals tended to adopt a more "emotional" approach, anxious for the process to be over quickly and more reliant on advice from professionals and/or family. Moreover, the research reported that many relied on their own, or reported, perceptions of a provider's name and reputation (that is, trust). Consistently the FSA's own research has found that while private investors endorse the concept of product disclosure in the KFD, written information in fact plays only a limited role in any investment decision, with personal contacts being the most trusted source.[76] In other words, brand name and trust, rather than information search and processing, provide the basis for decision-making (something product providers and their marketing teams are well aware of).

Non-cognitive factors such as trust and emotion are increasingly being recognised in research as playing a fundamental, and necessary, part in decision making.[77] Orthodox economic analysis tends to regard

---

[73]See further D Campbell (ed), *The Relationship Theory of Contract: Selected Works of Ian Macneil* (Sweet and Maxwell: London, 2001).

[74]FSA Consumer Research 5, supra, para 3.44, n 57.

[75]Consumer Research 18, *The Development of More Effective Product Disclosure*, March 2003, paras 5.5, 5.6.

[76]See especially FSA Consumer Research 1, *Better Informed Consumers*, April 2000, but see also Consumer Research 2, 24, and 31, all available at http://www.fsa.gov.uk/Pages/Library/other_publications/consumer/2000/index.shtml.

[77]See, e.g., R Muramatsu and Y Hanoch, Emotions as a Mechanism for Boundedly Rational Agents: The Fast and Frugal Way, *Journal of Economic Psychology*, 2005, 26, 201–221.

emotions such as trust, as an "add on" to exchange transactions, a useful "lubricant to exchange" but which is unnecessary where the parties have adequate information. Attention has been drawn to the neglect by the influential behavioural economics movement of emotions such as trust, and their impact on behaviour. Elster, for example, calls for the need to understand how emotions interact with other motivations to produce behaviour, and suggests that emotion is an inevitable component of decision-making, and should not be discounted as "irrational" behaviour.[78] Others suggests that the proliferation of information actually increases, rather than decreases, the importance of trust as parties strive to make sense of the complexities and uncertainties revealed by increased information.[79] Some go so far as to suggest that in making decisions about the future – and investment decisions are inevitably decisions about the future – emotion is an absolute requirement for decision-making.[80]

Even those private investors identified as "highly sophisticated" in FSA consumer research (claiming to have a good knowledge and understanding of financial matters, like reading the financial pages and making their own financial decisions) admitted to ultimately basing their strategies for assessing risk levels of various products on "gut feel or judgement". While the focus of much research has been into consumer decision-making, Pixley has recently studied the role of emotions in financial markets. As a result, she suggests that no matter how rational firms' calculations of past information are, or how sophisticated their risk modelling, ultimately future outcomes are simply unknowable. It is only through emotions such as trust and distrust that firms are able to

---

[78] J Elster, Emotions and Economic Theory, *Journal of Economic Literature*, 1998, Vol 36, 47–74. It is also worth noting that the role of emotion specifically in financial organisations and markets has been examined in a recent book, J Pixley, *Emotions in Finance* (CUP: Cambridge, 2004).

[79] G Ingham, Critical Survey: Some Recent Changes in the Relationship between Economics and Sociology, *Cambridge Journal of Economics*, 1996, Vol 20, 243–275, at 250.

[80] See, e.g., T Chorvat and K McCabe, Neuroeconomics and Rationality, *Chicago-Kent Law Review*, 2005, Vol 80, 101 (available at: http://ssm.com/abstract_id=748264); J Elster, supra, n 78.

suppress the uncertainties about the future, and hence to act.[81] Firms, too, inevitably use emotions in decision-making.

Information and its implications

What does all this suggest for information disclosure in the retail financial market? First, it suggests that the model of the rational consumer is neither an accurate nor an adequate model of consumer decision-making and behaviour.[82] Second, it suggests that the effectiveness of information disclosure as a regulatory technique intended to empower consumers, and through that empowerment to regulate markets, may be limited.[83] It also suggests the need for caution over attempts to link information disclosure with greater consumer responsibility for the outcome of consumers' decisions. The industry is currently pushing for a more robust role for caveat emptor.[84] The FSA has stated in its 2004–05 Annual Report

> Once consumers have the information they need, we expect them to use it and to take responsibility for their own decisions. *In addition, if, while in possession of appropriate information, they make a decision which turns out to be incorrect or unwise, they should have no redress through the regulatory system.* The regulatory system cannot protect consumers from performance risk, providing that the risk has been appropriately explained at the outset. We believe that, just as firms can mis-sell, consumers can mis-buy and this sense of responsibility must be present in our work with consumers... At the same time, we are clear that firms must

---

[81] J Pixley, supra n 78.

[82] For a discussion of the (various) meanings of "rational" from various theoretical perspectives, see T Chorvat and K McCabe, Neuroeconomics and Rationality, supra, n 80. W H Redmond, Consumer Rationality and Consumer Sovereignty, *Review of Social Economy*, 2000, Vol LVIII, No 2; and J Jacoby, supra, n 69, for a very thorough (and entertaining) refutation of the rational choice theory prevalent within the US Law and Economics movement.

[83] Although it is recognised that there is always the potential for the "marginal consumer" to discipline the market.

[84] See, e.g., speech by Jonathan Bloomer, chairman, Financial Services Practitioner Panel, FSA Annual Public Meeting, July 2005, available at http://www.fs-pp.org.uk /docs/speeches/sp_21072005.pdf.

not use the "buyer beware" principle as a justification for misleading consumers, either wilfully or accidentally (Emphasis added).[85]

If information disclosure is to form the basis of consumer responsibility for outcomes which have great significance for consumers' longer-term financial security, then the link between disclosure and consumer behaviour needs to be grounded in a sufficient understanding of decision-making, and the information disclosed must be effective in the context of that decision-making process. The key lies not in the constant tweaking of documents in the hope that this time they will work to encourage rational and informed decision-making, but requires a return to "first principles" and a reassessment of the aims of, and potential for, information disclosure. In fact the Sandler Review of medium- and long-term savings in the UK,[86] although focusing on different issues, concluded that a well-functioning, efficient market providing consumers with good quality and good value products is probably not attainable, given the intrinsic characteristics of the "products" and the structure of the market.[87] In other words, no amount of information disclosure is likely to produce the desired outcomes. Sandler concluded that the solution lay in product regulation. As a result of this review the government has introduced a suite of "stakeholder" retail investment products (a deposit account, a medium-term investment product, a child trust fund and a modified stakeholder pension), produced by the industry and sold by the industry, but whose features are regulated. Whether the industry will have sufficient incentive to market these products remains moot.[88]

---

[85] FSA Annual Report, 2004–05 Section C.
[86] Supra, n 2
[87] Supra, Chapters 9 and 10, n 2.
[88] The Association of British Insurers reports that stakeholder products appear to be making little impact – http://www.abi.org.uk/Newsreleases/viewNewsRelease.asp?nrid=11942, part of the reason apparently being the costs of regulation and the imposition of the price cap (and see further Treasury Select Committee Report supra n 27, para 68 – 27.) However, a new sales regime for stakeholder products came into force in April 2005 – see FSA Annual Report 2004/05, s 2, available at http://www.fsa.gov.uk/pubs/annual/ar04_05/ar04_05sec2.pdf, and FSA Consultation Paper 04/11, A Basic Advice Regime for the Sale of Stakeholder Products, November 2004 and this may impact upon sales volumes.

For the FSA, however, "process" rather than "product" regulation will remain the norm and information disclosure, despite its limitations, will remain an important component of consumer protection strategy. It is perhaps ironic that in the one financial area where significant numbers of consumers have been very successful at using information to shop around, compare product features and switch providers to obtain a better (or zero) rate of interest, the credit card industry, those consumers have been pejoratively branded "rate tarts" by the industry which has responded by introducing moves to clamp down on card holders who switch cards to "avoid" paying interest.[89] While the credit card industry might want consumers to shop around, it doesn't want them to shop around too much.

But of course information disclosure does not stand alone in the process-based regulatory toolkit. To enhance consumer capability the FSA together with other bodies is developing a national strategy for financial capability. It has produced learning materials for use in schools, and has developed its website to include, for example, a consumer "learn online" section which it believes will improve knowledge and understanding.[90] The FSA states "it is widely accepted that in the UK the overall consumer understanding of financial matters is at a worryingly low level. It is agreed that, without this understanding, consumers are not well placed to discharge their responsibility for their own financial decisions".[91] It is hard not to conclude that these initiatives are as much about convincing citizens of the need to enter the retail investment markets, as they are about improving investor knowledge of the markets. These strategies, while promoting awareness of generic types of products currently available, will probably be of limited assistance in negotiating the myriad of complex and opaque products on the market and selecting the "best" product. As the FSA Consumer Panel have stated, "for

---

[89]See The Death of "Mr O Percent" is on the Cards, *The Independent on Sunday*, 5 June 2005, p 24; and Rate Tarts hold the Trump Card, *Money Telegraph*, 8 June 2005, available on line at http://sport.telegraph.co.uk/money/main.jhtml?xml=/money/2005/06/08/cmcard08.xml.

[90]http://www.fsa.gov.uk/consumer/11_LEARN/index.html.

[91]Evidence to Treasury Select Committee, Treasury Select Committee Report, supra para 100, n 27.

large groups of consumers no amount of simplification, education and information will obviate the need for accessible, independent and good quality help, generic advice, in understanding their financial needs and how to meet them".[92]

The role of advice

More important arguably than information or education for the private customer attempting to navigate the maze of the retail investment market is the role of the financial adviser. The regulation of advice complements the information disclosure regime. Just as regulators have been concerned to ensure that consumers have sufficient information to make "informed" decisions, so too they have been concerned to ensure that where consumers obtain advice that advice is best, or at least suitable, advice. As McMeel and Virgo suggest,[93] the distinction between information and advice is one of degree only. Assessing the impact of information disclosure for consumers is insufficient without considering the effectiveness of the advice that will often accompany it, particularly given the importance of trust and reputation for investor decisions.

Advice can come from a number of different sources, but is primarily provided by product providers themselves, or financial advisers. Issues surrounding the accessibility of advice for certain groups, particularly for low income earners, have been recognised and are being addressed through government proposals to allow Citizens Advice Bureaux as well as employers to provide financial advice.[94] At the same time the FSA argue that the reform of the polarisation regime, including reform of the adviser remuneration system, will bring further improvements in access (though this is disputed by some[95]). But access to advice is one

---

[92] FSA Consumer Panel evidence to Treasury Select Committee on restoring confidence in long-term savings, Treasury Select Committee Report, supra, para 100, n 27.

[93] G McMeel and J Virgo, *Financial Advice and Financial Products: Law and Liability* (Oxford University Press: Oxford, 2001), at para 1.59.

[94] See FSMA 2 year review: changes to secondary legislation, HMT, February 2004, http://www.hm-treasury.gov.uk/media/F6C57/fsma_2yrrev_vol1.pdf.

[95] O McDonald, More Mis-selling to Come?, *Journal of Financial Regulation and Compliance*, February 2005, 6–8.

issue, the quality of the advice received another. Just as the quality of investments themselves is difficult to assess and only becomes apparent, if at all,[96] some time after purchase, so the quality of advice can only be assessed, if at all, with hindsight.

Regulation of advice has been a feature of the UK financial services industry since the 1970s, and particularly since the Gower Report into Investor Protection in the mid 1980s.[97] The quality of advice is controlled primarily through the FSA's authorisation requirements, its training and competence requirements, and through its "conduct of business" rules. These rules are intended to ensure that the product recommended for a consumer is "suitable", or the "best", product available. These rules, together with the polarisation regime (itself subsequently abolished), were introduced because of concerns over the effect of adviser incentives (such as commission payments). It was believed these incentives did not always produce optimum outcomes for consumers, and that the law in this area was not sufficiently clear to protect consumers.[98] Prior to the introduction of polarisation in 1988, it was recognised that the real competition in the retail packaged product sector was between product providers competing for adviser outlets, and not between product providers competing for consumers. In addition, the payment of commission by product providers to advisers had the potential to skew the recommendations advisers made to consumers.[99] Consumers on the other hand found it difficult to determine which advisers were truly independent and which were tied to product providers. In other words where potential investors sought advice, there was a danger

---

[96] Even when the final value becomes apparent the investor will not necessarily be able to judge whether another product would have produced a better return.

[97] See further J Black, *Rules and Regulators* (Clarendon Press: Oxford, 1997).

[98] J Black, ibid., pp 54 and 142; A Hudson, *Law on Financial Derivatives* (Sweet and Maxwell: London, 2000); see also the Law Commission Report, *Fiduciary Duties and Regulatory Rules*, CM 3049 (HMSO: London, 1995).

[99] See J Gray, Insurance Brokers and the Financial Services Act, in F Rose (ed) *Current Legal Problems in Insurance Law* (Sweet and Maxwell: London, 1987). J Black, *Rules and Regulators*, supra, n 97.

that the advice was not truly independent but was tainted by adviser self-interest.

Polarisation required financial advisers to be either fully tied to one product provider so that they only sold that provider's products, or to be completely independent in the sense that they could not be contractually tied to any provider. Independent advisers should then have been able to provide advice across the market. At the same time commission controls were introduced to control adviser bias. The controls on commissions did not survive long for the OFT declared them anti-competitive and they were removed in 1990.

In November 2000 the FSA announced that it was reviewing the polarisation regime. Although a number of options for reform were considered, in 2002 it was decided that polarisation would cease altogether. The rationale given by the FSA for removing the regime was the now familiar "competition leads to consumer benefits" argument: "consumer benefit and protection is enhanced through competition, and competition leads to innovation and a fairer deal for consumer".[100] Polarisation prevented banks, building societies and other tied agents from recommending the products of providers, other than the one to which they were tied. This, the FSA argued, was inhibiting consumer choice and hence competition,[101] particularly when FSA research revealed that 80% of consumers purchasing packaged products did so via tied agents (trust, rather than status – independent or tied – being the key driver in choosing an adviser).

Given that most consumers buy through tied agents and, in the light of what FSA saw as consumers' "persistent and widespread failure to

---

[100]See, e.g., FSA newsletter issue 41, February 2002; Howard Davies letter to Hon Gordon Brown, 1 November 2000 – FSA Consultation Paper 80, Reforming Polarisation: First Steps, January 2001, Annex A. It is clear that there were other pressures on the FSA to reform polarisation. The Office of Fair Trading had recommended a partial relaxation of the regime on competition grounds. There were also concerns that polarisation would not survive the introduction of the European directive that aimed to liberalise cross-border barriers to insurance intermediary services.

[101]But see NCC, *Consumer Empowerment & Competitiveness*, a report prepared for the NCC by J Bush, October 2004, which finds little direct evidence of the link between consumer choice and empowerment, and competitiveness.

shop around",[102] removing the restrictions on tied advisers offering the packaged products of other providers will, claims the FSA, at least give those consumers the benefit of increased choice of product provider. The FSA recognise that there will still be room for consumer confusion over whether the adviser is truly independent or not, for its research identified that while consumers understood the concept of independent advice, they were less clear about what was meant by "tied advice".[103] Likewise there will continue to be scope for commission bias to continue to undermine the suitability of advice, particularly in the case of advisers who are now "multi-tied".[104] However, the FSA, and the OFT,[105] believe the solution lies in yet more disclosure. In order that consumers in the depolarised market will not be confused about whether an adviser is truly independent or not, advisers must provide consumers with an "initial disclosure document" setting out the range of product providers the adviser deals with. In addition, in order to reduce the risk of commission bias for packaged products, all advisers (independent or otherwise) must provide a "menu" document to private customers at the point at which they first make contact. This "menu" document must contain an indication of the cost of advice, and whether it is to be paid by fee, commission or both. Where payment can be by commission, it must also be accompanied by an indication of the market average commission.[106] Advisers who wish to remain "independent" are required to offer private customers the option of paying for advice by fee. Multi-tied or tied advisers are not required to offer the fee option (FSA research revealing that consumers are not prepared to pay a fee to tied advisers, believing them to be salespersons of providers[107]).

The stated objectives of the "menu" disclosures are to reduce the opportunity for commission bias, to exert downward pressure on

---

[102]FSA Consumer Research 9, *Polarisation*, January 2002, at para 4.10.

[103]Ibid., at ES.5.

[104]See FSA Consultation Paper 121, *Reforming Polarisation: Making the Market Work for Consumers*, January 2002, at para 4.28.

[105]OFT letter to the FSA, OFT 774, available at http://www.oft.gov.uk/nr/rdonlyres/6c2f6e09-ec91-4d3c-bb1d-d58c3d10d7d8/0/oft774.pdf.

[106]See FSA Policy Statement 04/27, supra, para 18, n 39.

[107]FSA Consumer Research 9, supra, para ES.9, n 102.

commission levels, to promote consumer awareness, and to encourage shopping around. [108] But again this information disclosure is only likely to exert pressure on commission and fee levels if private investors do use it to shop around. As the evidence from the KFD research has already revealed, private customers do not shop around, trust, being the dominant driver in their decision-making rather than the information on charges and other information currently disclosed in the KFD. [109]

The retail financial services sector is a sector where market forces are strongest at the level between product provider and distribution outlets (advisers). This is the level where there is greatest opportunity for competitive pressure to be successfully applied to secure better value retail products. But where advisers are paid by product providers primarily on the basis of the size of the sum invested, rather than on fund performance, advisers are unlikely to have much incentive to exert this pressure. [110] The fundamental issue remains, where do advisers' obligations lie? In order to try to ensure that advisers put the interests of consumers first, the Conduct of Business regulations require that advisers only recommend products on the basis that they are suitable. [111] Yet suitability is essentially "against the natural grain" of advisers' incentives, and there are difficulties around its meaning:

> Suitability and its counterpart, mis-selling, are crucial concepts in defining industry compliance and hence costs. Yet "suitability" is not defined in the regulations. Industry participants have therefore formed their own views of what is required to meet the suitability standard by reference to how regulators have in practice

---

[108] FSA Policy Statement 04/27, supra, n 39.

[109] And, for those consumers who do shop around, the market average figure is only likely to be useful if it provides a realistic basis on which to compare actual commissions (depending on how the commissions are calculated).

[110] Sandler and Myner, in their evidence to the Treasury Select Committee on restoring confidence in long-term savings, identify inefficiencies within the industry that reduce the value of products resulting from various factors including the opacity of fund performance; commission rebates paid by stockbrokers to fund managers; poor asset allocation decisions; the failure of actively managed funds (with their higher commissions) to outperform tracker funds; and high total charges negating the better performance of riskier products over less risky products. Supra, n 54.

[111] FSA Handbook, COB5.3.5.

supervised their businesses. In particular their notion of mis-selling has been substantially shaped by the Pensions Review.[112]

In other words, the industry has not sought to proactively define suitability from the perspective of what is best for the consumer, but rather from the perspective of "what is the minimum the regulator demands". Adviser focus arguably remains directed at avoiding mis-selling, rather than ensuring that the consumer buys the most suitable product available. The Treasury Select Committee in its report into restoring confidence in long-term savings has observed:

> Across the industry there is a danger that companies and trade bodies are ab-rogating their responsibilities in relying so heavily on the FSA to police and deliver good standards of behaviour. External regulation by a body such as the FSA should not be seen as a substitute for effective self-regulation... All the major trade bodies in the long-term savings industry should have clear codes of practice which take the standards of behaviour laid down by the FSA as a minimum but aim to improve on the FSA's requirements in those areas where the industry feels better standards will do most to help its customer base.[113]

But even this, inherently ambiguous, "suitability" requirement will not fully apply where a private customer is sold a stakeholder prod-uct (also commonly referred to as "Sandler" products[114]). Stakeholder products were introduced by the government in order to attract more low and middle income earners into the market. However, the govern-ment also believes that the current advice process (requiring advisers to engage in a "fact find" before recommending a product) is too long and costly and is inhibiting growth of this market.[115] Therefore, in order to encourage citizens to buy, and the industry to sell stakeholder prod-ucts, the advice process has been deregulated so that these products can be sold by salespersons who provide only basic advice.[116] Sales inter-views are pre-scripted, with the salesperson following a series of filtered

---

[112]Sandler Review, supra, para 5.34, n 2.

[113]Treasury Select Committee Report, supra, para 55, n 27.

[114]See n 88 and accompanying text.

[115]O MacDonald, supra n 95.

[116]Stakeholder products (except for the smoothed investment) can be sold by advisers who have received "basic" training only. FSA Press Release FSA/PN/086/2004.

questions (the FSA has produced a model script, although firms will be expected to produce their own versions). Sales staff can administer the script without formal training and competence qualifications, but must take customers through the filtered questions. Any recommendation made must be "suitable", but only on the basis of the answers given to the scripted questions. No other "fact find" is required, and staff are not permitted to give "advice".[117]

The FSA already has experience of designing and implementing a basic advice regime, in the context of the stakeholder pension introduced in 1999. This sales process centred around the use of "decision trees" (a form of filtered questions). Evidence from FSA research into the decision tree process revealed that advisers themselves believed "fundamentally decisions trees are focussed on a balanced, logical, non-emotional decision making ... in our experience as advisers people are not any of these things when it comes to finance".[118] Only 6% of customers thought it played a substantial role in the buying process.[119] Initial road testing of the filtered questions for the expanded stakeholder suite of products has revealed that the new basic advice process is not delivering optimum outcomes for customers. Over 30% of overall product recommendations were identified as below the standard of a "good" recommendation, rising to 46% for pensions.[120] The script was subsequently revised and road tested again, although some problems remained.[121] Only time will tell whether the outcomes from the unregulated advice sector will, in the real world of commercial pressures and sales targets, prove to be in the customers' best interests. Effectively,

---

[117]See Policy Statement 04/22, *A Basic Advice Regime for the Sale of Stakeholder Products*, November 2004, and see also FSA Handbook COB 5A.

[118]Per product providers and intermediaries, FSA Consumer Research 20, *Review of the Regulatory Regime for Stakeholder Pensions – report on research with product providers and intermediaries*, April 2003, at para 3.3.4.

[119]Per consumers, FSA Consumer Research 19, *Review of the Regulatory Regime for Stakeholder Pensions – Report on consumer research*, April 2003, para 1.20.

[120]See FSA Consultation Paper 04/11, *A Basic Advice Regime for the Sale of Stakeholder Products*, June 2004.

[121]FSA Consumer Research 32, *Consumer Testing of a Filtered Questions Approach to the Selling of Stakeholder Products – stage 3*, November 2004.

in order to encourage the industry to sell these products, the risk of misselling is transferred to the customer as a risk of misbuying.

But the significance of information and advice for the private investor does not end at the point of sale. Unlike goods and other products whose value usually depreciates after purchase, savings and investments are expected to appreciate in value. But after purchase, the consumer's circumstances might change, with the result that the investment is no longer suitable, or the fund might not perform as well as anticipated at the time of purchase. Despite this, the extent of any obligation on firms (providers or advisers) to inform the consumer that a product may no longer be suitable, remains nebulous. Concern remains that the industry is still too focused on the sale process, with little concern for consumers after the point of sale. The FSA is addressing the need for ongoing information by proposing to require all packaged product providers to provide annual statements to consumers after the point of sale[122] (although what, realistically, investors will be able to do with this information, without advice to give it context and meaning, is uncertain). The FSA is currently introducing proposals to require firms (providers and advisers) to "treat customers fairly", including after the point of sale.[123]

The proposals are likely to require providers and advisers to critically review relevant parts of the product lifestyle that are relevant to their business, including: whether products developed meet consumer needs; whether communications given before, at and after the sale are clear, fair, balanced and not misleading; to balance commercial objectives with the need to treat consumers fairly; to consider the need to honour consumer expectations.[124] The FSA has said "fairness is not just about process it is about outcomes" and ensuring the consumer does not experience a "nasty surprise" as the result of being treated unfairly.[125] It remains to be seen to what extent the FSA might develop, in effect,

---

[122] FSA Insurance Sector briefing, April 2005.

[123] FSA Discussion Paper 7, *Treating Customers Fairly after Point of Sale*, June 2001.

[124] C Briault, *Teaching, Communication and Temperance – A Regulatory Perspective*, speech to the Association of Friendly Societies, Annual General Meeting, 14 October 2004, SP205.

[125] Supra, Annex A, n 123.

a concept of a "duty to care" that will require firms to accept additional responsibility to individual consumers for post sale performance of the product. More likely, a focus will be on requiring firms to provide consumers with post sale information that, it believes, will enable consumers to make their own decision about the continued suitability of the product purchased.

In summary

There is a temptation in the modern "information society" to view information as communication. Disseminating information becomes equated with creating knowledge and understanding. But effective communication is a two-way process and requires the reflexive monitoring of each recipient's responses. Information dissemination on the other hand is acontextual, non-reflexive and impersonal, it requires interpretation to give it meaning.[126] Advice is the form of communication that, for many, provides the bridge between information and knowledge and understanding. In an environment where consumers are to be made more aware of, and given a greater sense of ownership of, their responsibilities to secure their own longer-term financial well-being, access to advice assumes a greater significance.

Yet the most recent misselling episode, involving the sale of precipice bonds by firms including "trusted" high street building societies to retirees,[127] suggests that, despite the various conduct of business rules, advisers do not always serve the interests of the citizen investor well. Market and product structures, as well as remuneration methods, undermine FSA attempts to ensure investors' interests come first, and the introduction of retail products whose features are regulated may yet be undermined by the quality of "deregulated" advice. The solution is believed to be more information. But underpinning information

---

[126]H Tsoukas, supra, n 36.
[127]See FSA/PN/112/2004 in which the FSA publish notice of the imposition of a fine of £650 000 on Bradford & Bingley Building Society, the largest IFA in the UK, for misselling precipice bonds.

disclosure is an assumption that citizens can, *and should*, conform to the model of the rational decision-maker. Much regulatory effort is directed at encouraging and educating citizens to conform to a model which, we argue, is more myth than reality. The danger for citizens is that, as more information is provided to them, they are increasingly expected to take responsibility, *as if* they do conform.

As part of the political desire to shift the responsibility for long-term individual financial security downwards, from government to the individual citizen, the boundary between collective and personal responsibility is being redrawn, and citizens are increasingly expected to look to the marketplace for that security. It has been recognised, however, that many citizens face particular difficulties in participating in financial markets, hence the imposition of the statutory objectives of public awareness of the financial system and protection of consumers. The FSA has sought to put these two objectives into practice by focusing on regulating processes, including imposing disclosure rules on the industry and on improving citizens' financial awareness and literacy, rather than regulating products. In so doing, FSA and government policy have become intertwined in their desire to promote the concept of the financial citizen.

But underlying this concept of the financial citizen are issues that remain obscured from public view. Talk about the "savings gap", measures to improve consumer competence, measures to enhance disclosure, all leaves unasked one crucial question – where should responsibility for citizens', longer-term financial security lie? This public policy debate has been largely circumvented by government devolving responsibility for regulating the financial services industry and "consumer protection" onto an independent regulator who, despite its extensive powers and apparent independence, is effectively constrained by a statutory framework that imposes an economic model of regulation through the underlying statutory principles and the competition scrutiny role given to the OFT. The opportunity for these broader policy debates has been lost. Regulatory policy is effectively removed from the political sphere. This is exacerbated by the sheer number and rate of proliferation of government and government sponsored initiatives into the pensions and longer-term savings "crisis" and political evasiveness surrounding this "crisis". For example, the Pension Commission's first report was delayed until after the recent general election, and there has been further suggestion that no reform will take place until after the next general election.[128] This further illustrates the obfuscation, confusion and reluctance to face what for politicians with short-term incentives appears an intractable issue. Hence the issue is shifted further down through product and process design onto the individual citizen. As this chapter has sought to illustrate, regulatory tools such as information disclosure are, in this instance at least, about far more than merely redressing imbalances of information between supplier and consumer, but are part and parcel of a broader, but largely unacknowledged, political, agenda.

---

[128]See http://neweconomist.blogs.com/new_economist/2005/04/pension_reform_.html.

7

An illustrated critique of meta regulation and concluding comments

Introduction

The regulatory strategies examined in Chapters 3 to 6 have themselves been spawned as a response to what the first two chapters showed was a governmental and regulatory switch in focus and toolkit from rules to risks. These "meta-regulatory strategies" seek to increase the penetration within regulated firms and individuals of regulatory goals and objectives. Those goals and objectives are themselves defined through the prism of risk. This concluding chapter asks how such strategies can be seen against more theoretical work relating to the way in which law and regulation attribute responsibility to and within business organisations. It argues for the need for a more explicit analysis of the use made by the FSA of notions of senior management responsibility and compliance/ethical culture. It asks how useful these concepts really are to the attainment of regulatory objectives in a competitive commercial environment such as the financial services industry. It questions how legitimate it is for financial regulation to offload real substantive policy, goal and value conflicts onto the shoulders of individual firms and key individuals within such firms under the guise of elaborate mechanisms of regulatory enrolment and decentred proceduralisation.[1]

The legislative and regulatory initiatives examined in Chapter 3 are designed to enrol regulated firms and individual actors therein to the FSA's own regulatory mission. That mission is in turn defined in terms of risk to its statutory objectives. To that extent, these initiatives can be seen as part of a much broader trend which has been apparent for over a decade now whereby regulation (in its many different manifestations – not just financial regulation) is shifting its focus downwards into firms and its gaze on the efficacy of their own internal systems and controls.[2] That downward shift extends, within firms, onto the shoulders of individuals.[3] Power provides an insightful critique of aspects of this trend. He has described this downward and inward reach of regulation as being nothing short of the natural consequence of societies', governments' and the public's desire to know, manage and somehow neutralise real risks and uncertainties. This, he argues, must inevitably result in the translation of such risks and uncertainties into reassuringly measurable outcomes and traceable processes to be devolved into the language of systems, controls and strategy familiar to regulator and regulated:

> Organisational translations of risk into internal controls are necessary conditions of possibility for risk-based regulation, and hence for the successful operation of the risk management state. *Internal control is thereby the state in organisational miniature.*[4] (Emphasis added)

---

[1] J Black, Decentring Regulation: Understanding the Role of Regulation and Self-Regulation in a "Post-Regulatory" World, *Current Legal Problems*, 2001, 54, 103–146, J Black, *Mapping the Contours of Contemporary Financial Services Regulation*, ESRC Centre for Analysis of Risk and Regulation (CARR) Discussion Paper No. 17. (CARR: London, 2003).

[2] I Ayres and J Braithwaite, *Responsive Regulation* (OUP: 1992), Chapter 4, M Power, *The Audit Society* (OUP: 1997), Haines and Gurney, The Shadows of the Law: Contemporary Approaches to Regulation and the Problem of Regulatory Conflict, *Law & Policy*, 2003, 353–380, C Parker, *The Open Corporation: Effective Self-Regulation and Democracy* (Cambridge University Press: 2002).

[3] R Baldwin, The New Punitive Regulation, *Modern Law Review*, 2004, 67(3), 351–383.

[4] M Power, *The Risk Management of Everything* (Demos: 2004), at p 24.

What is also becoming clear is that the same policy and priority conflicts, and uncertainties about the future that exist within societies (and indeed within all ourselves), and the need to confront and make political choices with which societies are faced can, through the adoption of risk-related regulatory techniques to enrol business organisations into the task of government, neatly shift, obscure and bury these conflicts and uncertainties. This is achieved in ways that are convenient to government, but which may yet pose serious concerns. Haines and Gurney describe the role played by regulatory laws in the shift to what Power has memorably termed as "the audit society":

> [T]he conflict – and the juridification that accompanies it – is delegated to the regulated organisation through the regulatory innovations of performance standards and manipulation of organisational culture through audit processes and requirements. Juridification is not restricted to law and ancillary legislation; it reaches deep within the company itself – to encourage self-regulation of micro-level behaviour. To give effect to this regulatory goal, codes of practice, accreditation, and auditing regimes are brought into play and become essential tools by which companies seek to assure regulators and courts [and the Financial Services and Markets Tribunal] of their commitment to compliance.[5]

In the context of UK financial regulation, the FSA's SYSC regime, the sheer range of individuals subject to the need for approval under Part V FSMA 2000 (despite the FSA's recent initiative to reduce the number of functions comprised therein[6]), and the growing focus on compliance culture discussed earlier in Chapter 4, all serve to illustrate this juridification. The roles, constitution of tasks, nature of obligations and mode of discharge of the responsibilities of specific individuals within regulated organisations are, as has been shown in Chapters 3 to 5, being increasingly juridified and subject to penal sanction ostensibly to aid and abet the effort to secure organisational compliance.

Baldwin's research into the efficacy of increased regulatory powers of sanction, including the individualisation of regulatory responsibility, provides useful insights here. He illustrates his argument about the increasingly punitive nature of regulation with examples ranging

---

[5] Haines and Gurney, n 2 p 368.
[6] FSA Consultation Paper 05/10 discussed in Chapter 3, see text accompanying n 42.

from the FSA's emphasis on senior management responsibility for compliance, the existence and incidences of use of the FSA's powers to prosecute individuals, seek redress against them on behalf of investors, and discipline them under Part V FSMA 2000, through to a host of other criminal offences and deterrent sanctions of individual liability under the competition, health and safety, environmental, UK company directors disqualification legislation and other individual directorial liabilities. He refers too to the potential for subtly different individual responsibilities for NEDs that is sometimes mooted in corporate governance debates.[7] He too cites the Sarbanes-Oxley Act 2002 as providing the most visible example of sharp-end "individualisation" for organisational failures in its introduction of criminal offences for chief executive officers (CEOs) and chief financial officers (CFOs) of US public companies.[8]

The United States congress' response to the collapse of the Enron group is in global terms the most significant example of regulatory enrolment in the pursuance of the urge towards what Power has termed "the risk management of everything".[9] Its key provisions show the dominance of risk-based, meta-regulatory technique. They include empowerment of the SEC under the Securities Exchange Act 1934 to prescribe rules whereby companies subject to its annual reporting requirements shall include in their annual reports an internal control report which shall

(1) *state the responsibility of management for establishing and maintaining an adequate internal control structure and procedures for financial reporting; and*

(2) *contain an assessment, as of the end of the most recent fiscal year of the issuer, of the effectiveness of the internal control structure and procedures of the issuer for financial reporting.*[10]

---

[7]See text in Chapter 5 accompanying nn 57–65.

[8]Sarbanes-Oxley Act 2002 (HR 3763).

[9]M Power, supra, n 4.

[10]Section 404 (Management Assessment of Internal Controls), Sarbanes-Oxley Act 2002.

Interestingly, the UK Financial Reporting Council ("FRC") has issued guidance which highlights how the UK's own Turnbull guidance on internal control (considered in Chapter 5) may be used as an evaluation framework by those US registrant companies that are subject to section 404 and the UK Combined Code.[11] This illustrates the emergence of an acknowledgement of multiple and overlapping compliance requirements that is the inevitable result of the growth in meta regulation. However, both the FRC and the SEC are a very long way from providing safe harbours for such overlaps.

In an attempt to influence the normative climate within firms' financial reporting culture, ethical issues too are juridified by section 406 of the Sarbanes-Oxley Act 2002. That provision requires issuers to comply with the requirement to adopt and make public a code of ethics for senior financial officers, or explain their non-compliance. Such a code should incorporate

> such standards as are *reasonably necessary* to promote (1) honest and ethical conduct, including the ethical handling of actual or apparent conflicts of interest ... (2) full, fair, accurate, timely and understandable disclosure in [required] periodic reports ... (3) compliance with applicable governmental rules and regulations. (Emphasis added)

The Sarbanes-Oxley Act 2002 represents a sharpening of the individualisation of regulatory responsibility. Power sees this individualisation of responsibility as fuelling a spread of "second order risks". Such risks are themselves derived from the primary "real risks" facing the business, but are socially and institutionally amplified and visited on the shoulders of individuals through mechanisms of individual accountability, sanction, punishment and reputational damage.[12] The Sarbanes-Oxley legislation has taken this amplification to a new dimension by the effect of the certification requirements and individual criminal penalties introduced by sections 302 and 906, which have the effect of making

---

[11] The Turnbull Guidance as an evaluation framework for the purposes of s 404(a) of the Sarbanes-Oxley Act (Financial Reporting Council, 16 December 2004).
[12] M Power, supra, n 4 p 49.

CEOs and CFOs personally (and potentially criminally) responsible for their companies' financial results and controls, risking fines of up to $5 million and up to 20 years imprisonment for non-compliance with certification requirements.

Attractions of regulatory enrolment of organisational internal controls, culture and officers into the regulatory enterprise

There are undoubted attractions to this diffusion of enrolment in the regulatory mission and the permeability of the line between regulator and regulatee considered in this work. There is intuitive appeal to many in notions of "co-regulation", "cooperation", "mutual dialogue", the obfuscation of the divide between collective/public/regulatory goals and private ones, and the promise of a greater degree of compliance with the normative goals of regulation. Parker, in arguing for a more democratic and self-regulating model of the corporation that is open to the absorption and internalisation of a much wider range of external political, economic and social goals and values, uses words that could easily have been adapted to form part of the FSA's original justification for SYSC and its increased emphasis on the role of senior management and managers in delivering compliance:

> Regulation within the new regulatory state is aimed as much at reinventing regulation within "private regulatory space", such as corporations, as at reforming external regulatory agencies. The experience of command and control shows that it is not reasonable, practical or efficient for external legislatures and regulators to be solely responsible for determining how organisations should manage social issues. The design and enforcement of regulation to govern every potential social dilemma [or risk and uncertainty] facing businesses is simply not achievable. And even if it were, it would not make businesses better citizens, since citizenship implies an internal capacity to respond with integrity to external values. The new regulatory state uses enforced self-regulation and incentives for voluntary compliance in its attempts to steer corporate conduct towards public goals without interfering too greatly with corporate autonomy and profit."[13]

---

[13] Parker, supra, n 2, p 29.

Both SYSC and the Approved Persons regime with its accompanying principles and code of practice can be seen as examples of such "enforced self-regulation". The most striking feature of this analysis is the enthusiastic support for deployment of regulation, its techniques and tools in the attempt not only to shape and influence what happens in the internal "private" domain within a business entity but also to *internalise* rather than *impose* regulation's own normative values within management decision-making and within individual senior managers' decision-making. Parker takes enrolment analysis a stage further as she argues for such enforced self-regulation of firms to be seen as key to the achievement of what she terms: " 'the open corporation' ... a marriage between management, democracy and law".[14] Haines and Gurney highlight how regulation has been adopting techniques of individualising regulatory responsibility across a wide range of areas with a view to influencing firms' internal cultures, but foreshadow their sophisticated critique of such efforts:

> [I]ndividual liability is seen as a way of ensuring strong leadership within companies with respect to compliance by "nominated officers"... In an apparently deft move, the need for senior management to "champion" compliance within a particular regulatory regime (and engender a compliance culture) and the need to make criminal [and quasi-criminal] regulatory penalties feared by those who are in a position to make meaningful resource allocations are solved by a single policy initiative.[15]

If this analysis is applied to UK financial regulation it is possible to hear echoes of the discussion in Chapter 6 of how FSMA 2000 and the FSA envision individual consumers as responsible, rational and informed "financial citizens". Government and society more generally are unable and/or unwilling to face certain macro-economic realities, and chary about explicitly confronting them, which sow the seeds of the contemporary pensions crisis. Hence, as a quid pro quo for the metamorphosis on the part of individuals into "financial citizens", government, through the medium of the FSA's regulatory technique, seeks to effect cultural

---

[14]Parker, supra, n 2, preface.
[15]Haines and Gurney, supra, n 2, p 361.

and organisational reorientation within the financial services industry itself as well as within individual firms and even within individual
managers.[16] This reorientation being necessary to bring about the transformation of those industry participants engaged in helping constitute
the new financial citizenship into better, more responsive and open
citizens themselves. Those qualities are then to be judged in terms of
achievement of the FSA's own regulatory goals as laid out in its statutory objectives.[17] Those statutory objectives must in turn be translated
through the FSA's toolkit into values, which permeate the decision-
making and inform the strategies and actions of those subject to its writ.
The techniques being employed to do this include those considered in
this work: risk-related supervision (examined in Chapter 2); initiatives
like SYSC and the Approved Persons regime and enforcement action
in support (outlined in Chapter 3); and ratcheting up the pressure on
senior management to engage fully and proactively with the FSA's own
goals (as examined in Chapter 4).

Other examples of such analyses abound in the vast literature on corporate social responsibility and corporate governance, to which reference was made in Chapter 5.[18] What is also striking about such analyses
is the belief that regulation has the ability to achieve these ends, and to
the extent to which it can, the assumption that benefits outweigh any
potential negative incentive effects. Those negative incentive effects
might bear upon any or all of the regulated firms, individual managers
within them, the regulated industry itself and the regulated industry's
own ability to deliver other goals of social and economic policy. Several
criticisms may be made in response to the attractions of meta regulation
and regulatory enrolment and the discussion will now turn to some of
these in the first part of this chapter. In the following part of this chapter, examples from the UK financial services industry, in the form of
recent decisions of the courts and the Financial Services and Markets
Tribunal, are used to illustrate this critique.

---

[16] I Ayres and J Braithwaite, *Responsive Regulation* (OUP: Oxford, 1992) at p 31.
[17] Section 2 FSMA 2000.
[18] See references at n 9, Chapter 5.

A critique of meta regulation: problems with regulatory enrolment

Does it necessarily work?

Power has examined the introduction of operational risk charging as a regulatory tool in international banking regulation within the context of the second Basel Capital Accord, which of course has been and will continue to be of critical influence on UK regulatory design and implementation.[19] He views it as yet one more expression of "a general climate of regulatory attention to organisational internal control systems and cultures of control".[20] Such attention has been accompanied by the development of a vast array of overlapping regulatory and legal frameworks, and standards and codes of the type considered in Chapters 3 and 5; many of which apply directly to designated individuals at work within regulated firms as well as the firms themselves.

"Enforced self-regulation" despite its oxymoronic nature has become a reality for firms, managements and managers that, on one analysis, ought to result in greater openness, responsiveness, purchase and "buy-in" by firms and individuals to the democratic values that engendered the vast plethora of regulatory law at work in business today. "Enforced self-regulation" and its agents *ought* to be the vital marriage broker in Parker's union of management, democracy and law. Seen in the abstract, and as Power also has pointed out, all regulatory projects (ergo laws) begin life as visionary, abstract, aspirations to control and order. They are easy to agree at the most general level. It is only at the level of concrete implementation that messy realities intrude and problems with this regulatory (and one might argue democratic) downward shifting of responsibilities and responsibility emerge.[21]

---

[19]Basel Committee on Banking Supervision, *International Convergence of Capital Measurement and Capital Standards: A Revised Framework*, "Basel II Capital Accord" (www.bis.org).
[20]M Power, *The Invention of Operational Risk*, ESRC Centre for Analysis of Risk and Regulation Discussion Paper No 16 (CARR: London, 2003).
[21]Ibid.

Taking just some of these problems in turn, first, in his consideration of a number of aspects of the "Audit Society", Power postulates that the shift towards "regulation of others' regulation" may be little more useful than the seeking of forms of collective comfort for collective anxiety about risk and uncertainty.[22] He asks whether it might simply be providing "deluded visions of control and transparency which satisfy the self-image of managers, regulators and politicians but are neither as effective or as neutral [in effect] as commonly imagined".[23] A common way of dealing with anxiety is through displacement activity and Power has argued that the history of regulatory initiatives to counter and contain operational risk (such as that of a rogue trader) has all too often resulted in fruitless and positively damaging classification, proceduralisation, and the spread of secondary regulatory responsibility and reputational damage (and fear thereof) to individual decision-makers.[24] Yet, he argues, when it comes to the really important task of having any effect whatsoever on the "killer events" that are the real source of primary risks, the "unknown unknowns" (as Rumsfeld put it with more acuity than he is often credited with[25]) and the uncertainties which are not easily measurable and calculable, then regulation's current "benign big guns"[26] – the meta-regulatory enrolment of firm's own internal controls, systems and risk management capability – are little more than a comfort blanket. They give rise to "fantasy policy documents which project comforting images of controlling the uncontrollable".[27]

---

[22]M Power The Audit Society, supra, n 2.

[23]Ibid., p 143.

[24]M Power, The Risk Management of Everything, supra, n 4 at Chapter 4.

[25]"Reports that say that something hasn't happened are always interesting to me, because as we know, there are known knowns; there are things we know we know. We also know there are known unknowns; that is to say we know there are some things we do not know. But there are also unknown unknowns, the ones we don't know we don't know. And if one looks throughout the history of our country and other free countries, it is the latter category that tend to be the difficult ones." Donald Rumsfeld, US Defense Secretary, 12 February 2000, Department of Defense Press Briefing.

[26]I Ayres and J Braithwaite, supra, n 16.

[27]M Power, supra, n 4, p 30.

Drawbacks of individualisation of responsibility

Baldwin's recent empirical research into FTSE 250 UK companies' responses to the risk of regulatory sanction, especially individual managerial liability through the imposition of individual deterrent sanction (of the type, inter alia, imposed on approved persons), bears out that point. He questions whether or not such individualisation of regulatory responsibility for the firms' "good citizenship" (in regulatory terms) really does encourage such behaviour and stimulate compliance.[28] His survey and interview findings showed that individuals within firms do not necessarily have the clearest of pictures of corporate and individual regulatory risks, or how a particular behaviour might result in either level of liability (organisational or individual) and should not therefore be assumed too readily by regulators to be capable of a "rational" (in regulatory terms) compliance response to the threat of such liabilities.

However, he draws a sharp distinction between "punitive", deterrent individual liability for regulatory risk, as one potential compliance-inducing tool on the one hand and "meta regulation", "enforced self-regulation" and "responsive regulation" as argued for by Parker on the other hand. He sees the latter as an alternative proactive regulatory approach that should be considered as capable of bringing about substantively compliant behaviour within organisations. But this distinction between "individualised" and "organisational" regulatory responsibility is far more blurred than he portrays. To take the FSMA/FSA regulatory techniques considered in Chapter 3 as an example, it will be recalled that the whole point about the interrelationship between a firm's liability under SYSC and its designated senior managers' liabilities under the Approved Persons regime is that they are designed deliberately to incorporate punitive *and* proactive elements. Indeed, Parker's analysis appears to leave ample room for individualised managerial liability for self-regulation.[29]

Insofar as regulatory responsibility for organisational failures in systems and controls can have an impact upon both the regulated firm

---

[28] R Baldwin, supra, n 3.
[29] Parker, supra, n 2, p 242.

and its individual senior managers, Baldwin's findings of confusion as to the distinction drawn between corporate and individual regulatory risks on the part of relevant individuals "in the frame" may in fact be explicable. Indeed the FSA's continuing emphasis on the links between individual senior managers' own responsibilities and their responsibility for organisational compliance show that individuals *should* see the two levels of responsibility as intertwined. The arguments put by Sir Philip Watts, former chairman of the Royal Dutch/Shell Oil group, in his challenge to the FSA's 2004 enforcement action against the Shell group for market abuse and misleading the market in breach of the listing rules, have considerable resonance here.[30] He referred the FSA's use of its enforcement machinery against the Shell group to the Financial Services and Markets Tribunal, arguing that it was procedurally unfair to him, the then CEO of the group, as it failed to give him full notice of the proceedings as a third party, who, he argued, was identified in the context of the FSA's decision notice in respect of the companies.[31] The essence of his argument was "what a company has done or not done" is so indivisibly and closely intertwined with the CEO's responsibilities and the ship she steers, that a finding of fault on the part of a corporate entity, especially where it involves the serious integrity issues involved here, namely market abuse arising from failings in internal business controls, must *inevitably* be seen as being a finding of fault on the CEO's part or at the very least be capable of causing her prejudice.

Sir Philip pointed to the press furore surrounding the Shell oil reserves affair and how he was so often portrayed as a villain of the piece, along with his chairmanship of Shell at the time. He argued that this meant that, even though the text of the FSA's decision notice did not name or

---

[30]The original enforcement action, which resulted in a financial penalty for the group of £17 million, was taken in relation to false and misleading statements made by the group between 1998 and 2003 as to the amount of hydrocarbon reserves which FSA determined were market abuse under s 123 FSMA and in breach of continuing obligations requirements under the Listing Rules. See FSA, Final Notice Royal Dutch/Shell Group, 24 August 2004.

[31]*Sir Philip Watts v. Financial Services Authority* (Financial Services and Markets Tribunal: 7 September 2005).

identify him by any description of his role, he was still identified by it and therefore deserved the procedural protections he had been denied by the FSA. The FSA argued, however, that there was a sharp and clear distinction between the firm's responsibility and that of any individual senior manager, and that the two should not be seen as congruent or coterminous for the purposes of applying procedural protections in the enforcement process. The Tribunal agreed, but regulated firms and their senior management (who are becoming increasingly used to the type of rhetoric and message from the FSA considered in Chapter 4 on the key links between firm and senior management responsibilities) might well be forgiven for finding the FSA's argument here at odds with its overall message in most other contexts. Sir Philip Watts' argument provides a practical example of how, as Power has argued, primary risks to the firm spill over into secondary reputational risks for themselves as key decision-makers, especially in the kind of "media and law-intense" context that would surround the calling to account of a multinational oil giant.[32]

Unintended effects?

Another element to the lack of effectiveness of such meta-regulatory/enforced self-regulatory strategies may be the effects in terms of achievement of "public" or regulatory goals actually produced, as opposed to those into which it was intended to enrol the regulated firm, its managers and its culture. In other words, do such techniques even achieve their stated purposes? Not necessarily. Baldwin finds that responses other than straight compliance-seeking may result. Such responses include outsourcing, risk-sharing (insurance against regulatory fines and liabilities) and increased resilience (tolerance and contingency strategies for enforcement action).[33] Power voices even more cautionary warnings about the possible behavioural effects of the explosion in organisational systems audits that has accompanied enforced

---

[32] M Power, supra, n 4, p 14.
[33] R Baldwin, supra, n 3, p 373.

self-regulation:

> An important critical theme is that the growth of auditing, and of systems that
> seek to represent performance in such a way as to make it readily auditable, leads
> to a decline of organisational trust . . . The audit explosion is associated with elab-
> orate games of compliance (e.g. the construction of public "consultation"), and
> leads to an excessive concern with representations of individual and collective
> performance by specialist officers . . . and to defensive strategies and blamism that
> stifle organisational innovation and lower employee morale.[34]

Effects on the corporate mind (and soul)?

One of the most trenchant recent critiques of the effects of the growth
in regulatory and government embrace of risk management, and its tools
of intra-firm and individualised regulatory responsibility, is provided by
Hunt.[35] In a sweeping and provocative work, he examines the effects
of what he terms greater "self-regulatory" initiatives within business,
although actually his examples also include the techniques of meta regulation and enforced self-regulation under discussion here. He argues
that many of the re-regulatory initiatives which have led to new internal organisational frameworks within business modelled around ethics,
risk management, corporate governance, sustainable development, corporate social responsibility (to name but a few) have been triggered by
waves of "irrational pessimism" about the future on the part of governments and societies. Further, he argues that one of the most fundamental
effects of these changes within business has been to entrench a culture
of caution and risk aversion which stifles innovation and growth.[36] Cultural change has indeed been wrought by regulatory penetration within
business and its senior management, he concludes, but he does not describe the outward-looking, responsive and democratic culture of the
open corporation in the same terms as Parker. Instead, he states:

> In the name of accountability, responsibility and transparency, corporations have
> institutionalised a bewildering array of codes of conduct, ethical regulations,
> internal controls, risk management procedures, board reforms, new types of board

---

[34]M Power, Evaluating the Audit Explosion, *Law & Policy* 25(3), 185–202 at 190.
[35]B. Hunt, *The Timid Corporation* (John Wiley & Sons Ltd: Chichester, 2003).
[36]Ibid.

position, audits and reporting obligations, and sustainable development and corporate social responsibility regulations. The problem with this huge increase in regulation is not that it somehow impedes a mythical free market from operating properly but rather that the combination of government regulation – and self-regulation – operating in tandem, entrenches an irrational cautiousness and restraint. It is institutionalising risk aversion. Just like in the world of science, where scientists are now counselled to adopt the "precautionary principle" – do not experiment unless the outcome is safe and poses no risks – businesses have adopted similar principles.[37]

Cross-overs and clashes

Leaving aside the effectiveness and unintended effects of meta-regulatory techniques, another (but related) criticism may be made. As the analysis explored in Chapters 3 and 5 above showed, it is all too easy to gloss over and disguise the very real problem of inherent conflicts in substantive regulatory objectives between different regimes. This is happening in consequence of the overly enthusiastic and uncritical adoption of what are often termed "meta regulation" techniques, which have been referred to throughout this work variously as "enforced self-regulation", "de-centred regulation" or "regulatory enrolment". Haines and Gurney point to how much of regulatory scholarship is now directed towards improving compliance per se. So, compliance as a global goal wherever a regulatory regime demands it, is considered as both desirable in itself and achievable. Specific practical conflicts and dissonances between individual regulatory and legal regimes that face subject businesses are ignored or skated over:

> Conflict when recognised is most often understood as the conflict between compliance and self-interest or profit. . . with the moral rightness of improving compliance assumed [although Hunt and many others would disagree strongly with that lexical ordering] . . . Conflict is glossed over by delegating responsibility for reducing all risks onto the regulated – without due consideration of the incompatibility of risk reduction in competing areas.[38]

Chapter 5 of this work has already considered examples of such conflict in the specific context of conflict between the Approved Persons

---

[37] Ibid., p 42.
[38] Haines and Gurney, supra, n 2, p 355.

regime and SYSC and more general company law and corporate governance requirements. Haines and Gurney's own work uses the example of dissonance between health and safety and competition regulatory legislation. Interestingly, they argue that some of the more fashionable "meta-regulatory" techniques now in use, such as juridification of an organisation's own internal systems and controls, increased individual responsibility for nominated officers within the organisation and a shift to generally expressed regulatory standards and rules (all of which are evident in UK financial regulation) can lead to overcompliance with a particular regulatory regime which may inhibit the achievement of competing and conflicting substantive regulatory goals. The example they give is a business's outsourcing work to a contractor, prompted more from fear of falling foul of trade practices legislation than any other economic motive, with a resultant cost to the achievement of health and safety goals.

Black too, in her thoughtful recent contribution on the interaction of "law" and "regulation", which she grounds in a financial services context, picks up on the possibility of conflicts between regulatory obligations and those of the common law, yet is more optimistic than Haines and Gurney about the effects of such tensions. She argues that, where common law and regulatory standards traverse the same territory, courts may come to employ a hybrid model of conflict resolution, whereby one system may borrow and import the other's norms where it finds them useful.[39] The common law, however, has centuries of "form" in developing its standards by importing and borrowing from trade usage, market practice, sector- and profession-specific guidelines and other such influences. This is of course one of the common law's greatest virtues. Hence it is easy to argue that it has an innate capability to resolve conflicts with specialist regulatory regimes, over time. But that is of little ex ante assistance to those faced with reconciling (to use Bamford's example considered in Chapter 5) the conflict between the different commercial courses of action dictated by, on the one hand regulatory obligation

---

[39] J Black, Law and Regulation: The Case of Finance, in C Parker, C Scott, N Lacey and J Braithwaite (eds) *Regulating Law* (Oxford University Press: Oxford, 2004), pp 33–59.

and regulatory objectives under FSMA 2000 and, on the other hand, those dictated by considerations of the interests of shareholders which still predominate in the general fiduciary duty company law test of what constitutes the "interests of the company".[40]

Burying the bodies of political timidity and disingenuity

Haines and Gurney point out that the problem of hiding and obfuscating substantive regulatory conflicts operates well beyond the territory of one specific regime overlapping with the common law (which, in some ways, is the least problematic conflict to resolve). Their critique is largely directed at the problem of different public policy goals, which cut across, compete with and impede each other, being shifted downwards by politicians and governments into regulatory regimes which, in turn, shift them downwards even further onto and into the regulated entity and its individual managers. Their criticism resonates strongly with the discussions in Chapters 5 and 6 about the political convenience of such downward shifting both into regulated firms and onto individual consumers as financial citizens:

> [G]overnments are keen to embrace methods of resolving conflict in a manner that reduces political risk. Regulatory reform promoting generic compliance processes rather than open political debate on the goals to be achieved is seen as one such method.[41]

This raises a point of much greater importance as to whether the employment of modern meta-regulatory techniques to ostensibly "secure compliance" and "promote good citizenship and ethical/compliance

---

[40]Bamford, Directors' Fiduciary Duties and the Approved Persons Regime in E Ferran and C Goodhart (eds) *Regulating Financial Services and Markets in the 21st Century* (Hart: 2001), discussed in text accompanying nn 4–9 and nn 30–32, Chapter 5.

[41]Haines and Gurney, supra, n 2, p 355. One of the authors has argued previously that real substantive policy conflicts between the FSMA 2000 agenda of consumer protection and governmental fiscal goals in relation to savings policy are also being buried in technocratic re-regulation of retail financial products in the wake of the Sandler initiative – J Gray, Sandler Review of Medium and Long-term Savings in the UK: Dilemmas for Financial Regulation, *Journal of Financial Regulation and Compliance* 2002, 10(4), 385–392.

cultures" in fact amounts to a certain abdication of democratic responsibility on the part of government. Governments and societies that are unwilling to face up to unknowns, uncertainties and real substantive policy conflicts may conceal such in technocratic efforts to secure compliance with some non-specific global goal. As Douglas' work would suggest, risk as an organising concept for government action, and the regulatory techniques risk-related regulation has devised, are tailor-made for such apparently neat de-politicisation.[42] The attractions of meta-regulatory strategies are easy to see for both governmentality theorists, who view the shift to risk as an organising concept for government action as a guise for constituting and exercising power in an apparently neutral manner, and for "Risk Society" theorists.[43]

Viewed from either perspective, meta regulation takes the political sting out of risk, uncertainty and the hard choices they throw up. It is the ideal neutering technique. But harsh political choice cannot be wished away. The question needs to be raised as to how fair, democratic and politically legitimate it is to proceduralise and delegate substantive policy conflicts onto the shoulders of regulated firms and individuals within such firms. How right is it to leave these policy conflicts to be resolved in situations where those faced with them may face sanctions, disincentives and individual liability under a number of differing regulatory regimes, all of which employ similar techniques to promote compliance with each regime's own isolated goals? How should firms and managers be expected by the differing regulatory regimes to which they are subject to be "enrolled" in promotion and pursuance of conflicting regulatory objectives without more explicit acknowledgement of the reality of the value conflicts between these regime's goals, and guidance as to how to order and prioritise objectives where they do conflict? This raises a much broader question of whether this downward shifting of regulatory responsibilities represents a degree of abdication and obfuscation of political responsibility that is both democratically unattractive and potentially economically harmful.

---

[42]Douglas in Chapter 1 text accompanying n 37.
[43]See discussion of alternative perspectives on "Risk" in Chapter 1 accompanying nn 15–37.

The generality of meta regulation

Another specific criticism may be made of the techniques of meta regulation. Generally phrased and "outcome-oriented" standards leave questions of how best to secure and show compliance with them to firms' own internal systems and controls, which in turn leads to greater uncertainty in implementation for the regulated. Rule design and the respective advantages and disadvantages of general and specific regulatory rules have, of course, long featured in the literature on regulation.[44] Three dimensions have been identified that formal regulatory rules should possess in order to maximise regulatory precision (or accurate matching of regulatory action with policy goals):[45] "transparency" of meaning by the use of clear, commonly understood language; "accessibility", in that the intended audience for the rules should be able to apply them easily to concrete fact situations; and "congruence", in the sense of whether or not the message carried in the rule's words produces the desired behaviour.

In their analysis of lessons to be learned from the saga of personal pensions misselling in the UK, Black and Nobles argue that the financial services industry failed to "think through the implications of the broad duties [such as the 'suitability' and 'know your customer' Conduct of Business requirements] in the particular context of pensions business, and that this was a critical element in the mis-selling process".[46] However, they do not conclude from this, by now, iconic failure of general rules to achieve the delivery of either transparency, accessibility or congruence (to use Diver's terminology) in the context of personal pensions sales and advice that the indeterminacy of general rules themselves are the problem. Far from it. Instead, they argue that the factors which led to the introduction of general, as opposed to specific, rules in the first place (industry resistance to regulatory incursion into the business space) would have worked to prevent specific rules from ever having

---

[44]C Diver, The Optimal Precision of Administrative Rules, *Yale Law Journal*, 1983, 93, 65, Ogus, *Regulation: Legal Form and Economic Theory* (OUP: 1994), Baldwin, Scott and Hood, *A Reader on Regulation* (OUP: 1998).

[45]C Diver, ibid.

[46]J Black and R Nobles, Personal Pensions Misselling: The Causes and Lessons of Regulatory Failure, *Modern Law Review*, 1998, Vol 61, 789 at 818.

been introduced. Hence, the alternative to general rules was no regulation, and hence no remedy for investors to whom pensions had been missold. The very fact that the SIB and PIA regulatory guidance as to what exactly constituted misselling under the broad and general Conduct of Business duties was able to operate as a basis for assessing and awarding investors' compensation for past business on an industry-wide basis is hailed by Black and Nobles as evidence of the superiority of general rules as a means of achieving investor redress. But they acknowledge that general rules are not without inherent limitations in terms of "congruence", i.e. their ability to achieve the desired regulatory outcomes. Thus, in the pensions context, such an outcome would have resulted in only suitable business having been advised and transacted by firms in the first place. But, this failed to happen to a significant extent across almost the entire retail financial services industry.

The essential indeterminacy of general rules expressed in terms of desired outcomes or performance standards, and the fact that they often require the exercise of judgement and discretion rather than mechanistic compliance, means that

> they are only as good as the context in which they operate... To operate effectively the rules have to be supported by a shared understanding of what it is they require, such that they can be applied appropriately to new or changing situations without the need for further specification or explanation.[47]

General rules, which as Black and Nobles quite rightly point out, firms themselves prefer at the point of rule design, therefore, demand an "interpretive community" in order to develop concrete meanings in any given situation. Moreover, they argue that the responsibility to form that community and develop those meanings (i.e. actually do the "thinking through" that was lacking in pensions misselling) should be shared between firms and regulators, as well as being developed within firms themselves. Some of the comments made by firms in the most recent Financial Services Practitioner Panel survey of the FSA's regulatory performance, considered in Chapter 4, reflect the difficulties firms may find operating in a climate of generally expressed "performance" and "outcome-oriented" rules and standards. The FSA's unwillingness to

---

[47] Ibid., p 819.

provide what firms saw as effective interpretive guidance emerged as the strongest negative indicator in the survey. The comment (highlighted already in Chapter 4) of one head of compliance at an IFA network revealed the difficulties some firms faced in "thinking through" what their regulatory responsibilities might be:

> There is no such thing as informal guidance. There is no-one at the FSA who is willing to give you informal guidance. They put it back on you. That's the rule, you interpret it as you want.[48]

In reply to such criticisms, it is possible to see the repeated call from the FSA for stronger and more pervasive "compliance culture" within regulated firms, and especially the emphasis on senior management responsibility for that cultural tone, as an attempt to develop and embed an effective and vigorous interpretive community within firms themselves. Indeed the shift towards meta-regulatory techniques such as SYSC and the way in which they combine with the Approved Persons regime can be seen as introducing a new level of generality to general rules in an attempt to improve awareness, appreciation and active pursuance of regulatory goals within the firm through an internal interpretive compliance culture which continuously promotes what Bovens termed "active" responsibility[49] across the range of the firm's business.

Seen like this, the undoubted attractions of using regulatory techniques of enrolment and enforced self-regulation to impose responsibility on firms and senior managers for internal systems and controls become apparent. It gives them a direct incentive to think, talk about and actively promote regulatory goals and objectives by setting the tone of their organisation's culture, and so give life and meaning to general rules and principles.

However, Power highlights how more general regulatory rules and standards that inevitably arise from the increased shift towards responsibility for "systems" designed to bring about desired regulatory

---

[48]Third Survey of the FSA's Regulatory Performance (Financial Services Practitioner Panel; December 2004) at p 69.

[49]M Bovens, *The Quest for Responsibility: Accountability and Citizenship in Complex Organisations* (Theories of Institutional Design Series: Cambridge, 1998) see discussion in Chapter 3 at text accompanying nn 77–79.

outcomes (as opposed to responsibility for specific prescribed actions or omissions) limits a regulator's ability to use its enforcement techniques. He argues:

> Where the external emphasis shifts from compliance to the "effectiveness" of systems for determining compliance there is a corresponding shift in the knowledge base and focus of the external monitor [regulator].[50]

One consequence of this is that regulators will be in a weaker position when it comes to their ability to clearly establish actual instances of regulatory breaches for the purposes of discipline and enforcement. So the question of what is and what is not non-compliance with a generally expressed rule will be far more contestable. To some extent comments, by the Financial Services and Markets Tribunal in the course of its recent decision in relation to endowment misselling claims by the FSA against the Legal & General Assurance Society,[51] bear out Power's point on the enforcement dangers (from a regulator's perspective) of overreliance on general standards.

Illustrating this critique of aspects of meta-regulatory techniques in a financial services context

Comments made by the House of Lords and the Financial Services and Markets Tribunal in two very different decisions illustrate the very different ways in which private law and financial regulation decision-makers can view the significance of "systems failure" for the purposes of determining liability.[52] Neither decision entailed firms' liabilities under the FSMA regime of SYSC. Instead, they were concerned with liability for misselling of retail financial business under standards imposed by the PIA under the then applicable Financial Services Act 1986 regulatory

---

[50]M Power, *The Audit Society*, supra, n 2 p 133.
[51]*L & G Assurance Society v. FSA* (Decision of the Financial Services and Markets Tribunal: 18 January 2005).
[52]*L & G Assurance Society v. FSA* (Decision of the Financial Services and Markets Tribunal: 18 January 2005) and *Lloyds TSB General Insurance Holdings Ltd and others v. Lloyds Bank Group Insurance Co Ltd* [2003] 4 All ER 43.

regime. Nonetheless, the decisions and comments made therein bear out aspects of the critique of meta-regulatory techniques outlined so far.

Standards of regulatory responsibility in Legal & General Assurance Society v. FSA

In this reference the Financial Services and Markets Tribunal was called upon to determine whether Legal & General Assurance Society Ltd ("L&G") had, as claimed by the FSA, committed breaches of applicable regulatory rules in the period from 1997 to 1999 in relation to L&G's sales, and its procedures governing the sales, of a type of mortgage endowment policy known as a flexible mortgage plan ("FMP") to 'low-risk' customers. The latter were defined by L&G as those customers who required certainty that their mortgage would be repaid at the end of its term. The Regulatory Decisions Committee ("RDC") of the FSA had issued a decision notice imposing a £1.1 million financial penalty on L&G for rule breaches it found were established in relation to missales themselves and the procedures that ought to have been in place to prevent such misselling.

The FSA had made two basic claims before the Tribunal that were referred to throughout both of its two decisions which arose from this reference (in January and July 2005) as the "procedures case" and the "misselling case". The FSA claimed the procedures case was established by deficiencies in L&G's procedures as evidenced by its failure to ensure through its sales and compliance procedures that L&G advisers sold FMPs only to customers for whom they were actually suitable. The misselling case concerned the extent of actual misselling by L&G. The FSA claimed that the incidence of misselling was unacceptably high and it relied on a report of a sample size of 250 of FMP sales prepared by PricewaterhouseCoopers (referred to in the decisions as the Endowment Sales Review "ESR") to assert that plans were missold to customers for whom they were not suitable, either because they did not understand properly the risk of capital shortfall inherent in the plans, or because the customers to whom they were sold were not in fact prepared to accept such a risk.

The FSA claimed that the ESR showed that 60 of the 250 sample sales reviewed by it were missales. From this, it extrapolated the conclusion that the level of FMP misselling by L&G was unacceptably high. L&G had argued that the FSA's extrapolation had overstated the ESR's conclusions, which, in reality, were not nearly so clear as to whether the claimed missales had taken place. L&G argued that the RDC's overall finding was thus erroneous since it was based solely on extrapolation from erroneously represented results from a statistically insignificant sample size. The Tribunal held in its decision on January 2005 that the claims comprising the procedures case were borne out by the evidence in front of it and were therefore justified, but it did *not* agree with the view of the FSA and its Regulatory Decisions Committee in relation to the misselling case. In its decision in July 2005, the Tribunal considered the issue of appropriateness of penalty and ruled that a financial penalty of £575 000 should be substituted for the original £1.1 million.

These decisions received widespread attention throughout the industry and its advisers as they were seen as totemic, despite the Tribunal's caveat that they should not be viewed in this way. The level of interest resulted from the fact that L&G's reference was the first challenge to disciplinary action by the FSA before the Financial Services and Markets Tribunal which related to large-scale retail business misselling liabilities. L&G's challenge captured the industry's lingering sense of grievance over the way in which (on one view) huge costs and disruption were imposed on the retail financial services industry in the form of the pensions review, which was a systemic root and branch retrospective review and compensatory exercise of past business. Some in the industry argued that the pensions review used liability standards that were by no means clear or apparent and were informed by regulatory hindsight.[53] Although the L&G reference related to enforcement action taken by the FSA as result of L&G's implementation of the review of endowment misselling, the industry's malaise at the conduct of the pensions review

---

[53] See Black and Nobles, supra, n 46 for a rebuttal of that view and a picture of the scale of the pensions review. See also J Gray, The Legislative Basis of Systemic Review and Compensation for the Mis-Selling of Retail Financial Services and Products, *Statute Law Review*, 25(3), 196–208 for discussion of the genesis and politics of the pensions review as well as examples of judicial considerations of the pensions review in case law.

explained the considerable interest and comment in the conduct of enforcement action arising out of what was widely perceived as another widespread regulatory scandal.[54]

In the course of its decisions, the Tribunal made various comments that provided insight into how meta-regulatory techniques may stand scrutiny in the future when under consideration as liability standards in enforcement contexts. It is these comments made by the Tribunal that are of interest here, rather than the substantive outcome of the decisions itself.

The FSA had alleged that L&G had been in breach of SIB Principles 2 (skill care and diligence), 5 (information for customers), 9 (internal organisation – the forerunner of what is now the FSA's Principle 3, supported by SYSC's requirements) and 10 (relations with regulators). It also claimed that L&G had been in breach of more specific PIA and Adopted LAUTRO rules in force at the time, which governed the establishment and review of compliance procedures, including training and competence procedures, staff monitoring and conduct of business requirements, such as suitability, risk warnings and explanations and key features disclosure. In relation to the "procedures case" (which the Tribunal actually found was supported by the evidence), the Tribunal rejected L&G's argument that the FSA could not, in its attempt to establish liability under more generally expressed rules and principles, rely on evidence of instances of breaches of specific rules, unless those specific rules themselves were also the subject of enforcement charges against it. The Tribunal said that

> FSA is free to rely on whichever rule or rules reflect what they perceive to be the gravity and extent of the alleged mischief. It would be undesirable, and potentially oppressive to an applicant, for FSA to be required to *clutter the indictment*" unnecessarily with a whole range of extra charges.[55]

This, then, appears supportive of the FSA's ability to take, and its practice of taking, enforcement action in relation to breaches of standards which are more generally expressed and meta-regulatory in tone than

---

[54]See J Gray, ibid.

[55]*L & G Assurance Society v. FSA* (Decision of the Financial Services and Markets Tribunal: 18 January 2005) at p 9.

other more specific standards and requirements. The FSA may use breaches of such specific standards and rules as evidence to support the establishment of more general failures (for example, a failure to establish efficacious compliance systems), but will not be put to proof of breaches of these specific rules.

More generally expressed standards carry a stronger normative message, so the graver the alleged mischief (in terms of regulatory objectives) the more appropriate general standards as a basis for discipline become. However, Power's suggested difficulty with meta-regulatory generality of rule design in terms of its implications for ease of enforcement is borne out by subsequent comments of the Tribunal. It stated that the more generally expressed the rule or standard, the greater the difficulty in coming up with an objective compliance standard against which to measure a firm's liability. It cautioned against the dangers of regulatory hindsight in applying general standards in such a way as they took no account of a lack of clarity about what was compliant practice at the relevant time or indeed that the standard expected might have shifted and evolved over time:

> L&G have to be judged against the compliance standards as they applied in the Relevant Period. The fact that procedures are changed and improved as they were in the latter part of 1999 does not mean that prior conduct was necessarily inappropriate or in breach of the rules. Such an approach would inhibit firms from improving their standards. So what were the standards in the Relevant Period? . . . [I]n civil litigation it would be common to prove practice at a particular time with evidence from witnesses from other organisations involved in the industry. We were told that such evidence was not now relied on in financial services discipline cases. In this case there was no evidence to help us judge what other firms were doing or how L&G's performance related to them apart from indirect reports received by [its compliance director] or relayed to L&G by Coopers and by Deloitte [who had provided compliance consultancy services]. This creates no difficulty when a firm is being judged against an objectively measured standard or where there is explicit guidance indicating in reasonable detail what should or should not be done. It is more of a problem when we are considering the broader requirements of "best endeavours", "due skill care and diligence" or the obligation to establish procedures directed at all the "Rules and Principles" particularly where, as we see it, standards may have changed over the course of the Relevant Period.[56]

---

[56]Ibid. at p 45.

In L&G's particular case the Tribunal said that the defects it found in L&G's procedures were basic. Consequently, it found that L&G was liable for the failure to have, review and maintain procedures adequate to ensure compliance; a finding that was unaffected by any doubts about a lack of clarity of the standards or temporal shifts in what was expected of firms. However, in any future determination of liability of a firm for breach of the requirements of SYSC, the caveat entered by the Tribunal may have more force than it did on the facts in the L&G case. This is because the SYSC requirements are even more generally expressed than those at stake in the L&G challenge. SYSC had no direct equivalents under the previous regulatory regime and hence what is a reasonably acceptable management practice, system or control arrangement may now be a far more indeterminate and contestable concept. Having sounded this general warning in the L&G case, the Tribunal may well take a different view on these questions to that taken by the FSA.

Another feature of particular interest in the L&G decision is how the more holistic focus that meta regulation has on systemic failures on the part of firms, rather than their specific acts or omissions, is beginning to influence ways of approaching issues of causation in the context of regulatory responsibility. The Tribunal in this particular case agreed with the view of L&G that the FSA and its Regulatory Decisions Committee had read too much into the findings of the PWC Endowment Sales Review and had extrapolated erroneous conclusions from a sample size that was statistically insignificant for the purposes for which the FSA sought to use the review. It took the view that it was only possible to say with any certainty that misselling had been established to have occurred in a much lower number of cases (only eight) in the review than was claimed by the FSA. Hence, the extent of misselling was not, the Tribunal thought, "unacceptably high" on the evidence before it and so the FSA's misselling case largely failed. However, what the Tribunal was most certainly *not* doing in this part of its decision was curbing the ability of the FSA to use such self-evaluative wholesale reviews of past business by firms as representative evidence for the purposes of establishing responsibility for non-compliance that stretches beyond the terms of the cases comprised in the review of past business itself.

The Tribunal will allow findings of fault in a limited number of cases to be extrapolated more widely throughout a firm's business:

> Our reservations about the ESR are about its particular features not about the use of sales reviews in general. FSA has difficult and important work to do in the public interest. Companies engaged in financial services have to accept that enforcement, particularly in large scale matters, may involve approximation and what is at times a "wholesale" approach to investigating and establishing fault.[57]

Viewed solely in the specific context of attributing regulatory responsibility within the financial services regulatory regime, this type of approximation may seem unproblematic and simply an illustration that meta regulation's emphasis on systemic, as opposed to specific, approaches can be used by regulators evidentially in an enforcement context in support of enforcement action taken for breaches of more specific rules. The language of regulatory enrolment of firms in the "public interest" work of the FSA with its emphasis on their need to "accept" this fact-finding practice is clear here.

However, as Haines and Gurney have argued, it is not realistic to view regulatory regimes in isolation either from each other or, as Black has recently acknowledged, from the values and standards of private law too.[58] An example of potential conflict between this type of meta-regulatory, "systems-based" approach to "fault" and regulatory responsibility on the one hand and that of private law's traditional approach on the other, surfaces in another recent decision in the financial services regulatory liability context – this time in the sphere of private law of insurance contracts. It is to this we now turn.

Insurance contract construction in pensions misselling context

In contrast to the FSA's willingness to use holistic approaches to fact finding to establish regulatory responsibility and the Tribunal's above noted acknowledgement of its need so to do, in *Lloyds TSB General*

---

[57]Ibid. at p 65.
[58]J Black, Regulating Law: The Case of Finance, supra, n 39.

Insurance Holdings Ltd and others v. Lloyds Bank Group Insurance Co. Ltd [59] the House of Lords sounded a warning note as to the acceptability of taking an overly holistic approach to establishing the "cause" of regulatory responsibility for the purposes of determining civil liability as between insured and insurer under an insurance contract. The case concerned the appropriate construction to be given to the term "act or omission" in the insuring clause of a professional indemnity insurance policy taken out to insure the claimant companies against liabilities arising from pensions misselling. The determination of that point of construction had a significant impact on whether or not the policy's aggregation clause applied to the claims which gave rise to the insured companies' liabilities, which, in turn, determined the subsequent application of the policy deductible to those claims and hence the amount the insurers would have to pay out on the policy.

The claimant companies, Lloyds TSB General Insurance Holdings Ltd, TSB Life Ltd, TSB Pensions Ltd, TSB Bank plc and Lloyds TSB Life Assurance Co. Ltd ("the TSB companies") had incurred significant compensation liabilities to investors between 1988 and 1994 in relation to breaches of a specific LAUTRO Rule which required them to "ensure" that their sales representatives complied with the LAUTRO Code of Conduct in relation to sales and advice of personal pensions. The LAUTRO Code was at that time the financial regulatory code applicable to the companies concerned. The 22 000 individual compensation claims that the TSB companies received in the wake of the review of past personal pension business led to some £125 million in compensation payments made, although no individual claim exceeded £35 000. A group-wide policy to which the companies were party insured the risk of liability under the Financial Services Act 1986 for misselling. The relevant insuring clause provided:

> This Policy ... provides an indemnity to the Assured in respect of the Assured's legal liability to third parties for any third party claim ... which meets the following requirements:-

---

[59] [2003] 4 All ER 43.

Any third party claim must:

(i) be for compensatory and/or restitutionary damages; and
(ii) be first made against the Assured during the policy period; and
(iii) ... (g) be for financial loss caused by a breach on the part of the Assured or an Officer or Employee of the Assured of the provisions of the Financial Services Act 1986 (including without limitation any rules or regulations made by any Regulatory Authority or any Self Regulatory Organisation pursuant to the provisions of the Act) ... in respect of which civil liability arises on the part of the Assured.

An aggregation clause in the policy provided:

If a series of third party claims shall result from any single act or omission (or related series of acts or omissions) then, irrespective of the total number of claims, all such third party claims shall be considered to be a single third party claim for the purposes of the application of the Deductible.

The pensions misselling claims against the TSB companies were clearly within the scope of the insuring clause, but there was a question as to the appropriate interpretation and application of the clauses relating to the level of the deductible. The level of the deductible applicable to third party claims was set at £1 million in the policy. Could a series of third party claims be aggregated so as to constitute a single third party claim for the purposes of the application of the deductible? If not, then 22 000 individual claims would have to be seen as individual third party claims for the purposes of the deductible clause. Since each and every one of them was far exceeded by the £1 million deductible, no liability to pay any of the claims would arise for the insurers. If, however, the 22 000 individual claims could be seen as a single third party claim by their characterisation by the aggregation clause as resulting from a "single act or omission" or "a related series of acts or omissions", then the situation was far less bleak for the assured TSB companies since the £1 million deductible would be applied against the aggregate figure for pensions misselling compensation liabilities of £125 million. Liability to bear that £124 million was therefore at stake in this litigation.

At first instance, the High Court had taken the view that the TSB companies' admission of breaches of those LAUTRO Rules which required them to establish employee training systems and monitor employees in order to ensure employees did not breach the LAUTRO Code of Conduct meant that this failure to train and supervise employees was the cause of all the individual claims, and was therefore itself a "single act or omission". The Court of Appeal, however, ruled that "act or omission" must be something that constitutes the investor's cause of action underlying the pensions misselling claim. Consequently, since the cause of action in these claims arose upon the contravention by a TSB company representative of the LAUTRO Code of Conduct, these contraventions could not be seen as a "single act or omission". However, the Court of Appeal interpreted the words "or a related series of acts or omissions" used in the aggregation clause and ruled that acts or omissions could be related if they had a common origin or "single underlying clause".

For these purposes, then, the Court of Appeal thought that the TSB companies' failure to ensure LAUTRO Code compliance arose from their breaches of rules relating to staff training and monitoring. Therefore it concluded that the individual acts or omissions behind the pensions misselling claims could be seen as a related series for the purposes of the aggregation clause. Both lower courts reached the same conclusion that the aggregation clause did apply to the pensions misselling claims. On appeal to the House of Lords, however, a very different approach was taken, resulting in a different outcome. The Lords ruled unanimously that the phrase "act or omission" was not to be read as allowing for a unifying causal factor that was more remote than the specific act or omission which was the cause of action of each individual claim.

It agreed with the Court of Appeal's analysis of "act or omission" up to a point, namely that the cause of action underlying each of the 22 000 individual pensions misselling claims against the TSB companies arose when the relevant individual company representative failed to give an individual investor "best advice" under the LAUTRO Code. The TSB companies' failure in respect of their monitoring and training systems was therefore not the cause of action to these claims and hence could not be seen as a single "act or omission". Lord Hoffmann considered the nature of the TSB companies' liability:

> It is a contravention of [LAUTRO Rule] r 3.4(4)(a) to "ensure that" company representatives comply with the code of conduct. A duty to "ensure that" something does or does not happen is the standard form of words used to impose a contingent liability which will arise if the specified act or omission occurs. Even if the act or omission is that of a third party, such as a company representative, the liability is not vicarious. The company is not liable for the representative's act or omission: that is simply the contingency giving rise to the company's own liability. Nor should one be misled by the word "ensure" into thinking that the effect is to impose upon the company a duty to do something. No doubt the company will be well advised to take whatever steps it can to prevent the contingency from happening, but the question of whether it took such steps or not is legally irrelevant to its liability. It is liable simply upon proof that the contingency has occurred.
>
> It follows that the absence of a training or monitoring system, even though an independent breach of the rules, was legally irrelevant to the civil liability of the TSB companies. Even without any such system, they would not have been liable unless their representatives actually contravened the code. Likewise, any such contravention would have given rise to liability whether they had a training and monitoring system or not. It cannot therefore have been an act or omission from which liability resulted.[60]

The Lords thought the Court of Appeal had been wrong to construe the words "(or related series of acts or omissions)" in the aggregation clause so loosely as to allow for the linkage of a multitude of discrete acts or omissions if either the acts had a single underlying cause of common origin (which the Court of Appeal saw here as the training/monitoring systems failures) or if they were "the same omission" occurring on more than one occasion (which they saw as presenting the same misleading documents to investors). Lord Hoffmann ruled that this construction was incorrect since it yielded an interpretation that lacked any logic in terms of the parties' manifest intentions. He explained it this way:

> This result seems to me paradoxical. It means that the parties started by choosing a very narrow unifying factor: not "any underlying cause", not "any event" or even "any act or omission", but only and specifically an act or omission which gives rise to the civil liability in question. Having chosen this as the opening and, one must assume, primary concept to act as unifying factor, they have then, by

---

[60]Per Lord Hoffmann, op. cit., supra, n 59.

a parenthesis, produced a clause in which the unifying factor is as broad as one could possibly wish. It is sufficient that all the claims have a common underlying cause or (on the view of ... [the Court of Appeal]) the breaches of duty are the same, which I take to mean sufficiently similar. In my opinion this construction is allowing the tail to wag the dog. I do not think that it is reasonable to understand the parties as having intended the parenthesis to stand the rest of the clause on its head.

When one speaks of events being "related" or forming a "series", the nature of the unifying factor or factors which makes them related or a series must be expressed or implied by the sentence in which the words are used. It may sometimes be necessary to imply a unifying factor from the general context. But the express language may make such an implication unnecessary or impermissible.

In the present case, the only unifying factor which the clause itself provides for describing the acts or omissions in the parenthesis as "related" and a "series" is that they "result" in a series of third party claims. In other words, the unifying element is a common causal relationship. But that common causal relationship is, so to speak, downstream of the acts and omissions within the parenthesis. They must have resulted in each of the claims. This obviously does not mean that it is enough that one act should have resulted in one claim and another act in another claim. That provides no common causal relationship. It can only mean that the acts or events form a related series if they together resulted in each of the claims. In this way, the parenthesis plays a proper subordinate role of covering the case in which liability under each of the aggregated claims cannot be attributed to a single act or omission but can be attributed to the same acts or omissions acting in combination.[61]

Perhaps, on one view, this decision seems of little wider note than another refinement of time honoured canons of appropriate legal construction of insurance contracts, helping clarify expressions used around causation and aggregation of claims, but with little value as regards regulatory technique. However, it is possible to see this dispute between insured and insurer (which was essentially all about allocation of risk and consequent cost of regulatory liability), and its eventual resolution by the courts, as indicative of the growing influence of "meta-regulatory" ways of thinking about the cause of multiple organisational liabilities. When looking for the point of causation of many different individual regulatory liabilities, all four lower court judges were comfortable with looking at what the Lords would have termed "upstream" within

---

[61] Ibid.

the TSB companies' internal organisational arrangements rather than merely the salesman/individual customer interface. It is testament to the widespread purchase of the systemic nature of the failures behind the pensions misselling that all four lower court judges saw the failures in monitoring and training systems within the TSB companies as sufficiently causally relevant to the 22 000 individual investor claims to be caught within the aggregation clause.

The House of Lords, however, did not allow what it agreed were indeed clear systemic failures (giving rise to LAUTRO rule breaches themselves in their own right) to cloud the causation and construction issues in this essentially private law dispute – albeit one about who should bear the cost of regulatory liabilities. In their refusal to look beyond the immediately proximate cause of a breach of duty (that was admittedly repeated many thousands of time) they also refused to accord legal relevance to what clearly were latent causes embedded within firm management structures and, interestingly, remuneration structures. The judgements, with a reference to commission bias, highlighted the role that distortionary remuneration structures played in stoking the pensions misselling episode. The Lords narrowed the issues down to a matter of classical private law construction of a commercial contract. No more, no less. The importance of the fact that the policy had used a tight and limiting form of wording in the aggregation clause, where other forms of words would have allowed for a more holistic, meta-regulatory and remote view of "cause", had become somewhat lost in the lower courts' analysis. The lower courts were perhaps too willing to examine the latent industry-wide "real" causes of pensions misselling and hence import them into the legal cause of the acts and omissions so carefully delimited by private law drafting techniques in this particular aggregation clause.

Implications

As meta-regulatory techniques proliferate and firms attempt to insure against regulatory financial penalties and liabilities in relation to breaches of SYSC and other regulatory codes concerned with systemic organisational acts and omissions as bases for liability, it will become all the more important to ensure that the contractual drafting private law techniques being employed to do this actually do allocate meta-regulatory liability risks as the parties intend and price them accordingly. In his consideration and critique of the consequences of "turning organisations inside out" by regulators' use of internal controls as a key meta-regulatory tool, Power too has picked up on the point that the pricing and hence insurability of these new organisational risks is problematic. The amount of litigation surrounding the appropriate allocation of risks between insured and insurer that arose out of the pensions review bears out that observation. It may well be that the insurance industry balks at the prospect of insuring against firms' own deficiencies in internal regulatory risk management, especially since such risk management will, as Haines and Gurney have pointed out, be addressed to a number of different competing and sometimes conflicting substantive regulatory regimes and breaches of meta-regulatory "systems and controls" requirements may well give rise to liabilities in each regime.

To insure against a range of such risks, whose source lies in the very risks that the different regulators themselves have chosen to shift downwards into the management of the firm rather than accident or error of employee, machinery, and the usual hazards of insurance, is to pass the problems inherent in meta-regulatory techniques (indeterminacy of standards and conflict between differing regulatory goals) onto insurers. As a result, the pricing and allocation of the risks and uncertainties surrounding the activities to which the regulatory regimes are addressed are passed back into the realm of private law and private lawyers, where they would have been all along in the absence of regulation at the end of the day. The difference is that the layers of meta-regulatory technique forming each regulatory regime will have added their own layers of complexity, uncertainty, potential competing conflicts and cost. Yet private law construction techniques will have the final say on the allocation of the costs of these conflicts between regulated firms and society. For, as Hunt points out, insurance is the ultimate "socialisation of risk".[62]

---

[62] Hunt, supra, n 35, p 98.

Concluding comments

The discussion of contemporary UK financial regulatory technique pro-vided in this work has sounded a series of cautionary notes as to the promise of meta-regulatory technique. It has argued that the growing use of regulation to "enrol" industries, firms, their internal cultures, their managers and staff in the regulatory enterprise by means of enforced "self-regulation" of systems and controls and the sharpening of indi-vidual responsibility for such systems, is not without problems. Meta-regulatory techniques may not be the best means for the achievement of "democratic" regulatory objectives. They may not represent the ef-fective enrolment of firms and the proceduralisation of democratic val-ues into the business sphere that they appear to promise. Rather they should be seen within the complex, interlocking and overlapping web that comprises the contemporary legal and regulatory environment for business. Viewed thus, these techniques compound the obfuscation of a much broader failure to reconcile and often even acknowledge compet-ing and conflicting values and ideologies underlying the regulatory and legal regimes from which they spring. The roots of this failure can only lie in a political timidity and anxiety besetting political institutions that must in turn reflect those of all of us.

As Haines and Gurney have argued with some force, the techniques of meta regulation "simply delegate the problem of the irreconcilable to the regulated entity".[63] Instead of society and government address-ing the hard choices between differing values and goals enshrined in different regulatory regimes, which would be the most open and most democratic way, meta regulation shunts them onto the shoulders of firms and managers. "Regulatory compliance cultures" within business are asked to make up for the shortfall in our wider democratic culture. As Power insightfully concludes:

> [t]he way societies call individuals and organisations to account says much about fundamental social and economic values . . . in [the Audit Society's] most

---

[63]Haines and Gurney, supra, n 2, p 374.

mundane regulatory techniques, it reflects a complex and not always consistent constellation of social attitudes to risk, trust and accountability. The motif of the audit society reflects a tendency for audit to become a leading bearer of legitimacy and this must be so because other sources of legitimacy, such as community and state, are declining in influence.[64]

Further, this work has sought to illustrate that risk-based regulation and meta regulation do not simply have implications for firms, but also have implications for citizens, in that they too are being enrolled into the regulatory process and remodelled under the guise of good citizenship – a remodelling that obscures political hard choices and devolves responsibility for their resolution onto citizens.

It is hoped that through critical scrutiny of some of the "mundane regulatory techniques" of UK financial regulation this work has helped bear out the force of this insight. Power has in fact gone on to argue that there exists the beginnings of an imaginative and positive agenda, whereby regulatory institutions, techniques and processes should acknowledge, rather than seek to bury, a "new politics of uncertainty", conflict, unknowns and hard choices.[65] Instead of bundling these eternal realities into risk categories, and seeking to tame, hide and dampen them through elaborate meta-regulatory strategies, government, regulators, firms (and ultimately all of us) should acknowledge that risk, failure, loss and fallibility are inevitable accompaniments to innovation, growth and change. To model regulatory technique exclusively around such values undermines trust in others' judgements and our own ability to face the future by employing reasoned calculation about "knowns" and courage, optimism and imagination about "unknowns". Without this, nobody can grow and thrive.

The challenge for regulatory scholars now is to take up that positive agenda called for by the politics of uncertainty. They can do so by employing emerging understandings in fields of disciplinary endeavour that

---

[64] M Power, *The Audit Society*, supra, n 2, pp 146–147.
[65] See Chapter 8, M Power, *The Risk Management of Everything*, supra, n 4.

appear to have something to say about belief, trust, cheating and fear,[66] and then by siting such understanding in practical processes, policies, industries, laws, individuals, and indeed their consciousnesses.[67] Such a research agenda may tell us far more about regulation in the future than we even know is as yet unknown.

---

[66]B Lange, The Emotional Dimension of Regulation, *Journal of Law and Society*, 2002, Vol 29(1) 197–225, J Pixley, *Emotions In Finance*, supra at n 68, Chapter 6, T Chorvat and K McCabe, The Brain and the Law (George Mason University School of Law Working Paper Series: 04-33), T Chorvat, K McCabe and V Smith, Law and Neuroeconomics (George Mason University School of Law Working Paper Series: 04-07).

[67]The need for regulatory scholarship to move from practico-descriptive work to understanding compliance processes too, has gained widespread currency. R Baldwin, H Scott and C Hood, *Reader on Regulation* (OUP: 1998), Introduction, pp 37–38. Practitioners too reached the same conclusion from a very different angle – see Newton *A Handbook of Compliance: Making Ethics Work in Financial Services* (FT Pitman Publishing: London, 1998), Chapter 5.

Index

Index compiled by Annette Musker